INDUSTRIAL EVOLUTION

LONDON : HUMPHREY MILFORD
OXFORD UNIVERSITY PRESS

INDUSTRIAL EVOLUTION

By N. S. B. GRAS
STRAUS PROFESSOR OF BUSINESS HISTORY
GRADUATE SCHOOL OF BUSINESS ADMINISTRATION
HARVARD UNIVERSITY

HARVARD UNIVERSITY PRESS
CAMBRIDGE, MASSACHUSETTS
1930

PRINTED IN THE UNITED STATES OF AMERICA

To

N. C. James

Scholar and Friend

PREFACE

This little book is a sketch of industrial evolution. Its brevity and lack of completeness are its merits, if it has any. The parts are of unequal value, some being founded upon first-hand materials and observations and some being based upon secondary and well-known sources of information.

My obligations are numerous, many of them being indicated in the notes appended to the chapters. Information has been freely given by Professor J. G. Callan, and two of the chapters have been read by Professor Georges Doriot. My obligations to Professor Edwin F. Gay are very great, particularly in respect to the Industrial Revolution in England. The manuscript has had the advantage of being read throughout by Dr. Henrietta Larson and Dr. Mildred L. Hartsough and in part by Mr. Sterling Popple and Mr. Ralph M. Hower. My secretary, Miss Emily B. Nichols, has given unstinted assistance in the preparation of the copy for the press. My wife has helped at all stages of the work, when time spared her from other duties.

N. S. B. G.

July, 1930

CONTENTS

ILLUSTRATIONS

PAGE

CHAPTER I

EARLIEST STAGE: USUFACTURE

THE earliest stage[1] or type of manufacture we may call usufacture,[2] or manufacture for use—not for sale. In this stage commodities are made for the user direct, in accordance with his ideals, and at his convenience. They are manufactured, moreover, from the raw materials that he provides. Although this is the earliest and most primitive kind of manufacture and although it has in large part yielded to other methods, historically it is the most important type known to man, not so much because it still survives, as because it has fed, clothed, housed, armed, and adorned so many generations—far more than any other type of industrial organization.

In the long period of its existence, usufacture has gone through many changes. We can best understand these changes by noting the various forms it has exhibited, the sub-stages through which it has gone. The first of these is the purely domestic phase. The family not only possesses the raw material, but does all the work, and, of course, ultimately consumes the finished products. This has been the predominant kind of manufacture among peoples in the collectional, cultural nomadic, and settled village economy.[3] Out of the skins of seals, the Eskimo makes canoes, thongs, nets, lassoes, and soles for boots.[4] From the buffalo, the North American Indian obtained not only meat but bones for weapons and hides for clothing, beds, tents, shields, boats, and saddles. The Veddas of far-off Ceylon manufactured a kind of rough pottery,[5] as did the prehistoric inhabitants of South and Central America.[6] The blankets of the Navajo Indians, once made only for use, not for sale, are well known for their warmth, durability, and decoration.[7] Among the Greeks and other peoples of the Homeric period, women were traditionally busy with the weaving of cloth. When the news of Hector's death came, his wife, Andromache, was "weaving a double purple web, and bordering therein manifold flowers;" and when she heard the shrieks, "the shuttle fell from her hands to earth."[8] Penelope faithfully awaited the return of Odysseus while weaving a web of pictured tapestry. Among the Greeks there was a well-developed textile workshop, part of the larger household establishment. In Odysseus' home at Ithaca, there were fifty women servants, taught to "card the wool and bear the servant's lot."[9] In this *gynaeceum*, women did most of the work in making cloth, all except perhaps fulling and dyeing.[10] In what was probably the household of Charles the Great, about A.D. 800, the women were to be provided with wool, dyes, and tools needed for the making of cloth.[11]

We know that usufacture in the home, although declining, occupies an important place in human economy even today. There may be a few of the oncoming generation living in apartment houses, however, who have seen none of the home industries. It is a fact, nevertheless, that the household is still an industrial establishment, in which many useful things are made, from doughnuts to preserves, from children's garments to women's hats. It is still strong as a repair shop, from the slavish washing of linen to the restful darning of socks. But all of these activities are rivaled by specialized establishments outside. Gradually, as the home loses its industrial prop, it is being compelled to stand totteringly on its other two legs, one biological and the other psychological. From the standpoint of efficiency gained through specialization, it would be a good thing to let household industry decline as fast as there develop outside agencies to take its place. If the ideal of individual development, however, involves the bringing out of all qualities, the manual as well as the intellectual and the social, then the complete loss of household industry is to be regretted. A good case can be made out for instruction in home crafts, offered alike in the Old World and in the New, notably in Sweden in the sloyd system, and in America in manual training for boys and domestic science for girls.

The second phase of usufacture, developing not later than settled village economy, sees outside labor brought in to assist the family in its manufacturing activities. Someone develops special skill in making shoes, in carpentry, building boats, blacksmithing, or tailoring. His neighbors send for him to help them, so that they may profit by his particular aptitude. Besides his wages, they provide his board and lodging. Many cases are recorded of princes sending not only for poets and jugglers, sculptors and architects but for armorers and masons, carvers and goldsmiths. Even down to the middle of the last century in Lombardy the tailor or shoemaker arrived in the midst of the old undivided type of family of large proportions and set up his shop for a week or even a month.[12] In this way he clothed or shod the whole family until such time as he could come again. At least until recently the system prevailed in the Styrian Alps, where the itinerant shoemaker was a welcome guest, for whom there was a special room set aside in even the humbler cottages.[13] In China various repair men go the round of the streets, each making his distinctive music—cabinetmakers with wooden clappers, smiths with an iron plate, and roofers and masons with bells and trumpets. This system is aided by the survival of the large family in China. The younger sons receive little or nothing, and have for sale only such skill as they have acquired. The capital in the form of tools is, of course, very slight.[14] In America we see it when the seamstress, caricatured as an ancient lady of slender proportions and inquisitive nose, is brought in to aid in making dresses for women and garments for children. Once I saw a small steamer built for three friends. They provided the material, workshop, and ideas, but employed a skilled workman to construct the ship. I want my house repaired and after buying the raw materials necessary—shingles, boards, tin, and paint, I hire a carpenter, tinsmith, and painter. If, however, instead of having the work done in this way, I let out the contract, another form of industry is brought into play, and, incidentally, my repair bill is ordinarily higher. In Varro's time blacksmiths (and fullers) seem to have gone out from the towns to the farmers like physicians;[15] and in our day umbrella menders and scissor grinders come to our doors seeking work—or alms. In Mexico even now itinerant weavers with a few ropes and sticks go from house to house weaving blankets and saddlecloths, their primitive loom being fastened to the nearest tree.

The ancient temple and the medieval monastery were like large families, held together, however, by religious rather than kinship ties. They had broad lands, flocks and herds, ample buildings, plenty of tools, and large stores of raw products. The religious devotees themselves often had industrial duties to perform, but like the kinship family the monastery came to employ outsiders. These might enter as servants or become tenants on monastic lands on the condition that they would render the manual service required. In the case of a certain French abbey, a holding of land was granted about 1100 to a painter on condition that he would paint the monastery or whatever else he was ordered to paint, and also on condition that he make window glass (small pieces leaded together). His son was to inherit his holding only in case he in turn was of his father's craft.[16] Another French monastery had three workshops, as set forth in a document of 822. In one of these shops there were three shoemakers and one fuller. In the second, there were six blacksmiths, two goldsmiths, two shoemakers, two shield-makers, one parchment maker, and three spindlemakers. In the third, there were four carpenters and four masons.[17]

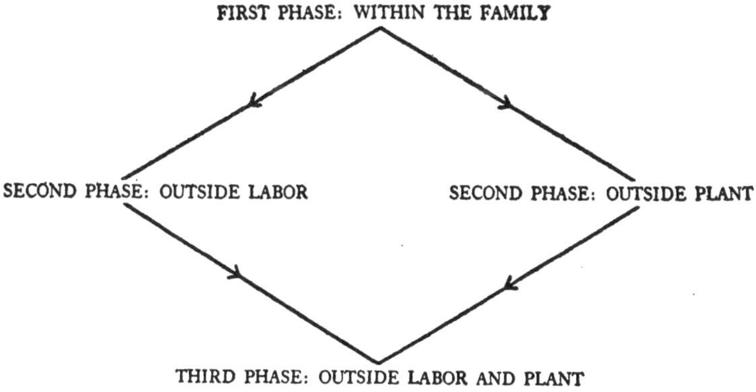

PHASES OF USUFACTURE

In the households of some medieval nobles and perhaps of the most important mandarins in China, skilled artisans were kept to manufacture various commodities out of silk and wool, wood and bronze. The material was given to the craftsmen, who were allowed to take their time. Some of the finest art treasures to be found in China to-day go back to the private workshops of earlier periods. Only the finest of the goods made were kept or at least treasured, and these were of inspired craftmanship.

There occurs another type of the second phase of usufacture, in which the aid of outside capital in the form of plant or equipment, is enlisted. Members of the family, or servants, take the raw material out to be made up in the plant of some outsider. Illustrations of this relatively unimportant phase are not very numerous. Olives would be made to give up their oil in another man's press. Kneaded dough would be taken to communal or other bakeries to be made into bread. A drawing of a primitive sugar press is found on the next page. The hand mills of more fortunate neighbors would be enlisted for the grinding of grain, the making of cider, and the preparation of flax. Favorable spots, notably along a neighbor's stream, would be employed for washing linen.[18] Since in all cases the actual labor would be done by the family owning the goods, or by the family servants, and generally in the immediate district, we may suspect that much of the service rendered by the loan of mill and press, oven and stream, was not directly and specifically paid for.

Much more important is the third phase, in which the raw materials are taken to some outsider who, with his own labor and his own tools, works them up into finished products. One of the earliest illustrations is the taking of metal to the village smith in ancient Greece.[19] In India the peasant takes gold to the goldsmith to have a nose ring made for his wife. This gives rise to the suggestive saying that "the jewell belongs to the wearer, but the gold remains with the goldsmith."[20] In ancient and medieval times cloth was taken to the fuller and the dyer to be carried a step nearer completion. Throughout the Middle Ages in many districts the villager took his grain to the lord's mill to be ground by the miller into flour or meal. Sometimes, indeed, he was actually compelled to do this by the custom of the manor or the highhandedness of the lord.[21] In our own time we find this form of industry well illustrated by the tailoring trade. Occa-

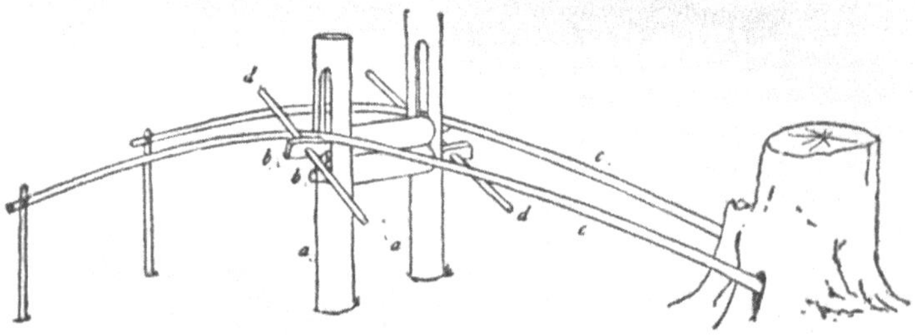

A PRIMITIVE SOUTH AMERICAN SUGAR PRESS

Roller press for squeezing sugar cane, upper Barama River. *a*, *a*, Upright posts with slits in which to rest the two rollers *b*, *b*. These are pressed together by the saplings *c*, *c* and turned in opposite directions by the handles *d*, *d*.

sionally we buy a piece of cloth, perhaps import it, and then employ a tailor to make it up. And of course our repair work commonly is done in this way.

Progress through all three phases of the stage of usufacture may be again illustrated, on the one hand by the making of shoes and on the other (probably) by the grinding of grain. First the family makes its own shoes; then it brings in outside help; and finally it sends the leather to a shoemaker who, working at his own home, provides both labor and equipment. It may be that it was at this early point in his history, at least in some parts of the world, that the artisan first became interested in gilds. If so, the gilds would be secret at first and aim more at general protection than at maintaining or raising piece wages. Along the other line of development, we see the peasant making his own flour with mortar and pestle; then he takes his grain to the plant of a neighbor who has a good hand mill for grinding grain between stones; and finally he uses the improved mill run by horse or water power and tended by the owner or lessee, the owner of the grain performing little or none of the labor. Thus we see that the resultant form is the same whether arrived at through the avenue of outside labor or of outside capital in the form of equipment.

Throughout the stage of usufacture, no matter what the phase, we observe that the goods are made to be consumed, not to be sold. There is no oversupply, for goods are made only in answer to a developed demand. The element of price does not arise, for there is no sale. Although this type of industry is at the bottom of the scale, still it makes a real contribution to subsequent progress in the development of some degree of specialized skill. This is found in the itinerant workman and in the artisan laboring in his own shop making up his customer's raw material into a finished article. The wage system arises when outside labor is employed; and in the third phase board and lodging are given up.[22] The element of interest is perhaps involved when an outsider collects a toll for the use of equipment. And yet there is no wage problem and no interest problem. A real issue does arise in cheating, when the consumer takes his homespun cloth to the fuller and gets back inferior cloth, not his own, or when he takes his gold to the goldsmith and gets back a jewel set in alloy.

All in all, this stage presents no mean accomplishments. It produced excellent wares, sometimes artistic, always durable, and as a reward received the patronage of the gods. In Egypt, woman's work, especially weaving, was done under the auspices of the goddess Tait; in Greece, Athena, and in Rome, Minerva. Hephaestus was the patron of crafstmen. Himself the god of fire, he kept his smithy on Mount Olympus. Egyptian Ptah, Roman Vulcan, Finnish Ilmarinen, Vedic Agni, and Teutonic Weland may all be compared with Hephaestus in one way or another. In Norse and Saxon literature, it is Weland, or Wayland, the Smith, who plays the largest part as the magic fabricator of coats of mail dear to the hearts of warriors.

Many have been the isolated efforts to revive or accentuate the system of usufacture. Most of the notable attempts have been connected with some larger form of idealism. Part of Gandhi's policy in India has been to induce his followers to use cloth made in their own homes or at least in India. In this way he would deal a severe blow to British factories. A much less pretentious effort has been made in the Province of Quebec by Mlle. Juliette Gaultier, of old French-Canadian lineage, to revive the making of fine woolens and linens at home and for home use. She has not urged all women to undertake this but has suggested that many with large homes, plenty of time, and aptitude for manual work should do so, especially if they wished to possess fine and desirable articles.

Some irate farmers in Minnesota, finding that they could sell their wool only at a low price in 1920 whilst, owing to the post-war scarcity of manufactured goods, they had to pay dear for woolen commodities, sent their wool to local factories to be made up into blankets, cloth, and socks. In St. Cloud, in the same State, is a small factory equipped to make woolen cloth out of medium-grade wool. It caters to farmers as far west as Utah. The farmers are invited to send in their wool to be washed, combed, spun, woven, and finished for use. To them are sent samples of the kinds of cloth made—from heavy material for overcoats to light flannels for underwear. The farmers pay cash for the work done. No guarantee is given that the goods sent to them will be made out of the identical wool received, but assurance is given that the quality will be approximately the same. Of course, manufacture is by means of modern machinery. Accordingly we may regard this as a commingling of a new and an old system rather than simply the revival of an old one.

The usufacture of goods has been shattered, yet it is bound to survive, that is, of course, as a type of industry rather than as a stage. And so it is commonly in economic history: one stage of production is supplanted by another, whilst the old form survives or is revived as a subordinate or temporary organization. Sharp distinction should be made between a stage and a type. A stage is always a type, but a type may be merely the shadow of a departed stage.

Even now we may expect to find usufacture under at least four circumstances. It has great vigor where people are isolated and therefore dependent upon themselves for manufactured wares. In many remote rural parts, notably in Kentucky and Tennessee, it has vitality, whilst on upper Manhattan Island it is almost nonexistent. Whenever people want fine wares of individual design and simple craftsmanship at low money cost, they may revert to usufacture. When we seek to boycott some other system of industry we may resort to usufacture. And we may do likewise in order to evade the laws under which we live. The most notable example of this is the manufacture of liquor and wine in the United States under the régime of prohibition. Of course the home distiller or fermenter does not rely upon himself alone. He buys bottles and kettles, stoppers and tools, made in modern factories. Thus does a rival form of industry aid an old competitor. At first there was little skill in the making of whiskey, rum, and wine, but now these can be made quickly and at least the wine can be made almost palatable. It should not be concluded from this, however, that illicit usufacture alone prevails. Those with skill or greed manufacture for sale to others. At this point our ancient type again disappears. It is interesting to note this making for sale is one of the forms of activity which the governmental authorities are most eager to combat.

NOTES TO CHAPTER I

1. For general treatment of industrial stages, see K. Bücher's article, *Gewerbe* in the *Handwörterbuch der Staatswissenschaften*, vol. iv (1892), pp. 922–950; K. Bücher, *Industrial Evolution* (1893, trans. by S. M. Wickett, 1901), ch. iii, "A Historical Survey of Industrial Systems;" G. Unwin, *Industrial Organization in the Sixteenth and Seventeenth Centuries* (1904), Introduction; G. Schmoller, *Grundriss der Allgemeinen Volkswirtschaftslehre*, vol. ii (1908), pp. 466–515, bibliographies, pp. 450–454, 491–494; G. I. H. Lloyd, *The Cutlery Trades* (1913), ch. i; Sir W. J. Ashley, *The Economic Organization of England* (1914), chs. ii and v; A. P. Usher, *An Introduction to the Industrial History of England* (1920), chs. i and ii.

2. K. Bücher (*Industrial Evolution*, 1893, 1901, pp. 154ff.) uses the term household industry; but this is ambiguous, for etymologically it would apply just as well to a later stage sometimes called domestic economy. Bücher's term could not be applied to the concept of the stage here set forth, because the work was not done in the home under all circumstances, as is explained later in this text.

3. For a description of the manufacture for use as carried on by various North American Indian peoples, see C. Wissler, *The American Indian* (1917), chs. iii–viii.

4. H. H. Bancroft, *Works, The Native Races*, vol. i (1886), p. 58, n. 50.

5. C. G. and B. Z. Seligmann, *The Veddas* (1911), pp. 323–324.

6. F. Ratzel, *History of Mankind* (1885–88, trans. by A. J. Butler, 1898), vol. iii, p. 67.

7. H. H. Bancroft, *op. cit.*, p. 502.

8. *The Iliad* of Homer, book xxii (trans. of Lang, Leaf, and Myers, 1903), p. 447.

9. *The Odyssey* of Homer (trans. by G. H. Palmer, 1891), p. 355.

10. G. Glotz, *Le travail dans la Grèce ancienne* (1920), pp. 270–271. For the Greek household, see the treatise called "The Economist," in *The Works of Xenophon* (trans. by H. G. Dakyns, 1897), pp. 199–290, for example, pp. 246–247.

11. For a translation of the capitulary *De Villis*, see *Translations and Reprints from the Original Sources of European History* (University of Pennsylvania), vol. iii, no. 2 (1912), p. 4.

12. Helen D. Irvine, *The Making of Rural Europe* (1923), p. 38, quoting A. Bezzozero.

13. K. Bücher, *Industrial Evolution* (1893, 1901), p. 164.

14. Nyok-Ching Tsur, *Die gewerblichen Betriebsformen der Stadt Ningpo in China* (Tübingen, 1909), pp. 42–43.

15. Varro, *Rerum Rusticarum Libri Tres*, i, 16, 4 (ed. of H. Keil, 1889), p. 35. It is really uncertain whether the *fabri* were smiths (T. Frank) or car-

penters (L. Storr-Best) and whether they were itinerant or stationary town workers.

16. *Documents relatifs à l'histoire de l'industrie et du commerce de France* (ed. by G. Fagniez), vol. i (1898), p. 68.

17. *Ibid.*, pp. 50–51.

18. See K. Bücher, *op. cit.*, p. 165.

19. G. Glotz, *op. cit.*, p. 53.

20. W. Cooke, *Natives of Northern India* (1907), p. 131.

21. R. Bennett and J. Elton, *History of Corn Milling*, vol. i (1898), pp. 211 ff.

22. See the ordinance of Diocletian (A.D., 301) published by K. Bücher, *Zeitschrift für die gesamte Staatswissenschaft*, vol. l (1894), pp. 704–717.

CHAPTER II

SECOND STAGE: RETAIL HANDICRAFT

WE HAVE now come to a stage in industrial development that is fairly well known under one name or another. It is the stage of the small worker in the town or country, making his wares in a shop or a room in his house. His wares are used by those in the immediate district. This type of industry has been called gild system, handwork, and handicraft. Gild system it is not. Handwork and handicraft it is, but these terms are not sufficiently distinctive. It is here called retail handicraft.

When the household, manufacturing primarily for its own needs, produced a surplus for sale, and when the artisan, hitherto working on his customer's goods, began to provide the raw materials himself and sell the finished product, the new stage of retail handicraft[1] was born. Usufacture may remain as a type but it is not the characteristically new and promising form of industry. It is still, of course, handwork that is being carried on, but it is work for sale to another person. The sale, however, is direct to the user.[2] It is a purely retail business, whether in town or country. It keeps many of the excellent qualities of the older system, usufacture, and is carried on under the oversight of the ancient gods. The worker, however, is henceforth also a trader. He is a profit taker as well as a wage-earner.

The origin of the retail handicraft was twofold, rural and urban. The rural handicraft was born before the town came into existence. When primitive man made more baskets or pots than he wanted, and exchanged them with a neighboring tribe for dried fish or red ochre, the first steps in this stage were taken. Life was not continuously strenuous for nomads depending chiefly on flocks and herds, and accordingly they could easily manufacture goods beyond their own needs. In the lone watches on the hills, the shepherd had ample time to spin the fine wool of his sheep. In her crowded tent, a woman of the clan wove this yarn into rugs, some used as prayer mats, some for bed coverings, and some for carpets. Such rugs have a history of thousands of years in western Asia. We know them still as Oriental rugs, distinguished alike by design and color. Such commodities the nomad sometimes offered in barter for other wares. Settled villagers also developed skill in manufacture and speed in producing beyond their own need. Doubtless this increased as commercial towns arose to take the surplus. Cloth beyond their own necessities was made for sale; also butter, cheese, and wine. In the Middle Ages the peasant had to pay a toll to his lord for making beer for sale.[3] In Russia the peasants have long engaged in bast-making and twine weaving.[4] They also make coarse linen cloth, felt shoes, and wooden ladles and plates for sale. In Staffordshire, in western England, two or three pottery works were found in a village, and here and there an isolated one on the moorlands. The equipment was wretched but adequate: an open tank for evaporating diluted clay, a shed for drying unbaked clay, and a hovel containing the oven for firing the pots. The mother or daughter peddled the wares made by the male members of the family. From her weary tramp she returned laden with goods purchased in the towns, goods not provided by the family's own meager agricultural activities.[5] In the highlands of Scotland the crofters wove cloth for a purely local market until factory competition began to disturb their old-time seclusion.[6] Even recently handmade tweed, blankets, and stockings were made on the island of Skye, Scotland[7]

AN ATTIC VASE FROM ORVIETO, SIXTH CENTURY B.C.,
SHOWING A BLACKSMITH'S SHOP

A SHOEMAKER'S SHOP FROM THE PRECEDING VASE

In Porto Rico there are many examples of the retail handicraft system in rural districts.[8] The poor countryman may have a small patch of ground on which he grows a little coffee, corn, or tobacco; or he may work as a laborer during the busy seasons on a large plantation. In either case he often uses his spare time to manufacture various articles which, on foot or on a pony, he will take to the towns for sale. He brings in huge crude cigars or chewing tobacco in long ropes for sale on the marketplace. He has dishes made of gourds and brooms of palm leaf. Straw hats, baskets, and hammocks as well as musical instruments are among his display. His cane-seated chairs may be crude but his walking sticks of wood and shark's vertebrae are very beautiful. Often he peddles his hats from town to town, sometimes selling to kinsmen or regular customers. Indeed he takes orders for certain styles and sizes of hats to be supplied on his next trip. We wonder how far American wares are supplanting such native manufactures.

Retail handicraft also grew up in the early towns and progressed there much farther than in the country. Tradition makes Theseus divide the people of Attica into three classes: nobles, peasants, and artisans. It was early said in Greece[9] that a man could enrich himself in maritime trade, agriculture, manufacture, poetry, prophecy, and medicine. The author of this statement, Solon, was both statesman and poet and had traveled much. We may assume, since he refers to manufacture as the arts of Athena and Hephæstus, that he wishes to convey the impression of skilled craftsmanship.[10] In a picture painted on an early Greek vase we see the close relationship between producer and consumer. A girl stands on a table, with her feet on a piece of leather. The shoemaker with knife in hand sits ready to cut the stock the shape of her foot.

On the wall are tools and leather.[11] Here we seem to have an example of the retail handicraft business. The artisan owns the tools and the raw materials. He manufactures at the order and for the use of customers whom he knows and deals with directly. In ancient Rome there were no bakers till relatively late, if we are to believe Pliny. Before they developed, the Roman women had done all the baking.[12] In time there were not only bakers but shoemakers, jewelers, and the makers of lead pipes and clay lamps.[13] So numerous and noisy did the artisans become in the ease-loving town of Sybaris that some of them (braziers, smiths, and carpenters) had to be relegated to the district beyond the walls.[14] In the Theodosian and Justinian Codes we find thirty-five trades exempt from public duty, such as lapidaries, silversmiths, blacksmiths, carpenters, and fullers.[15] By the end of the Middle Ages such crafts were to be numbered in the hundreds, but not all of them remained in the retail stage, as we shall see.

When we look closely into the retail handicraft we can distinguish two types which may be successive phases. In the first, the craftsman makes his wares only to order, that is, after he has been commissioned to do a definite piece of work. This is illustrated by the shoemaker in the town. He can nicely adjust his raw material to his business. He has no surplus manufactured stock. His chief assets are his skill, a few tools, and a one- or two-roomed shop. The same type is found when a householder gives a contract to someone to build a house for his use, or to make something for his benefit. This we may call the order phase. The second one may be called the chance-sale phase, for the craftsman makes up stock for sale to some undetermined person, who, he expects, will soon come along to demand his surplus. When we speak of this as

SHOEMAKER'S SHOP IN GERMANY, SIXTEENTH CENTURY, SHOWING THE CHANCE-SALE PHASE OF RETAIL HANDICRAFT

the second phase, we are thinking of developments in towns, where the shoemaker, the weaver, the saddler, the joiner, the goldsmith, and the cutler produced wares for future sale. On regular days this sale would take place in the shops themselves; on market days, and notably fair days, it would be in specially appointed booths on the market places or at the fairs.

When the artisan arrived at the phase of chance sale, his workshop became a shop for the sale of finished wares. Shopping for shoes, candles, bread, and other manufactured wares was henceforth possible. Hitherto it had been possible for the consumer to buy such wares at the weekly market or at the annual fair, that is, wares made locally and sold to the consumer. Of course, it was also possible to purchase goods made in another country under a more advanced system of industry. A shoemaker of Winchester, for example, would have as rival the fair of St. Giles held outside the walls. And other craftsmen would find that some of their customers bought country-made goods in the town market at the foot of the beautiful old cross. But regulations were made to assist the artisan, especially if he belonged to a gild. It is an interesting and unsettled question, however, whether there was a third rival—a general store. In the early American town the general store was a vitally important institution, like the inn and the blacksmith's shop. But we are not at all sure that there was a general store, such as the mercer's and haberdasher's, in the early European town. It is difficult to see how foreign wares could have been handled however unless there was some such store. In America, at any rate, this general store played a special rôle on behalf of a rival system: it was one of the agents for the introduction of a more advanced form of manufacture,[16] what we here call the wholesale handicraft system. An illustration of the retail handicraft system in the chance-sale phase may be taken from far western China. "There is [1915] a certain shoe shop in Leather Shop Street, Chengtu, which was opened over thirty years ago by the Family Yang. The capital is not more than a thousand taels and it earns at least three hundred taels a year. The building is a two-room structure, with the shop in front and the work-room behind. The entire front is open to the street during the day, but it is closed at night by movable shutters. Across two-thirds of the front is a counter with a glass case for exhibiting shoes. Beside the counter sits a man with a well-made shoe in his hand. He is waiting for customers. The room behind is fitted up as a workshop. There are only a few men. Some make the soles, of felt or paper covered with a thin layer of leather; others make the uppers, of silk or satin or both, using patterns. There is no difference between the right and left shoe. The daily wage of each workman is about 200 cash (five cents)."[17]

Although there is some evidence for the order phase in rural parts, as when a Russian peasant takes a commission for supplying beer at a neighbor's wedding, still it is the chance-sale phase that is all important in the country. Indeed the background of rural industries is the manufacture for use, and when we find sale introduced, it is ordinarily sale of a surplus. The surplus, whether cloth or shoes, butter or beer, is ordinarily taken to the neighboring market for sale to anyone who comes along. The country displays weakness in the first phase, just where the town is strongest. The difference in the last analysis, however, is in degree rather than in kind.

Rural and urban types of the retail handicraft system display contrasts other than in emphasis on order and chance sale. In the country there was less specialization than in the town, since manufacture and agriculture were much more combined than in the town. And also, there was in the country little more than a beginning made in the development of gilds and in many countries not even a beginning. The rural manufacturer sold at the homes of the consumers or more commonly on the open market, while the urban handicraftsman sold in his shop.

In the town, the retail handicraft had wide ramifications in the political, social, and religious life of the community.[18] This was brought about by the gild, which was the formal counterpart of the retail handicraft system. Although the craftsmen had been members of the merchant gild, their distinctive connection was with the craft gild. All handicrafts, except the lowest, had their laws and regulations, their officials, common chest, and a place of meeting. The apprentices were duly enrolled in a separate list, as were the journeymen and the masters. Regulations were set forth in the interest of the craft. Some crafts, notably on the Continent of Europe, required any journeyman who aspired to mastership to produce a masterpiece,[19] first as proof of his skill and later as evidence of his capital. Some also favored the *Wanderjahr*, that is, the pilgrimage of the journeyman from place to place, learning new methods and getting fresh experiences.

In medieval Europe craftsmen were generally free; and the more developed the town the greater the element of freedom. In ancient cities, however, slavery crept in, and with it the discredit of manual labor. Probably up to the sixth century in Athens, and up to the third century B.C. in Rome, artisans were generally freemen. As wars of conquest continued and expanded, the supply of slaves increased. Some of the slaves became domestic servants, some workers in fields, and some, often the ablest, artisans in households or in shops. Here were enacted some of the tragedies of the ancient world—a craftsman of great capacity was torn from his Asiatic home and, far from his family, was forced to labor in a Corinthian armory or a Roman lapidary's shop. Relief sometimes came in manumission after long and faithful service, but it was too late to heal the great wound of a sad life.

In the textile industry, at least in medieval towns and perhaps generally, there arose a peculiar situation.[20] Instead of selling directly to the ultimate consumer only, a craftsman often sold to another craftsman as well, taking either other goods or money in return. The weaver came to sell to the fuller, the fuller to the dyer, and the dyer to the cloth-worker (finisher, draper, or whatever he might be called). This exceptional condition arose from the fact that the textile industry came to be highly specialized in the towns,[21] no one man making a piece of finished cloth in the way that a shoemaker made a complete shoe, or a joiner a complete chair.

The essential of the retail handicraft is not the gild system, though many have dealt with it as though that were the case. It is not the making of a whole article, though some have so regarded it. It is not always sale to the ultimate consumer, for in the most important industry of textiles, the sale was often to another craftsman, a user, but not the ultimate consumer. It is not the absence of power machinery, as indeed the use of the word handicraft implies: the fulling mill was worked by water power and is an important illustration of the retail handicraft. As here conceived, the essential of this stage or type of industry is direct, retail dealing without the intervention of a special capitalist merchant or industrial entrepreneur.

As compared with usufacture, the merits of the retail handicraft system are very real. First and foremost was the fact that the artisan provided the raw material. This meant a wider choice of goods, not simply the taking of such wool or leather as the maker had himself produced. Here was discrimination which tended to raise the standard of work. Moreover, the entering wedge of capitalism was being driven in, first, in the artisan's ownership of raw material and, second, in his development of chance sale. In the latter there was a surplus of finished stock for sale. The retail handicraftsman was more specialized in his work than was the consumer-producer under usufacture. As the stage progressed, special skill came to be the largest diamond in the system's crown.

During the centuries of prevalence and of growth, in the ancient, medieval, and modern times, wherever town economy prevailed, there was no cessation in the effort to produce a genuine commodity. The artisan manufactured wares as if he was himself to use them. And indeed, if he did not use them, it was his neighbor who would consume his products. Badly made shoes, shoddy cloth, cracked spurs, and old cabinetware made over would soon come back to shame him. Apart from the carelessness of a few individuals, and the viciousness of others, good workmanship prevailed. It was the accepted ideal. The gilds wrote this ideal into their ordinances and had no great difficulty in enforcing it until the market expanded and another system came into being.

Such was the rule, but there were exceptions. Wherever sale enters in, there is temptation. The buyer is ignorant or careless—the opportunity for the seller. The victim may never discover the deceit. Hence the necessity for laws dealing with the weight of the penny loaf of bread. Indeed the assize of bread and ale was one of the most difficult laws to enforce. In its infraction both townsman and countryman had their parts.

The retail handicraft system was the first stage of mercifacture or the making for sale. All subsequent development has occurred under the same heading. And many of the defects of the system have come under the head of *merx*, leaving less and less room for *misericordia*. Still, as our experience has shown, the various defects of deceptive goods, false measures, and low wages have been evils of transition. The supreme defect in retail handicraft was really the local nature of the exchange of goods and services. The local sale—within the town or as between town and surrounding villages—meant a lack of variety in goods that could be purchased, from the standpoint of both raw materials and the methods of work. It meant also adherence to old methods and traditions. In these respects, the retail handicraft, though an improvement over usufacture, left much to be desired.

When industrial development reached mercifacture, business in manufacture was born. The artisan had become a buyer and seller. He might have his individual shop, but he nearly always had family assistance. Ordinarily he formed no other partnership. He used money either as a measure of value or as both a measure of value and a means of exchange. He kept no books, though he may have had scratch records. His greatest weakness lay on the side of buying and selling. He was a local trader, as we have seen. But he was also trying to carry on two operations, manufacturing and marketing. In doing these things he had no expert helpers. And accordingly when specialists in marketing came along, as they did come, his position became precarious. Here and there he was to survive even to the present, to perform important local services. But the stage of retail handicraft was to go, leaving behind only a straggling type of industry and a tradition of good work and decent living.

NOTES TO CHAPTER II

1. Like usufacture, this term, retail handicraft, is now used for the first time, so far as I know. It is meant to be an improvement over the older terms. Handicraft alone does not indicate anything different from the stage that follows. And gild system (used by Ashley, Lipson, and others) does not refer to industrial organization at all. The gild belongs to another subject, association, and it neither begins with nor ends with the retail handicraft system.

For pictorial representations of handicraftsmen at work, see Ernst Mummenhoff, *Der Handwerker in der deutschen Vergangenheit* [15th to 18th century], Monographien zur deutschen Kulturgeschichte, ed. by Georg Steinhausen (Leipzig, 1901).

2. The user need not be the ultimate consumer. See below, ch. ii, p. 20.

3. For example, *Historia et Cartularium Monasterii Gloucestriae* (Rolls Series), vol. iii (1867), pp. 98, 117, 121, 125–126, 184, 195, 197.

4. V. O. Kluchevsky, *A History of Russia* (trans. by C. J. Hogarth), vol. i (1911), p. 217.

5. E. Meteyard, *The Life of Josiah Wedgwood*, vol. ii (1865), pp. 97–99.

6. W. R. Scott, *Report . . . on Home Industries in the Highlands and Islands* (1914), p. 31.

7. *Ibid.*, p. 183.

8. This description I owe to a former student, a mature woman who in the year 1919 wrote out her observations of 1913–14.

9. For a study of ancient Greek industry, see the works of B. Büchsenschütz (1869), H. Blümner (1869, 1874–87), H. Francotte (1900), G. Glotz (1920), and P. Waltz (1922–23); also Rodbertus (1865), K. Bücher (1892), and E. Meyer (1895, 1898).

10. I. M. Linforth, *Solon the Athenian* (University of California Publications in Classical Philology, 1919), pp. 166–167; H. Francotte, *L'industrie dans la Grèce ancienne*, vol. ii (1901), pp. 122–123.

11. H. Blümner, *Technologie und Terminologie der Gewerbe und Künste bei Griechen und Romern*, vol. i (1874, 1912), pp. 285, 287.

12. Pliny, *Natural History* (Bohn's Classical Library), vol. iv (1856), p. 40.

13. T. Frank, *An Economic History of Rome* (1920), pp. 169–171, 184–189, 191–194.

14. *Hellenic Civilization* (ed. by G. W. Botsford and E. G. Sihler, 1915), p. 205.

15. G. Fagniez, *Documents relatifs à l'histoire de l'industrie et du commerce en France*, vol. i (1898), p. 28.

16. Harvey A. Wooster, "A Forgotten Factor in American Industrial History," *American Economic Review*, vol. xvi (March, 1926), pp. 14–27.

17. Written by Fuh Hai Yuin and supplied by Mrs. H. M. Carscallen, both of West China Union University, 1915.

18. See N. S. B. Gras, *An Introduction to Economic History* (1922), chap. iv.

19. See, for example, G. Fagniez, *Documents relatifs à l'histoire de l'industrie et du commerce en France*, vol. ii (1900), p. 101.

20. See G. Fagniez, *Etudes sur l'industrie et la classe industrielle à Paris au xiii*[e] *et au xiv*[e] *siècle* (1877), p. 234; A. P. Usher, *Industrial History of England* (1920), p. 217; E. Lipson, *The History of the Woollen and Worsted Industries* (1921), p. 27.

21. It has been found that before 1300 in Germany there were a few specialized dyers but no dyer's gilds. Commonly at that time a weaver dyed his own cloth or a shearman had a dyer do it. The specialization came later. H. Grunfelder, "Die Farberei in Deutschland bis zum Jahre 1300," *Vierteljahrschrift für Sozial- und Wirtschaftsgeschichte*, vol. xvi (1922), pp. 312, 318, 324.

CHAPTER III

THIRD STAGE: WHOLESALE HANDICRAFT
THE INDEPENDENT PHASE

IN THE third stage of industry, goods are made by one set of persons, marketed by another, and consumed by a third. In other words, the artisan manufactures the wares which are disposed of by merchants or industrial entrepreneurs. This may develop to some extent in the local market; but more commonly it is to meet the needs of inter-urban trade, and later to cater to the metropolitan market. Manufacture is still characteristically by hand, but sale is no longer direct to the consumer. It is still handicraft, not retail but wholesale, involving not only large amounts of goods but small as well. What is specially implied in the word wholesale is not so much size as indirectness.

The common failure to dwell upon the stage of wholesale handicraft[1] is hard to understand—now that we really know about it, because there are so many references to it in travels, history, and anthropology. Whenever an advanced trading people comes into contact with a tribe in a primitive condition, the question of trade arises. In case primitive peoples have developed some skill in manufactures, their wares are sought by merchants. Numerous are the instances of this, such as the moccasins of North American Indians, the blankets of the Navajo Indians, and, best known of all, the Oriental rugs of Persia, Turkey, Afghanistan, and India. The wares of all of these peoples were made by hand and with simple tools, and then sold to merchants who disposed of them in trade, far or near.

Many Greek towns early became distinguished for their

manufactured wares: Chalchis for swords, Miletus for fine woolens, Megara for coarse cloth, and Corinth and Athens for their pottery. The pottery of Corinth was so excellent (650–550 B.C.) that it was in demand all over Greece, in the islands, Asia Minor, on the Euxine coast, in Italy, and on to the north and west.[2] Then Athens came (about 550 B.C.) to surpass Corinth in the ceramic art and its wares went to the distant parts of the civilized world.[3] Apparently in both cities the vases and other clay products were made chiefly by small masters who sold to merchants traveling abroad. It was these small masters, at first free men later slaves, who perfected styles and set the fashion in ceramic art, imitated by other cities of the ancient world,[4] and almost worshipped by students in our day.

In medieval towns we find a similar situation. Arras, Lille, Valenciennes, Bruges, Ypres, Chalôns, and Cambrai, were famous cloth towns, all members of the Hanse of London.[5] It is said that about 1300 in Ghent there were 4,000 weavers in addition to other cloth workers, out of a total population of 50,000. In 1431 over 51 per cent of all workers in Ypres were manufacturers of cloth.[6] Although retail handicraft flourished in medieval Paris, there came a time (in the fifteenth century) when that city relied less on its own cloth industry than on the wholesale handicraft of Normandy, Flanders, and other provinces.[7] In London the apprentices and journeymen were so incensed on one occasion (1 May, 1517) that they rose against foreigners resident in the city, for the haberdashers who had formerly handled the work of London artisans had now turned to foreign sources of supply, especially Flanders. The pin workers, girdlers, and glovers of London had themselves been engaged in making wares for the haberdashers, and now they saw themselves undersold by cheaper goods imported from abroad.[8] Whenever we read of an early trader dealing in a great variety of commodities, as in the case of the London haberdasher; wherever we find evidence of an early store without a workshop, as in the hardware store unearthed in Pompeii;[9] and whenever we learn of an early industry carried on in small shops, the products of which were sold far and wide, as was the case with Corinthian vases and weapons; we may be certain that we are dealing with the wholesale handicraft system.

In America, at least in the eastern part of the United States, the general store seems to have played its part in developing an independent wholesale handicraft system in the late eighteenth and early nineteenth centuries. The storekeeper in the rural center received some manufactured wares from distant towns and from abroad. In the absence of money he could sell these only for goods. The farmers could give their raw products but they also found it profitable to exchange the products of their winter labor. We should remember that many American farmers had been carpenters, saddlers, shoemakers, and the like in Europe. Extra shoes—those made beyond the needs of the farmer's family—were bartered for imported wares. Of course butter, pot and pearl ashes, knitted socks, and other such commodities were traded in the same way. In addition to this development, there was also this counterpart: the artisan in the incipient town was sometimes forced to establish a general store in order to sell his wares. Under a system of money-barter economy, the artisan was forced to take goods in exchange for his products. A shoemaker might take cloth which he would sell to customers who themselves made no cloth but did make iron tools or wooden wares. Such a storekeeper would often find himself obliged to employ others in finishing some of the wares received and might find it convenient to pay his outworkers in goods.[10] Of course, here we are slipping into a somewhat more advanced form of economic organization.

When we look more closely into the wholesale handicraft system, we discover two phases of development, two

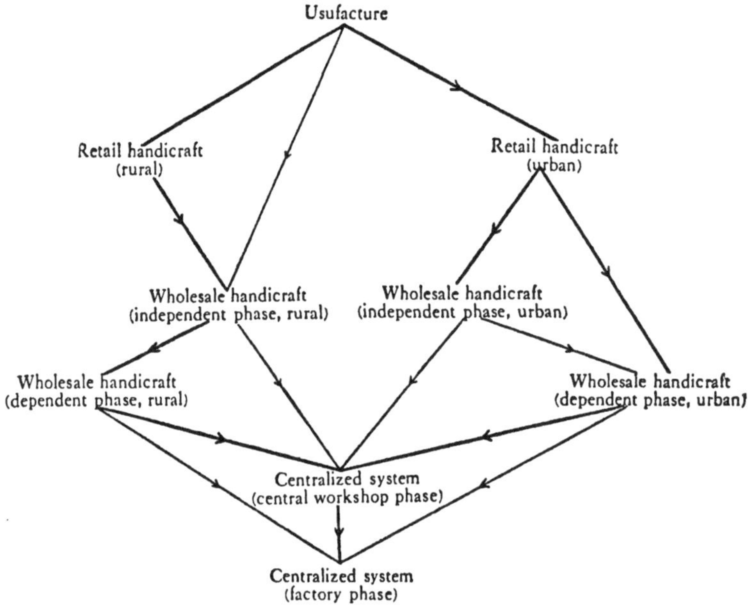

STAGES OF INDUSTRY

No attempt has been made to draw all the lines of development and filiation; only the most significant are here shown. Heavy lines indicate normal genesis.

sub-types of the industry. These we may call the independent and the dependent. Probably the earliest instances of the independent phase came from the countryside. Wine had been made for the use of the owner of the vineyard and for sale locally. When it came to be so well made that it was handled in inter-urban trade, and was sent long distances, it entered the wholesale handicraft stage. The peasant gathered the grapes, stemmed them, and pressed out the juice by tramping with his naked feet or with his boots or with a hand press. Then he put the juice into vats or casks for fermentation. In due time he sold the product to an exporting vintner who sooner or later sent it to some town far or near, at home or abroad, selling it ultimately to an importing vintner, or to a taverner. The taverner in turn sold it to the consumer.[11] In some ways this is the most striking illustration of wholesale handicraft in the Middle Ages. Wine was a commodity of widespread use, in religious rites, for the sick, for recreation, and for health. The peculiar tastes of individuals could be met to a nicety by the various kinds and varieties of dry or sweet and white or red. The real connoisseur distinguished wines not simply along these lines but he asked from what district they came—Rheingau or Moselle, Burgundy or Champagne. He went farther, inquiring as to the particular year of vintage and whether the grapes came from the top or the foot of the mountain.

In Sweden in the Middle Ages the country people made clapboards, barrel-staves, and osmunds (iron rods or bars), which were sent to many lands in western Europe.[12] In Kent thirty or forty men made wooden beads for sale to London haberdashers in the sixteenth century. Seeking a cheaper source of supply, the haberdashers took samples to Flanders and had them made up cheaply there by apprentices, to the ruin of the English workmen.[13] Such rural industries have survived the centuries and display great vitality in many parts of Europe. Elsewhere they are maintained with great difficulty.[14] We find in the toy industry of Germany a good illustration,[15] and until recently much hammered iron was made under this system. The peasants, when their field work had been finished, would mine and smelt iron ore, selling the iron to the hammer-master, who in turn made it into steel which he sold to the cutler[16] for manufacture into knives, scissors, and the like.

The independent form of this industrial system arose in the towns[17] not simply under the influence of traders but also when one craft came to sell only or chiefly to another craft. We have already seen how the weaver sometimes sold cloth in the gray, either to the consumer or to the fuller; and how the fuller sold the fulled cloth to the consumer or to the dyer, and so on. When the craftsman entirely gave up selling to the consumer, the old retail handicraft of the town may be regarded as having developed into the wholesale handicraft. Since the process was slow and gradual, no one can say just when that change came about, except that it happened when towns (ancient or medieval) were well developed, for example, toward the close of the Middle Ages, early in Italy late in France, early in Flanders late in England.

One of the traditional illustrations of the independent wholesale handicraft ("domestic system") is from northern England. It is the woolen industry of Yorkshire.[18] Here numerous small holders of land wove cloth in their houses. The yarn had been spun by their wives and daughters out of wool which they had raised or bought. The cloth was fulled in a nearby fulling mill and perhaps dyed by a local dyer with special skill. The peasant-artisan then folded and bundled his cloth ready for sale. On market day he drove to the Leeds or Halifax market where he exposed his piece or two of cloth at one of the booths. A traveling merchant, or a factor, perhaps from London, finally offering a price that he could accept, the weaver disposed of his cloth. He was independent in so far as he owned the raw material and tools, possessed his own little estate, worked at his own pleasure, and sold his finished product as he would. A similar situation exists in the highlands of Scotland in our own time. The crofters make Scotch tweed from the wool of their own sheep. This they sell to a local merchant who sells it to a wholesaler in a large center, especially London, the wholesaler in turn disposing of it to a nearby tailor or exporting it abroad. Sometimes, perhaps to an increasing extent, the crofter-artisan markets his product through an association.[19]

A notable example of the independent system was found in Ulster in the eighteenth century. The peasants with small holdings of land grew flax which they themselves retted, dried, and hackled. Their wives and daughters spun the fibers into yarn. Sometimes in Ulster, often in the rest of Ireland, the yarn was exported. The yarn, not sold, was woven by the men into linen cloth and sold in the brown to the linen drapers, at first at fairs, later in the regular markets in Belfast, Londonderry, and other towns. The linen draper would commonly have the cloth bleached either abroad, for instance in Holland, or in Ireland itself. The bleaching was a special process done successfully only by the well skilled. The drapers disposed of the cloth to exporters, commonly in London.[20] The climate of Ireland being favorable and the peasants being effective workers and having only small agricultural holdings, the industry become very important. It helped make the north of Ireland prosperous and distinguished. It was only about 1825 that the independent form of the wholesale handicraft system gave way to factory industry.

Many have found great merit in this independent phase of wholesale handicraft. Certainly the master artisan was independent economically (as well as legally). His apprentice or journeyman, if he had one, could look into the future with a fair assurance that he himself would become a master. And in some of the larger towns in the late Middle Ages and early Modern Period, this form of industry offered hope of mastery which had been denied under the retail handicraft system in its later development of gild exclusiveness. The journeyman working in the retail handicraft system, in other words, might rise to the height of mastership in the wholesale handicraft. Instead of having but one source of income, the independent worker, at least in the country, had two sources, industry and agriculture. Either was enough to provide a scant living if the other failed. Since the master worked when he wished, he felt free. Since he worked both indoors and in the fields, he had healthful labor. His goods were sturdy when for common use. And where aesthetic qualities were required, his output was at least individual, sometimes almost artistic.

In the independent phase of the wholesale handicraft system there was the class of business men or traders, already noted, who were intimately concerned with manufacture. Previously the masters—in the retail handicraft system—had been equally engaged in the processes of manufacture and the buying and selling of wares. Now there were such traders as woolen and linen drapers who did nothing but buy and sell manufactured products. Their special skill could go wholly into one aspect of the industry. Their work was to act as wholesalers and therein was specialized wholesaling born in industry. Of course such dealers had to have large amounts of capital in order to buy up and hold stock for catering to a wide market. Herein we find a differentiation between the commercial capital of the trader and the industrial capital of the small operating master. On occasion, however, the larger resources of the trader came to the rescue of the small artisan. As we might expect when more capital and greater knowledge and management were required, there was a tendency to form partnerships. Considerable family partnerships arose in western Europe in the period 1350–1550 for the purpose, at least in part, of managing the wholesale merchandising of manufactured wares. The Medici of Florence and the Fuggers of Augsburg are simply outstanding examples of this new class of traders. In these as in so many cases, successful merchants tended to take on additional functions of banking, but that was commonly later in the history of the family. Closely bound up with the necessities of a partnership, bookkeeping came into existence, partly in order to make certain the total profit or loss so that each partner might share according to his equity in the business.

There are, of course, aspects of the independent phase which are not to be set down as merits or contributions. Very commonly all members of the family, as well as the bread-provider, labored at the common task. Women had not only their household duties to perform and their babies to care for, but some manufacturing to do. Children at tender years were put to tasks when their growth demanded play. Any uncleanly habits of the family might pollute, possibly infect, the wares that were to be sold to others unwitting of the danger. Since two businesses, agriculture and manufacture, had to be cared for, one was frequently stressed to the neglect of the other, though in point of time much of the work dovetailed pretty well. The consumer and the merchant often found that the independent worker was too independent: he would neither hurry nor cater to the taste of a consuming public of whom he had little knowledge and for whom he had less sympathy. To the rural master there was little or no opportunity to form a strong association, unless benevolent outsiders came in to help with their time and money. The urban master had his gild, nominally independent, but really tending to sink into dependence on the merchants or employing masters.

NOTES TO CHAPTER III

1. The term wholesale handicraft is believed to be an improvement over others in use, each of which has drawbacks. Domestic system leads to confusion with household industry (our usufacture), and refers to only one phase (our independent wholesale handicraft). Putting-out or commission system applies to only one phase of the stage (our dependent wholesale handicraft). E. Lipson (*The History of the English Woollen and Worsted Industries*, 1921, pp. 5 and 36) uses the term domestic system but really describes the commission system. This is but one example of many confusions which seem to justify a complete change in terminology, unwelcome as that may be to those who have learned the old phrases.

Generally speaking, this stage of industry is as much neglected as usufacture. Common practice used to be to stress only two types of industry, the retail handicraft on the one hand and the factory on the other. One was the foil to the other. As usual, the transitional stage, wholesale handicraft, was passed over—until Karl Marx (*Capital*, vol. i, 1867, 1886, 1921, pt. iv, sect. 8d, pp. 509–514) called the attention of a wide public to its occurrence and importance (E. R. A. Seligman, *Economic Interpretation of History*, 1902, 1907, p. 69).

2. G. Glotz, *Le travail dans la Grèce ancienne* (1920), pp. 166–167.

3. *Ibid.*, p. 168.

4. H. Francotte, *L'industrie dans la Grèce ancienne*, vol. i (1900), pp. 65–67.

5. G. Fagniez, *Documents relatifs à l'histoire de l'industrie et du commerce en France*, vol. i (1898), pp. 205–206.

6. H. Pirenne, *Belgian Democracy* (1915), pp. 94–95.

7. G. Fagniez, *Etudes sur l'industrie et la classe industrielle à Paris* (1877), p. 241.

8. See R. Pauli, *Drei volkswirtschaftliche Denkschriften* (1878), pp. 38–40.

9. T. Frank, *An Economic History of Rome* (1920), pp. 180–181.

10. On this whole subject, see H. A. Wooster, "A Forgotten Factor in Industrial History," *American Economic Review* (March, 1926), pp. 14–27.

11. A. L. Simon, *The History of the Wine Trade in England*, vol. i (1906), pp. 301–303.

12. N. S. B. Gras, *The Early English Customs System* (1918), pp. 193, 214, *et passim*.

13. R. Pauli, *ibid.*, p. 32.

14. Cf. below, ch. xviii, p. 236.

15. *A Tour through Germany* (anon., 1792), p. 137.

16. J. H. Clapham, *Economic Development of France and Germany, 1815–1914* (1921), pp. 89–90.

17. We owe to George Unwin (*Industrial Organization in England in the Sixteenth and Seventeenth Centuries*, 1904, ch. ii) the first extended treatment of this subject in English history.

18. D. Defoe, *A Tour thro' the Whole Island of Great Britain* (1724–26),

vol. iii (ed. of 1742), pp. 108–112, 126–128; C. J. Bullock, *Selected Readings in Economics* (1907), pp. 114–124; W. Cunningham, *The Growth of English Industry and Commerce*, vol. ii, *The Mercantile System* (1903, 1912), pp. 497–503; Sir W. J. Ashley, *The Economic Organization of England* (1914), pp. 146–148.

19. W. R. Scott, *Report . . . on Home Industries in the Highlands and Islands* (1914), p. 65.

20. See Conrad Gill, *The Rise of the Irish Linen Industry* (1925), pp. 33–60, 138–139.

CHAPTER IV

THIRD STAGE: WHOLESALE HANDICRAFT
THE DEPENDENT PHASE

FORCES were at work to reduce the independent master to dependence. He might have been in either the retail handicraft system or in the independent phase of the wholesale handicraft: the result of the new forces was the same—the loss of economic advantage. Through incapacity, sickness, or misfortune, or because of trade depression, a small master might become indebted to a merchant beyond his power to pay. The rich trader was always ready to take advantage of the great number of masters, to reduce their remuneration to the point of mere subsistence. And often when the best raw materials were procurable only at a distance, the merchant had the advantage over the small industrial master: the English merchant could buy up large quantities, say of Spanish wool or Swedish iron, while independent masters had to use local inferior materials. In the long run, the independent small master was likely to see his output, made of inferior stock, rejected on the market and the goods, made out of the finer imported materials, readily purchased. Unless strongly entrenched, he had no other course than to bow his head. His submission was all the more abject when the merchant, or employer, was a member of a powerful association, while he had none or at best only a struggling gild of poor men. Dependent masters were dependent in varying degrees. The best-off might simply be commissioned to manufacture shoes (in the case of an Englishman or German, out of Spanish cordovan) at so much per pair. He might take work from any master, but in each case with the commission came orders as to how the wares were to be made and when they were to be ready. The worst-off might be hopelessly in debt to the merchant or, as we may now call him, the industrial entrepreneur. He might be laboring with tools owned by the employer and he might be eating food purchased with money advanced by the employer. Accordingly such a small master was a master in name only. The head of a household, he was not economically independent. There was left to him little choice: he had to work from sunrise to sunset; he had to follow orders as to time and quantity of output; and he had to accept about what wage was offered. Such a worker only waited to be driven into some such institution as a factory to become our modern industrial laborer.

While we may assume that the dependent generally supplanted the independent form, we can find instances where such was not the case. The Yorkshire woolen industry held its own in the face of the competition of the dependent system in operation in other parts. In northern Ireland the independent form in the linen industry held its ground and prospered in the eighteenth century, while the dependent could not be made to take deep hold in southern Ireland. In the latter there was in some respects a very favorable soil on which to grow the dependent system. There was insecurity of land tenure, improvidence, and a tendency to overpopulation. But there was also a lack of manual skill. The system was artifically stimulated, notably by large landlords who went both too fast and too far. Difficulties arose over the payment of wages, which were artifically put too high or too low.[1] One wonders, indeed, whether there have been many other instances of the artificial, or rapid, development of the independent form of this system in rural parts.

As the town developed from a small marketing center into an industrial community, the dependent phase grew slowly, not to oust but to supplement the other and older systems. Indeed the introduction of a new type of industry usually involved a struggle between industrial masters. Some became merchants and industrial entrepreneurs, rich and commanding, while others remained small masters, poor and declining. In Paris the richest weavers gave up working with their own hands in the thirteenth century. They even abandoned the direct supervision of manufacture, so as the more completely to devote themselves to marketing, the adjustment of demand and supply. They gave out the yarn to the poor master weavers working in their homes, paying them so much per cloth for manufacture.[2] In the copper trade of Dinant and the woolen industry of Flanders, we find early illustrations in the thirteenth century of the development of this dependent system,[3] in which rich masters put out materials on which the poor had to work. In the town of St. Omer, weavers, fullers, shearers, and dyers were almost completely at the mercy of the drapers who employed them at piece wages.[4] In Florence, dyers, shearers, and finishers about 1300 saw themselves robbed of their economic independence and of their direct relations with consumers.[5]

A good example of the dependent phase of the wholesale handicraft system comes from Douai in Flanders. Its early occurrence is explained by the fact that manufacture in this city was well developed, proceeding rapidly to the capitalistic form. The instance in question is the business of Jehan Boinebroke who flourished about 1270–1300.[6] Boinebroke was a rich patrician and an influential magistrate of the Flemish cloth town. Although he loaned money and owned considerable property in both town and country, his chief business was the manufacture and sale of cloth. He purchased his raw materials both at home and abroad. His wool came chiefly from England—for example from Lincolnshire, Cumberland, and Westmoreland. Both madder and alum were largely imported. In such foreign dealings he ran considerable risks, as when Edward I seized his property in England to satisfy long-standing claims against Flanders.

The business of manufacture *centered* in Jehan Boinebroke's own workshop, in which he had some of the dyeing done for him. But this central place was more of an office and a warehouse for raw materials and finished goods than a place of actual manufacture. From it he sent out raw wool to be washed, spun, woven, sheared, and dyed. This work was done by small masters using a room of their dwelling as workshop. At least nine different employments are mentioned, and about forty different masters are known to have worked for him in the later years of his life. These small masters (wool-beaters, weavers, dyers, and the like) were largely independent, legally and economically. That is, they were generally free to work for any person whatsoever. But it is clear that Jehan Boinebroke was fast robbing them of their independence. In some cases he owned the houses they occupied. To some he had loaned money. Some master weavers had been pledged to work for him exclusively. He did not hesitate to pay wages in truck, either in wool or in cloth. The small masters are the interesting part of the story, but in the background there were *valets* or journeymen who worked for these masters. About them we know but little. While the small masters were permanent residents and citizens of Douai, the journeymen were a less stable, even a migratory, element. We may infer that they were paid a piece wage, as were their masters, and a miserable one at that. It is likely that the journeyman dyers working directly for Jehan Boinebroke in his central shop were on the other hand paid on a time basis.

This is a pretty clear case of the wholesale handicraft industry passing from the independent to the dependent phase of its existence. The great advantage that the rich draper had over the small masters was that he could buy the excellent English wool at the lowest price right in England. His advantage in the purchase of dyes and mordants is no less significant. Moreover, he had a great advantage over the small masters in the sale of the finished product. He sold not only by retail at home but by wholesale abroad—in the fairs of Champagne and in England. It seems likely also that this rich draper used his position of magistrate to further his economic advantage over the unorganized small masters. Doubtless the poor were glad to see him exiled in 1298 and to see his goods confiscated. Certainly in the revolution of 1297 he had espoused the side of the rich patricians, and of the French party, against the poorer citizens and the Count of Flanders. Douai was fertile soil for a capitalistic industry. It had practically no gilds of small masters, or associations of journeymen, to check the growth of the new organization. It had industrial skill. And it was favorably located for the purchase of raw materials and the sale of the finished product.

Jehan Boinebroke was a hard, grasping man, high-handed, and disdainful of the rights of others. A tyrannous proprietor, a pitiless creditor, he beat down the wages of the small masters and boosted the price of his wares to the highest level. He possessed little moral feeling and less humanity. His fortune grew on the ruins of the small masters. And doubtless his nature deteriorated as his wealth increased. Another way of looking at the matter, however, is that in competition with Ghent, Florence, and other cloth towns, Douai was able to hold its own by the efforts of such men as Jehan Boinebroke and by them alone. Without such an entrepreneur the small masters might have been forced into the fields as peasants, and Douai might have been reduced to the proportions of a market village.

England was much more backward industrially than Flanders. The following instance seems to be a typical illustration of one of the prevailing forms of industry at about the time of the discovery of America. Although occurring later than the case of Jehan Boinebroke, it is earlier in its form of development. In other words, chronologically it is later while genetically it is earlier than the instance of Jehan Boinebroke. It was in the village of Coggeshall, Essex, not so far from London, where Thomas Paycocke lived; and there his house, once a residence and a workshop, stands today. This house is a splendid memorial both of the cloth industry and of the personality of the owner, who died as long ago as 1518. From an examination of the old homestead of Thomas Paycocke, a brass plate in the village church placed to his memory, and his last will and testament, we can derive at least a general idea of his life and work.[7] This well-to-do clothier gave out wool to women to comb, card, and spin. The yarn which he received from them he gave out to weavers to be woven into cloth. The cloth in turn was handed to the fuller and the dyer. Then it was packed and sent to a draper in London. It is a rather happy impression that we get of the total situation. Paycocke was in friendly relations with his outworkers. He was not grinding them down to penurious dependence, though he did tend to deprive them of their economic freedom. Whether he kept looms in his large house is unknown. Such a practice was common and threatening, for into the big workplace of clothiers and drapers many outworkers were induced, or forced, to go for work.

London cutlers in the late fifteenth century had been in the habit of commissioning small masters on the outskirts of the city to make knives for them.[8] Citizens of Norwich in the early seventeenth century put out yarn to their less fortunate fellows to make up into stockings which they sent to their factors in London, who sold the stockings to merchants shipping to Spain, France, and Portugal.[9] In Utrecht and Haarlem, we find apparently both the independent and the dependent phases of wholesale handicraft. As evidence of the dependent phase, we find regulations against paying wages in truck instead of money, providing a minimum wage, and limiting the artisans to certain masters for whom they must work to the exclusion of others.[10] When the small masters in London saw themselves threatened with loss of their independence, they fought hard against what now seems to us as the inevitable. They organized into formal associations or strengthened their old ones, and they tried to do co-operatively what the employing masters were doing singly. That is, they sought to provide raw material in large quantities and at low rates, and they sought to market it to advantage. They went so far as to enlist the aid of powerful companies and even the sovereign himself,[11] in this way rousing the merchants and employing masters against the monarchy and contributing something to the unpopularity and final overthrow of Charles I. All efforts to save themselves were in vain, for both economic and political forces were against them. Those who possessed capital had the upper hand. Those who employed their poorer brethren were the rulers of the land and not only allowed the system to develop but passed laws in favor of the masters. In the law of 1749, a late but clear example, the small masters in the textile, leather, fur, and iron industries were penalized for embezzling goods given out to them to work up, for pawning wares, and for taking new work before the old had been finished. The oath of the owners of the raw materials, that is, the industrial entrepreneurs, was to be sufficient to convict.[12]

The system has gone on in the towns till it has now become well recognized, often described, and given a definite place in remedial legislation. It is the sweat-shop system of the modern slums. Only one illustration of it in recent times need be given here. We are told that it was a frequent sight (in 1856) to see troops of women, laden with piles of canvas cloth, going to sew it up into sacks in their humble and often wretched homes, and then trudging back to the warehouse to receive a miserable pittance for their labor.[13]

A similar system grew up later in the country districts where the land was poor, where the raw materials had to be imported from afar, or where the population outgrew the traditional means of subsistence. It is found in England and Russia, in Sweden and France, in Flanders and Germany. It is today a well-recognized division of our small-scale industry. One of the best-known examples, coming from the period about 1650–1830, is the woolen industry of the southwestern part of England, the traditional West Country.[14] Here the rich clothier or industrial entrepreneur purchased wool from the woolgrower direct or imported it from Spain. The wool he gave out to spinners to make up into yarn. Then the yarn was handed out to weavers to make into cloth. After having the cloth dyed and finished, employing in all hundreds, it may be thousands, he either exported it abroad or sent it to a factory for sale in London. The wool-comber, once every second or third week in the early nineteenth century, gave out wool to his spinners and then yarn to his knitters. When the knitters delivered the stockings, gloves, or

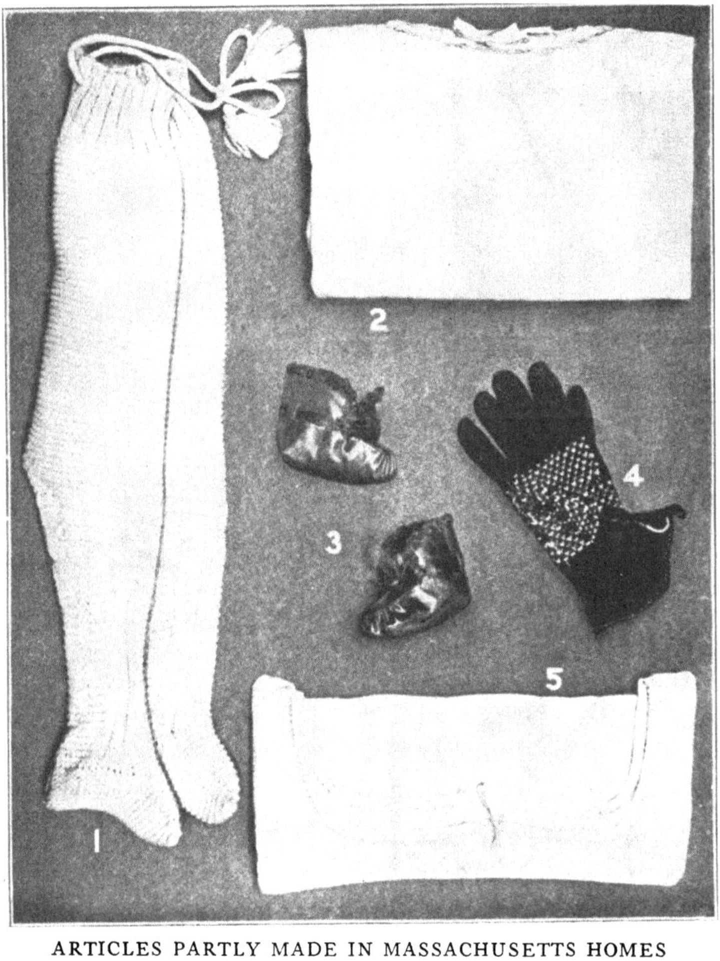

ARTICLES PARTLY MADE IN MASSACHUSETTS HOMES

1. Leggings on which "seaming" is done at home (43 cents a dozen).
2. Home-embroidered gown (embroidering on front and sleeves, $1.20 a dozen).
3. Baby's moccasins (making, 2½ cents a pair; trimming, 2½ cents a pair).
4. Hand-frame knit glove, "seaming" partly completed (seaming, 16 cents a dozen pair).
5. Hand-crotcheted edge on union suit (30 cents a dozen).

ULSTER EMBROIDERERS IN THE DEPENDENT PHASE OF WHOLESALE HANDICRAFT nightcaps, these commodities were dressed by the wool-comber and then sold to the hosier in some of the towns or in the metropolis.[15] In far-off Orkney, Scotland, in 1834, a merchant employer had 1,707 workers in 17 different places, 628 being in Kirkwall, plaiting straw for him. They owed him over £1,000 "for materials, advances [of cash], or provisions."[16] Married women in villages of Wiltshire, England, went in 1909 to factories for glove parts which they sewed together at 5d. per pair or less, and then, dim of eyes and empty of pocketbook, they wearily returned with their wares, glad to get the petty sums offered to them.[17] In 1915 there were 27 knitting factories, out of a total of at least 68 in Massachusetts, that reported out-work. While most of the manufacture was by machine, there remained special kinds of work better performed by hand. The women who did the various finishing jobs, as illustrated by the accompanying picture, were paid a piece wage.[18] Though the wage was low, the chance to earn it was eagerly sought. At the present time (1930) John S. Brown and Sons of Belfast, Ireland, having warehouses in London, New York, Toronto, Capetown, Wellington, and Melbourne, employ rural workers in Ulster at a piece wage. The firm supplies these workers with linen teacloths, bedspreads, and the like, which have been made in a factory and which have printed on them the designs which the workers are to follow. The task is simply to embroider these articles according to specifications given. The embroiderers are shown at work in the accompanying illustration.[19]

The various industrial stages arise, as we have seen, when certain general conditions come into existence; and here and there they manage to survive whenever these conditions continue to exist. It can hardly fail to be of assistance, however, to identify the growth of the various types more concretely—with chronological periods. In order to do this we must take some country, say, England. Up to about 1100 the stage of usufacture prevailed. From then till about 1500 the retail handicraft was the distinctively new system. And about 1500–1750 we find the wholesale handicraft existing as the typical form of industry pushing aside the older systems and giving rise to new problems. After about 1750 industry became highly centralized and faced fresh problems of health and happiness. It is a significant fact that all of these dates, except the last, show England behind such industrially advanced countries as Northern Italy and the Spanish Netherlands (Flanders). The exception, however, is significant: England's industrial advance has been as late in arrival as it has been conspicuous in attainment.

As usual, much that is good and much that is bad can be said about the form of industry under consideration. At last there had arisen a class of specialized industrial entrepreneurs, a class that has meant so much to the modern world of business. Such a person provided capital, standards, and management. Sometimes supervising certain processes himself, as when the clothier did the dyeing in his own establishment, he had general oversight of the actual work of production of his outworkers. He saw that goods were made according to certain standards and made on time. Of course, in the event of conflict or encroachment, the large industrial entrepreneur, well supplied with capital, was more than a match for the small master with his scant investment of capital in shop, tools, and perhaps hand machine. The dependent phase of the wholesale handicraft provided employment for those needing it, and often for those who could get it in no other way, such as the crippled and those forced to care for sick or infirm parents or children. It gave demand a chance to influence supply in the matter of tastes and time of production. And yet it allowed the worker some small vestige of personal (though not economic) independence, as long as he worked in the home. On the other hand, this phase had most or all of the demerits of the independent phase and some of its own. There was a tendency toward low wages and further exploitation through the payment for work in pepper, spirits, or other truck, which had to be sold before the worker could satisfy his regular needs. The worker was tempted not only to pawn but to steal his employer's goods, when he was in distress. Often he had little or no other support in the form of a garden or field, crops, or cattle. But most of all, his economic independence in the industrial world had disappeared. He had little, sometimes no, choice of employers; and when hungry, could not refuse work when wages were low. Without a strong association in the town, and without any at all in the country, the small master was helpless. He might migrate to the new countries of the world; he might join the army or navy; he might remain where he had been born, drinking his chief joy in life at the public inn.

When a new economic system comes into existence, fresh social differentiation takes place. When a market for land arose as the manorial system crumbled, some villeins, or former villeins, leased or sold their land to their neighbors. Some families came to have large holdings, while others retained only their cottages. In due time the latter were lost, the cottagers becoming out-and-out proletarians, living in tied-cottages, with nothing but their labor to provide for their daily needs and nothing to keep away the haunting specter of old age in a poorhouse. In industry a similar development took place. When the independent system gave way to the dependent, the ablest masters became industrial entrepreneurs, the least capable became small dependent masters or permanent journeymen working for small masters. We fear also that it was occasionally the most fortunate that rose and the least favorably situated that fell. At any rate the differentiation was marked. In many cases the industrial master owned the very houses in which the workmen dwelt. This is a close parallel to the agricultural laborers living in the rich farmers' cottages. In due time, these impoverished small masters and their journeymen turned to factories for relief—not from low wages but from unemployment.

NOTES TO CHAPTER IV

1. Compare C. Gill, *The Rise of the Irish Linen Industry* (1925), pp. 130–137.

2. G. Fagniez, *Etudes sur l'industrie et la classe industrielle à Paris au xiiie et au xive siècle* (1877), p. 226.

3. H. Pirenne, *Belgian Democracy* (1915), p. 93.

4. A. Giry, *Histoire de la ville de St. Omer* (1877), pp. 348–349.

5. A. Doren, *Die Florentiner Wollentuchindustrie* (1901), vol. i, pp. 22–23.

6. See the articles by G. Espinas in the *Vierteljahrschrift für Social- und Wirtschaftsgeschichte*, vol. ii (1904), pp. 34–121, 219–253, 382–412.

7. See Eileen Power, *Medieval People* (1924), pp. 156–158.

8. *Calendar of Letter Books of the City of London*, vol. l (1912), p. 224.

9. Lewes Roberts, *The Merchants Map of Commerce* (1638, 1677), p. 291.

10. O. Pringsheim, *Beiträge zur wirtschaftlichen Entwickelungsgeschichte der vereinigten Niederlände* (1890), p. 45.

11. G. Unwin, *Industrial Organization in the Sixteenth and Seventeenth Centuries* (1904), pp. 143–147, and ch. vi.

12. 22 Geo. II, c. 27. *Statutes at Large*, vol. xix (1765), p. 306. Compare 22 Geo. III, c. 58 and 24 Geo. III, c. 3. Compare also 4 Edw. IV, c. 1 (1464–65).

13. G. Dodd, *The Food of London* (1856), p. 186.

14. British Parliamentary Papers, *Report and Minutes of Evidence on the State of the Woollen Manufacture of England* (1806), *Report*, p. 8 and *Minutes*, p. 334.; G. Unwin, *Industrial Organization in the Sixteenth and Seventeenth Centuries* (1904), pp. 235–236; R. B. Westerfield, *Middlemen in English Business particularly between 1660 and 1760*, Transactions of the Connecticut Academy of Arts and Sciences, vol. xix (1915), pp. 273 ff.; E. Lipson, *The History of the English Woollen and Worsted Industries* (1921), pp. 52–59.

15. *The Book of English Trades and Library of Useful Arts* (12th ed., London, 1824), pp. 372–373.

16. W. R. Scott, *Report . . . on Home Industries in the Highlands and Islands* (1914), pp. 179–180.

17. M. F. Davies, *Life in an English Village* (1909), pp. 126–127.

18. *Industrial Home Work in Massachusetts*, Women's Educational and Industrial Union, Boston (Boston, Mass., 1915), pp. 74–76.

19. This information has been obtained from the firm in question by correspondence.

CHAPTER V

EARLY ASSOCIATION IN INDUSTRY
GILDS AND YEOMANRY

SO FAR we have been considering the organization of industry, whilst now we turn to association in industry. By organization is meant the way in which the whole business is carried on: the demand for the goods, the actual manufacture, and the final supplying of the demand. Or, we may express organization as the buying of raw materials, the combination of all elements necessary for manufacture, and the sale of the finished product. Such organization, so far as we have gone, has passed through three stages. Association in industry is something very different. It is the coming together of the producers for mutual advantage. The masters may form associations of their own, as may the workmen. Or the two may be members of the same association.

We cannot be certain about the very first type of association in which industrial workers played a part. The issue seems to be between village gilds of workers in one craft, such as are still found in India, and the merchant gild[1] of the towns, such as we find in the medieval urban centers of western Europe. The merchant gild was a group of merchants, artisans, and others who had a monopoly of local trade and who commonly dominated the town government. Such a gild apparently did not exist in ancient Roman towns, in China,[2] or in medieval London or Paris. But in many towns of medieval Europe, particulary in England, the merchant gild was a conspicuous institution.[3] Although this type of association was called a merchant gild, nevertheless, it contained craftsmen, who were, of course, buyers and sellers. For instance in

1196, the merchant gild in Leicester, England, had as members four or five dyers, one miller, one soapmaker, as well as one mercer, one leech, and one villein.[4] In some towns artisans were excluded from the merchant gild. In 1226 we find that a charter granting a merchant gild to the burgesses of Stirling, Scotland, stipulated that the walkers and weavers were not to be included in it.[5] But even in those cases in which the artisans were included, the artisans were probably not a dominant group.

In the craft gilds the artisans, as well as the traders, found associations which would look after their peculiar needs. The craft gild was a one-craft or a one-trade gild, to which the town ordinarily entrusted the right to regulate important matters of buying and selling or manufacture. It is found in the ancient as in the medieval period.

Although such craft gilds probably did not exist in Greek cities until the Roman occupation,[6] they were found in the Roman state. There were in Rome at the time of Numa (about 700 B.C.) eight craft gilds. These were the flute blowers, goldsmiths, house-builders, dyers, shoemakers, tanners, coppersmiths, and potters.[7] At first these craft gilds were just tolerated by the state; later they were given official sanction, and even made the servants of the state. The gilds in Rome seem to have been open to anyone, never had a monopoly of the trades or industries they represented, and never controlled apprenticeship. To the craftsman there were advantages of a religious and social nature in belonging to these gilds. Of course indirectly there were economic advantages also. At least by the fourth and fifth centuries A.D., not a trade was left without its association.[8] But with the fall of the Roman Empire almost all of these gilds seem to have disappeared, possibly an occasional one having survived' such as the water merchants' in Paris.

The historic craft gilds, about which we have a great deal of detailed information—from their ordinances and from legal cases, arose in western Europe not later than the close of the eleventh century. They sprang up to serve the special needs of each trade. At first they were generally religious fraternities, formed ostensibly to maintain a candle in a church, or for other such purpose, but really to help the members of the trade. They gained public recognition where they could. In 1130 in England the weavers of Oxford, Lincoln, and London paid considerable sums to the king for their gild.[9] In 1180 there were eighteen unauthorized gilds in London alone which paid varying sums to the king for moral support if not for protection. The first was that of the goldsmiths, the fourteenth was the clothworkers', and the fifteenth the butchers'.[10] Gradually they gained the official recognition of the towns; on the Continent this often occurred only after a bitter contest with the merchant gild. Ultimately, that is, by the fourteenth and fifteenth centuries, every artisan was required to enroll in a gild and every gild had more or less influence in the government of the town. By 1376 the crafts were in possession of the government of the City of London, a position which they or their successors have practically maintained down to the present day.

A member of a craft gild expected to gain many advantages through his membership. He was one of the few entrusted with the regulation of his occupation. He could prevent competition from craftsmen just outside the walls or from abroad, from craftsmen who sold inferior wares, and from craftsmen who reduced prices unduly. He could get help in his business through the gild's activities, and through the regulation that a gildsman could ask a fellow member to share his raw materials. Of course, there was the advantage of social intercourse and civic honor. The gilds provided the personnel and regulated the millinery for processions and shows, rather notably on Corpus Christi day. In Beverley, England, there were thirty-eight crafts participating in the Corpus Christi procession in 1390. Among them were masons and plumbers; tanners, skinners, saddlers, glovers, and girdlers; tailors, weavers, fullers, coverlet-makers; goldsmiths, smiths, cutlers, latteners, and furbishers; bowlers, turners, spooners, ladlers, coopers, arrowmakers, and bowyers; butchers, bakers, fishmongers, chandlers, and vintners.[11]

Some of the handicrafts were split up into rather special occupations. In Paris in the late thirteenth century there were, besides the cobblers, the makers of silk and linen shoes, of cordovan shoes, and of basane shoes.[12] As might be expected, there was incessant trouble between the handicraftsmen of close kinship, particularly between the shoemakers who made new shoes and the cobblers who were supposed to repair old ones; as also between the turners and joiners, coopers and carpenters, and leatherworkers and harness makers.[13] Each handicraftsman tended to stretch over into the field of his neighbor's work, the disputes being settled by arbitration or by the municipal authorities. In Châlons in 1411 the tanners, the richest people in the town, wanted also to be curriers. The tanners, however, were ordered to be only tanners and to deliver leather in a public place to the curriers and to stand a fine for poor leather sold.[14]

The wares made by gildsmen were either for use by the customers who provided the raw material or for sale. When for sale they were to be disposed of in the workshop where made or on the public market—and not on the streets. It is an important point to note that craft gilds arose in some crafts when industry was still in the usufacture stage, but in the second and third phases of that stage.[15] Examples of this are the weavers, the tailors, blacksmiths, dyers, and various house-builders. There was a tendency for these artisans to develop into the retail handicraft system, but some of the tailors and house-builders have come down to our day in the usufacture form of organization. Some trades had very early reached the retail handicraft stage, such as the chandlers, pewterers, cutlers, bowyers and fletchers, armorers, shoemakers, and skinners. The bakers, however, baked the bread made in the homes at so much a loaf, and also sold their output to the consumers; the goldsmiths also made jewelry out of customers' gold and out of their own for sale.

Normally the craft gild contained three degrees of members, reflecting always the conditions that prevailed in the craft organization. At the bottom were the apprentices, then the journeymen or day workers, and thirdly the masters. Of course, it was the masters who controlled the gild, just as they controlled their own workshops. The tyranny of the master was tolerable because, in the early towns at least, every normal apprentice had a reasonable expectation of becoming a journeyman, and every journeyman of becoming a master. Sometimes the journeyman was expected to spend a period of his laboring years in travel and sometimes he was expected to produce a masterpiece as proof of his skill and accomplishment.

It is a matter of interest to note that the modern Masonic Order, which officially is supposed to go back to the building of King Solomon's temple, probably had its origin in the gild of operative masons of the late Middle Ages. Arising before 1600, possibly in Scotland, the Masonic Order reflects the conditions prevailing in a medieval craft gild with its apprentices, journeymen, and masters, and its emphasis upon symbolism and ritual, so dear to the hearts of the simple minded.

There came a time when the opportunity of advancement for all the workers was lost (see the shortening of

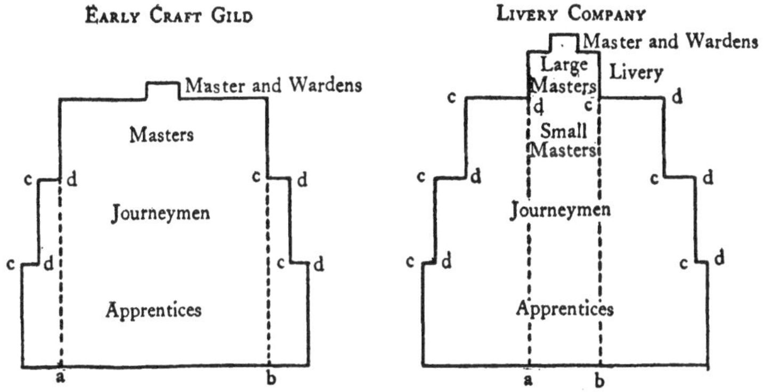

CLASSES IN THE MEDIEVAL CRAFT GILD AND LIVERY COMPANY

Note the shortening of the line ab, a tragic circumstance for the poor man. All persons below the lines cd failed to rise to the top.

the line ab in the accompanying diagram). When the towns had become more highly commercialized, when the peasants had flocked in to engage in industry, and when trade betweens towns and even between nations was increasing, a relatively large amount of capital, as well as skill, was required. This capital was needed, not so much for tools as for the buying of raw materials and the holding of finished goods. Accordingly it became no longer possible for every journeyman to become a master. A few journeymen were kept back—held in the ranks of permanent workers. These remained in their masters' shops without any expectation of setting up shop for themselves. In order to make their mastership the more difficult some gilds imposed high entrance fees.[16] In this way the association reflected and accentuated the organization of industry.

Not only were there few journeymen who could become masters and a great many who could not, but there was an increasing number of masters, in the fifteenth and sixteenth centuries, who had to remain in a humble position while few of their number rose to positions of dominance. In other words, for example, some of the goldsmiths, drapers, and saddlers became commercial masters employing others of their craft to do the actual work. Of course some of the small masters, losing their economic independence, cried out against their degradation. They even rose in arms and spilled the blood of their oppressors. This happened very dramatically in Florence, Ghent, and London.[17] A noteworthy example of conflict in London occurred in 1327 when the saddlers were beaten publicly by the small masters who had been forced to work for them alone and were forced to do it under unfavorable conditions. They were the lorimers, the joiners, and the painters.[18] Of course, as we have seen, the organization of industry was changing from a retail handicraft to a wholesale handicraft system. In the latter, commercial capitalists were becoming dominant.

Corresponding to this internal differentiation in the organization of industry there arose slowly a new type of gild, the livery company. Or rather, we should say the craft gild entered upon a new stage in its history. The small industrial masters, no longer dominating industry, gave way in the gild to the merchants. The position of the merchants, themselves former industrial masters, was recognized in the gild by their exclusive right to wear the livery of the gild—particularly on great festive occasions. A more solid privilege was their right to control the gild and through the gild the regulation of the craft itself. The commercial masters formed a governing group called the court of assistants. From these the masters and wardens were chosen. The differences between the old craft gild and the new livery company are illustrated by the preceding diagram.

Those handicrafts that had a strong commercial element rose to positions of great strength and power. Their gilds came to rank alongside of the great gilds of traders. And in various large cities these rich industrial and commercial groups gained a position of dominance. In London there were twelve great livery companies, in Paris six, and in Florence seven. In sixteenth-century London the goldsmiths, drapers, skinners, and tailors ranked with the grocers, mercers, fishmongers, haberdashers, and salters.[19] But generally the industrial crafts lagged behind in the race for wealth and power. This was reflected within the individual handicraft as well as between trades.

When the rich traders came to dominate the organization of the industry and the gild or livery company, the permanent journeymen and the small industrial masters working for the traders sought their own salvation in separate associations. The journeymen of different trades had often been allowed separate meetings. They were called the yeomanry. When conditions became hopeless for them, they sought to meet secretly to consider their own welfare. They went so far as to advocate better conditions for themselves. In England, the livery companies were too strong to permit any such independence of action.[20] The yeomanry were whipped into subordination and dependence. But on the Continent the story is different, particularly in German towns. The journeymen's associations there were so strong as to wage economic warfare upon the rich operating masters—the traders and the industrial entrepreneurs. In Colmar a strike was carried on by the journeyman bakers for ten years, 1495–1505, with the help of the journeymen of the same trade in neighboring towns. The result was somewhat of the nature of a draw but on the whole it seems to have been chiefly a victory for the journeymen.[21] This, however, was by no means a typical instance.

Of greater significance than the protests of journeymen were the efforts of the small masters to save themselves from hopeless dependence upon the traders or the industrial entrepreneurs. Much of this story is as yet unknown, but enough has been made clear to enable us to distinguish the main outline of the story. The small masters sometimes joined with the journeymen or acted independently to form a separate yeomanry of their own with their own livery.[22] They even went to the extent of enlisting powerful persons at Court to aid them in their fight against the wholesale handicraft system. And it is thought that Charles I raised enemies to himself by espousing the cause of the small masters.[23] At this point the economic struggle in England merged with religion and constitutional controversy. But Charles I lost his head and the small masters their ambition.

The livery companies had won: in reality it was the victory of capital and commerce, or, as we should say, commercial capital. The livery companies have lived on to the present day in London as among the richest, most benevolent, and most extravagant of metropolitan institutions. They provide charitable insurance or active relief for their poorer members; they support schools now as once they provisioned London with corn and helped to colonize Ulster. They elect the lord mayor, sheriffs, and until recently the members of parliament. Outsiders pay large sums to become members. Some of their halls, mostly modern, contain rich plate and fine carved panels. Their daily luncheons are adequate; their periodic dinners at the Guildhall are as sumptuous as they are famous. There has been a movement to revive the livery companies, to put meat into the empty shells. The Brewers' Company has been made up wholly of brewers, but there are few parallels. The Fishmongers' Company has long carried on the inspection of fish, but few of these companies have any connection with trade. And yet after a careful inquiry into the affairs of these liveried gilds about 1880–84, the British government decided to allow them to continue to operate.[24] And thus they occupy some of the choice sites in London which might be better employed. Long ago their functions of regulation were practically all taken over by the state and the form of industrial organization, the wholesale handicraft, was supplanted by a later system—centralized industry, a form which knew them not.

Although the medieval associations had their day and ceased to be, at least as effective organisms in trade and industry, they have had an enduring influence upon business combination. The diagram that follows indicates the development of both association and combination and the influence of association upon combination through the regulated company.

In tracing the development of combination in industry—the formation of business units—we must begin with the individual artisan possessing his own shop and equipment. Then came partnership, with slow and unsteady pace. While evidence for partnership in commerce is plentiful, it is scant for partnership in industry. Three interesting examples have come to my attention. In 1292 in Lucca we find a partnership formed between a dyer and two silk merchants. The latter were to furnish the capital (500 lire) and were to receive one half of the profits. The other half was to go to the dyer, who was to enter into no other partnership and was to do no work for other people.[25] Here we have, in effect, the dependent phase of the wholesale handicraft system. It is not unlikely that there was more of such partnership than we would expect from the scant evidence. In Prato, also in Italy, a partnership agreement was entered into by a merchant, a wool-washer, a wool-carder, and a wool-dyer. The date is 1396. The merchant agreed to furnish the shop, tools, and other equipment, and to pay the workmen (or, it may be, the master artisans). The three master artisans agreed to work in the shop and to keep careful accounts. At the end of a year a trial balance was to be made; and, if the profits were sufficient, the merchant was to be entirely repaid and what still remained was to be equally divided among the four partners, who, it should be noted, shared equally in paying the expenses.[26] The third instance comes from Florence and is dated 1525. Rafaello de'Medici and two others agreed to articles of association for three years or longer. Two were to invest capital, the third skill and management. The purpose was to make soap to sell to wool and silk merchants in Florence.[27]

The joint-stock principle, an extension of partnership, developed in mining and commerce long before it did in industry. In the formation of the joint-stock company, at least in English commerce, the regulated company played a part. This regulated company was a craft gild of merchants trading abroad at their own risk. The orthodox illustrations are the Merchant Staplers and the

Merchant Adventurers, both prominent in fifteenth-century England. In the sixteenth century we find some new trading companies taking the form of regulated companies and some the form of joint-stock companies. There are instances, indeed, of companies changing from one to the other form. Certainly the new joint-stock companies carried over some of the organization and several of the terms of the regulated companies.

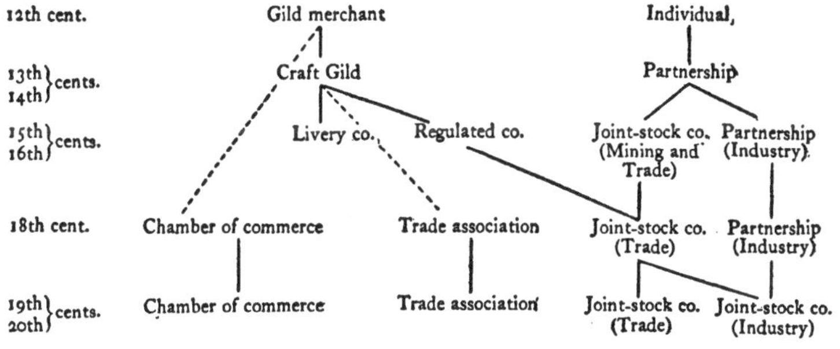

DEVELOPMENT OF ASSOCIATION AND COMBINATION

The joint-stock principle was not generally applied to industry until the nineteenth century when the developing factories required so much capital to build and to operate that two or three partners were ordinarily unable to meet the situation. The S. U. M., or Society for Useful Manufactures, formed in New Jersey in 1791 under the leadership of Alexander Hamilton, William Duer, and others, is an early example.[28] It is interesting to note that this company still exists. The Boston Manufacturing Company, established in 1813 and referred to below,[29] is another example. It is an interesting fact that in both these instances the industrial concern was established by merchants or by men interested in trade.

The example of the commercial joint-stock company was potent in the formation of the industrial joint-stock company. And in the formation of the former the craft gild, working through the regulated company, played its part.

NOTES TO CHAPTER V

1. There were two other kinds of merchant gilds, the gild of general dealers or mercers, and the gild of various *traders*, such as vintners, grocers, iron-mongers, and drapers.

2. See H. B. Morse, *The Gilds of China* (1909), pp. 49–85.

3. See C. Gross, *The Gild Merchant*, vol. i (1890), p. 283.

4. Mary Bateson, *Records of the Borough of Leicester*, vol. i (1899), pp. 12–15.

5. D. B. Morris, *The Stirling Merchant Gild* (1919), p. 48.

6. See J. P. Waltzing, *Les corporations professionnelles chez les Romains*, vol. i (1895), p. 71; and A. E. Zimmern, *The Greek Commonweath* (1911), p. 264, n. 1.

7. See J. P. Waltzing, *op. cit.*, vol. i (1895), pp. 62–63. In the place of tanners, K. Hoffmeister (*Die wirtschaftliche Entwicklung Roms*, Vienna, 1899, p. 15) puts walkers or fullers.

8. See Waltzing, *op. cit.*, vol. ii (1896), p. 101.

9. *Magnum Rotulum Scaccarii* (ed. by Jos. Hunter, 1833), pp. 2, 109, 144.

10. G. Unwin, *The Gilds and Companies of London* (1908), pp. 47–48.

11. *Beverley Town Documents* (ed. by A. F. Leach, Selden Society, 1900), p.33.

12. *Le livre des métiers d'Etienne Boileau* (ed. by G. B. Depping, 1837), pp. 138, 227, 231, and 233.

13. See H. Pirenne, *Belgian Democracy* (1915), p. 210.

14. *Documents relatifs à l'histoire de l'industrie et du commerce en France* (ed. by G. Fagniez,) vol. ii, (1900), p. 199.

15. See above, ch. i, p. 7.

16. See Stella Kramer, *The English Craft Gilds and the Government*, Studies in History, Economics and Public Law (New York, 1905), pp. 78–84.

17. See N. S. B. Gras, *An Introduction to Economic History* (1922), pp. 147–152.

18. See G. Unwin, *Industrial Organization in the Sixteenth and Seventeenth Centuries* (1904), pp. 22–24; and H. T. Riley, *Memorials of London and London Life* (1868), pp. 156–162.

19. See W. Herbert, *The History of the Twelve Great Livery Companies of London*, vol. i (1834), pp. 225 ff. and vol. ii (1836), pp. 3 ff.

20. See Sir W. J. Ashley, *An Introduction to English Economic History and Theory*, pt. ii (1893), pp. 106–124.

21. See G. Schanz, *Zur Geschichte der deutschen Gesellen-Verbände* (1877), pp. 78–92.

22. See the Letter Books of the City of London, for example, Guildhall, manuscript Letter Book, vol. i, fol. 136 ("yomen taillours").

23. See George Unwin, *Industrial Organization in England in the Sixteenth and Seventeenth Centuries* (1904), chs. v and vi.

24. British Parliamentary Papers, *City of London Livery Companies' Commission, Report and Appendix* (5 vols., 1884), vol. i, pp. 43–44, 69–71.

25. See *Atti della R. Accademia Lucchese di Sienze, Lettere ed Arti*, vol. xv (1854), p. 56.

26. See Enrico Bensa, *Francesco di Marco da Prato* (1928), pp. 313–315. Cf. also, p. 285, n. 1. For this and the preceding reference, I am indebted to Dr. Florence Edler.

27. Ms., Baker Library, Selfridge Collection 495, sect. Ab, pp. 100 ff.

28. See J. S. Davis, *Essays in the Earlier History of American Corporations*, vol. i (1917), pp. 349, 370–371; Arthur H. Cole, *Industrial and Commercial Correspondence of Alexander Hamilton* (1928), pp. 191–200.

29. See below, ch. ix, p. 111.

CHAPTER VI

THE MILL

SO FAR we have given little attention to the instruments of manufacture. Vital as these have been, they have not marked off one stage from another. It is only within the last century that power machinery has become a dominant factor. Because of the fact that tools and machinery have not generally been a key to industrial changes, we shall deal with the subject in summary fashion.

The axe, adze, hammer, and knife are among the oldest tools known to man. They are commonly the objects of study by anthropologists, partly because of their importance and partly because of the fact that their remains are discoverable in caves, graves, pits, and lake bottoms. Indeed, the development of early peoples is marked off by their tools—the eolithic, paleolithic, neolithic, bronze, and iron ages. Some of the other tools of great antiquity are the blowpipe, the hand bellows, the spindle, the frame loom without shuttle, and the mortar and pestle.

Very early in human history simple machines were devised. Instead of striking two flints to make fire, man used a drill. Whether the drill is really a machine or just a tool is a matter of difference of opinion, a fact which illustrates the difficulty of distinguishing tools from simple machines. Instead of winding threads in and out to weave a piece of cloth, man used reeds with pedals. Perhaps this is a clearer case of a machine. Instead of tramping grapes by the feet, man pressed them by means of a lever or a screw. And instead of molding clay by hand, he used a potter's wheel.

Much later came the spinning wheel, to take the place of the older spindle. It was in use at least as early as the thirteenth century.[1] The draw loom appeared somewhat earlier in China, much later in Europe. The printing press belongs to the fifteenth and following centuries. The knitting machine has been in continuous use in England, and possibly France, since the late sixteenth century. The cotton gin was invented in 1793. All of these, and a few others of no less importance, such as the spinning jenny and the sewing machine, were run by hand power. They helped man do his work, or actually did it for him, but not without his hand power and constant oversight.

The mill is the early consummation of machine production, brought about by the use of animal or natural power. To many of us the old mill is a lonely building neglected by day, weird by night, beneath whose friendly shadow owls and lovers seek seclusion. It has the glamor of romance about it, for it belongs essentially to the past. Near a mill a battle was lost and won. The more dilapidated the surviving structure is, the more attractive to the artist. A few mills should always be left standing for art's sake.

Hitch superhuman power to a simple machine and you have a mill. Today a plant run by power machinery is called a factory. No useful purpose is served by trying to distinguish categorically between a mill and a factory. Historically a mill came early to serve usufacture, retail handicraft, and wholesale handicraft. The development of the mill is a parallel course, not a deflecting circumstance. The factory came in as a modern organization, not unconnected with the growth of the mill but certainly not generally arising out of it.

The early mills were driven by water power and wind.

Sometimes it was the fall of water in a stream that was used, or the tide along the seacoast. The latter form existed since at least the early thirteenth century in Europe and may, of course, be seen there today. The tourist may see it on the Essex coast and elsewhere; we have all learned about the recent efforts along the west coast of France to use the tide waters. Near Boston, Massachusetts, Slade's Mill has been grinding spices since 1837, using the tidewater of the adjoining marshes. Of course, the use of waterfalls was long confined to small streams or to the flow between the abutment of bridges. The gigantic river-power plants of today go no farther back than the late nineteenth century.

There is much that is quite uncertain about the history of mills. We do not know whether animal power or natural power was used first. Possibly animal power was a later development, because of the fact that the early mill machinery would have offered such resistance to the horse or the ox that little would have been gained, particularly at a time when harness and other equipment were crude and inefficient. We do not know whether power was first used for economic or non-economic purposes. It is conceivable that Orientals first devised a windmill in order to say their prayers more conveniently. Into a hollow cylinder are sometimes placed prayer scrolls which when turned around make a plea to high heaven for the salvation of worldly men. This must seem to us like cheating the deity, to use his wind power to persuade his reason for human benefit.

We do not know whether power was first used for agricultural or industrial purposes, or whether devised by people of the Orient or of the Occident, or whether wind power or water power came first. We can only infer, perhaps wrongly, that a pretty strong claim can be made for the early use of wind power by Orientals for irrigation, while in Europe men first turned to water and for industrial purposes. Indeed, while the water mills were known to Greeks and Romans, windmills were probably not much used in Europe before the thirteenth and fourteenth centuries. Two Arab writers of the tenth century, however, seem to describe them as existing in Seistan (Persia).

The grinding of grain for flour and meal is one of the oldest purposes of the mill in European history. In place of the old mortar and pestle or the hand quern, came a crude water mill for pulverizing grain between an upper and a lower millstone. The stones used not only ground the corn but added to its weight by leaving some of its own particles in the product. And there are some today who would say that this is a wholesome product. Doubtless there is an argument here, that the plodding peasant consumer needed the stimulus of stony grit, while the modern overwrought city man would be irritated by it.

At first the grist mill may have been open to the use of neighbors, more or less without a charge, especially if co-operative efforts had gone into the construction of the mill. Later, especially in feudal Europe, a toll was charged and tenants were forced to patronize the mill of their lords.[2]

At first the grist mill was apparently made up of a wooden shaft with flat spokes for a water wheel at one end, the other end being attached to the millstones. These stones were directly above the water wheel, the shaft being in a vertical position. Of course, the wheel was right in the water of the stream, the sole source of power being the force of the flow of water. If the water went fast, the mill stones would move fast. And when

A WATER MILL FOR GRINDING GRAIN, ABOUT 1570

the supply of water was low, there was no use in trying to grind any grain. It was a great improvement when the wheel was attached to a shaft swung in an horizontal position, and especially when the water was allowed to drop into the paddles so as to give not only the force of the flow but the weight of the water falling. The horizontal shaft would have at the end opposite the water wheel a cog wheel which would fit into another cog wheel attached to a vertical shaft. This vertical shaft would ordinarly have attached to its upper end the stones that did the grinding. The use of cog wheels made gearing possible. A fast stream could be geared slow, and a slow one geared fast. Such an improved mill may have existed in ancient days, but was probably not in common use until the close of the Middle Ages.

Later, improvements came to the grist mill. Several sets of stones were used at one time. Iron parts took the place of wood. Various processes were hitched to the same central power, notably in the mills which followed the methods of the inventive American engineer, Oliver Evans.[3] When we find, at the end of the eighteenth century, grinding, conveying, elevating, and other processes all propelled by the same water power, we feel that the mill has actually become the factory. But then, this is after the Industrial Revolution had already got under way in England. It occurred only in the larger merchant mills and, although it greatly reduced costs, it was scoffed at when first made known. Still, it soon made rapid headway, in contrast, for example, with the contemporary rice mill. Although this integration of machine operation was confined to one type of industry, it is not to be passed over lightly. It showed at least what might have happened generally. The factory could have developed out of the mill.

Not only do grist mills but fulling mills go back to ancient times. Originally the fulling of cloth had been done wholly by hand and foot. That is, men had immersed the cloth in water mixed with chemicals and stirred it up, much as we wash clothes, until the cloth had become felted. When the felting had taken place, one could no longer see the warp and woof: the cloth appeared as a continuous piece of work. Power could be used to do the work by a rather simple device. A large mallet could be fastened to a shaft driven by water. The mallet could be raised and allowed to fall upon the cloth immersed in a large vat of water. It is said that when business was slack, the owner of such a fulling mill took in the washing of his neighbors. In the days of such strong household activity, however, such a proceeding would have been very improbable. It is unlikely that there was any such early anticipation of the modern steam laundry. It is not to be inferred that the fulling of cloth by power was accepted without a struggle. A little before 1300 an ordinance of the fullers of London was given official sanction to the effect that no fullers, dyers, or weavers of London should send their cloths out of the City to be fulled by mills in place of having the work done "under feet," or as we should say "by hand," within the City walls.[4] Gradually, however, in England and on the Continent generally, the new method gained headway, because it was a labor-saving device. As such it also was early accepted in America. Wherever the wholesale handicraft system dominated the woolen industry, we find the merchant capitalist or the industrial capitalist relying upon the fulling mill.

In a little town in western Massachusetts, as I know from some account books of the year 1822–23 in my possession, a fulling mill was used not only for fulling

A RICE MILL IN SOUTH CAROLINA, EARLY NINETEENTH CENTURY

Explanations of the Machine: A. The Windlass for raising the Flood Gate. B. Holes for a Pin by which the Windlass & Flood Gate are secured. C. The main driving Cog Wheel fixed on the Water wheel shaft. D. A large Wheel revolving on the same Axle with the small Wheel Y. E. A Small Lanthorn Wheel impelled by the large Cog Wheel D. F. Mill Stones. G. Hopper. H. Funnel through which the rough Rice falls from the Loft. I. Funnel from the Mill Stones discharging into the Wind-fan Hopper. L. A strap (worked by a Crank) for moving a riddle within the Fan. M. Hulls or Chaff passing through the Door. N. The Hulled rice discharging from the Wind-Fan into the Bin O. P. A Cog Wheel Moving the Axle S. Q. The Pestles. R. The Mortars. TT. Two Moveable Beams supporting the Axle S. U. End of the Cross Beam into which the Screw K. plays, and also supports the long moveable Beam VV. on which the upper Mill Stone rests raised at pleasure by Screw K. W. A Band which works the Pulley of the Wind-Fan. X. A long cross beam connecting the Beating & grinding Parts.

but for scouring, dressing, and dyeing. Sometimes the fuller sold logwood, Nicaraguawood, and alum used by the neighbors who did their own dyeing. In payment for the work done, the owner of the fulling mill received cider brandy, turnips, rye, beef, veal, pork, butter, sheepskin, and, of course, some cash. His labor was sometimes paid for by the services of his customers in repairing shoes for him and his family, in tailoring, and in threshing. He and his men were also employed in the building of houses for neighbors. Here was a complicated interdependence for goods and services, the center of which was the fulling mill.

It is worth pointing out that the fulling mill was used to full leather, that is, to make it soft and pliable. The scutching mill played a similar part in the linen industry. Comparable machinery was used for crushing bark for tanning and for beating clay used in the making of porcelain in China,[5] and for the hulling and cleaning of rice.

At least as early as the late Middle Ages in Europe water power was applied to the sawing of wood. The first sawmills were, of course, very crude affairs. A water wheel was made, by means of a crank, to pull down a sash saw which was then pulled up again by a sweep. In other words, a verticle saw was made to go up and down, somewhat after the fashion of a bucksaw. A log was brought to the saw on a carriage propelled by a heavy weight or by a cog wheel attached to the water-wheel shaft.[6] Very early this kind of mill was introduced into America. Indeed John Winthrop was given a subsidy to help him with his sawmill. Apparently both water and wind power were used. But it seems that there was less success with the hard woods than with the soft.

The paper mill both in Pennsylvania and in Massachusetts was an important part of colonial and early national industrial development. The rags were macerated by rollers and knives which were driven by water power. The pulp was then put through all the other processes by hand.

In some respects the iron mills are the most important of all. They made the metal and the parts that were of increasing importance for the making of all machinery. They integrated various processes after the manner of a factory. And later, in the works of Boulton and Watt, for instance, was made the steam engine that played such an important part in the growth of the factory. But still, the factory did not get its start in the iron industry, nor did it wait for the steam engine.

Power was used in the early iron industry in two principal ways. It was made to drive a bellows which blew air into the fire which smelted the ore (or reheated iron for later treatment). In the ore furnace there was a hearth and stack, in connection with which air was blown into the heated ore sometimes mixed with limestone flux. The output was used for pots and kettles and the like, and also for making pigs later to be heated for further fashioning. The bloomery performed a similar function but was little more than an open forge. Both of these used charcoal and accordingly gradually ate up the local supply of wood. The forge was sometimes worked by a water-power bellows, the output (in the form of pigs) being hammered upon an anvil until the desired bars or rods were produced.

Besides the power bellows there was the rolling and slitting of iron and the grinding of tools by power. When the iron bars were rolled thin they were slit by shears into small bits to be fashioned into nails.[7] Often we find a furnace, a forge, and a slitting mill, belonging to one

INTERIOR OF A MILL FOR SHARPENING AND POLISHING ARMOR ABOUT 1570

firm, situated on different water-falls in the same district. Of course, when several of these processes were integrated to turn out a finished or semi-finished product, when various small specialized mills were harnessed to a single water power, and when discipline and the division of labor were introduced, we have a factory in all essentials. But such a factory was not to assume leadership. An early illustration of some of the features of a well-developed mill appears on the opposite page.

It seems, as we look back into the part played by mills, that the mill stood as the embodiment of an idea of capital importance. This was the application of power machinery to industrial purposes. That it would have developed into a factory and led the way through an industrial revolution is not impossible nor yet improbable. But the fact is that it assumed no such general leadership. The mill had been the handmaid of industrial change: it was not destined to become the mistress. The factory developed in the textile industry, but it was in the manufacture of cottons rather than woolens. And the factory was introduced for the spinning of yarn and not for fulling or any allied process. Had there been as widespread a demand for flour and for standard iron products in the metropolitan trade of the early Modern Period as there was for cloth, the mill might have assumed leadership. But, in truth, it was not far behind. The use of "mill" for "factory" is no accident; it is indicative of a similarity, but not proof of a general filiation.

By some the mill is given a very definite place in industrial evolution. It is put after the tool and before the factory by one writer.[8] By others the mill stage is placed right after the handicraft.[9] And to some the mill is about the same as the factory, as our common use of the term today indicates. The position taken here, however, is that the mill does not constitute a stage at all. It is found alike in all of the first three stages. The lord's grist mill grinds for the lord's use, and for the benefit of tenants under the usufacture system. The fulling mill fulls cloth for the retail handicraftsman, and for the small master or the merchant and entrepreneur under the wholesale handicraft. In all probability it came into its own in the last-named stage as a separate part of the cloth industry, highly specialized and widely used. With the old mill went no very efficient machinery and with it we can identify no very large output. It was a labor-saving device but not on a large scale. It could be adapted to all of the early stages of industry. It might become a part of each stage but not the essential of any. The mill might be an incipient factory as in the case of early modern iron, lumber, and paper mills. The difference was largely of degree rather than of kind. The mill had less efficient power machinery, less division of labor and discipline, and a narrower market. In other words, these early modern mills are to be regarded as factories in the making.

NOTES TO CHAPTER VI

1. A. P. Usher, *A History of Mechanical Inventions* (1929), p. 231.

2. See, for example, F. W. Maitland, *The Court Baron* (Seldon Society, 1891), p. 123; Richard Bennett and John Elton, *History of Corn Milling*, vol. iii (1900), pp. 202 ff.

3. See C. B. Kulhmann, *The Development of the Flour-Milling Industry in the United States* (1929), pp. 96–99.

4. *Liber Custumarum* (Rolls Series), vol. ii, pt. i (1860), pp. 128–129.

5. See figure 2, plate xlii, in A. Brongniart, *Traité des Arts Ceramiques ou des Poteries* (Paris, 1854).

6. See V. S. Clark, *History of Manufactures in the United States, 1607–1860* (1929), pp. 174–177.

7. *Ibid.*, pp. 172–177.

8. D. H. Macgregor, *The Evolution of Industry* (n. d.), pp. 22–23.

9. Cf. G. Brodnitz, "Betriebskonzentration und Kleinbetrieb in der Englishen Industrie," *Jahrbücher für Nationalökonomie*, 3rd series, vol. xxxvii (1909), p. 178 (quoting Cooke-Taylor); V. S. Clark, *History of Manufactures in the United States, 1607–1860*, pp. 445–448 (stages set forth are: homespun, household and shop, mill and furnace, and factory).

CHAPTER VII

FOURTH STAGE: CENTRALIZED MANUFACTURE
THE CENTRAL WORKSHOP

AS THE inter-urban marketing increased in intensity, or later as metropolitan economy supplanted town economy, there arose a strong impetus on the part of merchants to get control of the process of manufacture. This was partly to produce such goods as the merchants knew they could sell and partly to have these goods ready when wanted. As we have seen, one way to meet this situation was to set up or encourage the dependent type of wholesale handicraft. Another method was to establish centralized manufacture, for, if the first should not prove wholly satisfactory on trial, the latter might then be adopted.

Centralized manufacture is done in large establishments in which many workmen labor under the direction of a single individual or firm, whose products are sold chiefly by wholesale. The first phase of development may be called the central workshop, the second the factory. The failure to distinguish between these two phases leads to a misunderstanding of some of the essentials of modern industry.

The central workshop was historically an establishment into which artisans hitherto working in their own homes or shops were invited or driven to labor under a single management. In ancient times it was easy enough to drive the slaves into such a workshop; in modern times the workers had to be induced by substantial gains, probably in the form of a greater yearly income or wage or more continuous employment. Large numbers of men and women were not rounded up because of any advantage in a large firm's ability to buy and use power machinery, for such machinery was not in use in this phase. It was partly for purposes of discipline, so that the workers could be effectively controlled under the supervision of foremen. Under one roof, or within narrow compass, they could be started to work at sunrise and kept going till sunset, barring periods for rest and refreshment. They could be kept working six days a week. And under the penalty of loss of all employment they could be kept going almost throughout the year. Under the new régime there was, at least at first, no time for fishing or hunting. There was no let-up in industrial activities in favor of field or garden. The goods were to be turned out just so fast and continuously. The employer could then make contracts to deliver goods at definite times and he could be certain to keep his word. Unfortunately he generally felt little or no obligation to his workpeople to keep them employed in slack seasons, even though they might have given up their other means of support to enter his workshop. Discipline, then, was to produce the goods on time. It was also to prevent the workmen from stealing raw materials, putting in shoddy, or otherwise getting the better of the employer.

A second advantage that the central workshop possessed, in varying degrees, over earlier forms of industry, lay in the division of labor. There were workmen on the one hand and foremen on the other. Some men did one kind of work, while others were put to something else. In time, considerable specialized skill would arise. Thus, partly through the division of labor and partly through discipline, the new form of industry could compete successfully with the old.

It has already been stated that genetically the central workshop was as old as the well-developed town and incipient metropolitan economy. Historically it probably dates from ancient Egypt, without, however, having a continuous existence. Probably Appolonius, the king's agent, owned such a workshop in the third century B.C., in which girls, free or servile, manufactured woolen cloth for their employer or master.[1] In so far as the temple workshops of Egypt and Babylonia produced goods for sale, they may be regarded as belonging to this stage, though their original purpose was usufacture, or the making of goods for the use of the temple inmates. In Greek history there are apparently many instances of central workshops, one of which may be mentioned. The father of Demosthenes had two such workshops about 377 B.C., one with thirty-two or thirty-three slaves, manufacturing weapons, the other with twenty slaves making sofas or bedsteads. Demosthenes sought an accounting of his father's goods: he demanded to know what had become of the stocks of raw material, ivory, iron, and wood which his father had been accustomed to sell in the raw state and also to make up into finished products.[2] The largest workshop known in ancient Greece, it is said, was established at Piraeus to make shields. At one time (404 B.C.) it employed 120 slaves. In these workshops the masters with their foremen must have had complete control over their workmen, since the latter were slaves. In the Roman Republic there were large potteries, clearly examples of central workshops. One firm had forty designers; a second and a third had twenty each. Every one of these designers kept many other workmen supplied, so that in each of the three cases the total number of workers was in the hundreds.[3] In the days of the Empire, the Roman government established large central workshops for the manufacture of arms and armor.[4] In the western Empire there were seventeen imperial weaving shops, and one in the East. In these, silk and cloth of gold were made. A linen workshop existed in Ravenna in Italy and another in Vienne in Gaul. In all of these instances the workers were both free and slave, and enjoyed the privileges of a gild.[5]

In so far as the medieval monastic workshops manufactured beyond their needs, notably beer and wine, they may be regarded as examples, though not important examples, of central workshops. Perhaps in some Italian and Flemish towns in the Middle Ages, many examples of central workshops might be found in the textile industry, especially in the dyeing and the fulling branches of the industry. Attempts to set up such workshops, however, were sure to meet with opposition from small and medium-sized masters, sometimes sufficient to block the plan.

A workshop for the making of tapestry was set up in Paris in the sixteenth century by the family of dyers called the Gobelins. In 1662 it was taken over by the king of France as a royal establishment. Here were manufactured some of the most elaborate pieces of tapestry, comparable to the work of Flemish masters. This institution has come down to the present day as a workshop with many looms leisurely operated by master weavers receiving as state employees a yearly salary from the French government. It is an object of interest to lovers of art and to the curious tourists visiting the French capital. A central workshop for the manufacture of hosiery existed in Orleans in the eighteenth century. It is said to have employed 800 persons inside and double that number working in the country. Another workshop with 150 artisans made printed calico cloth.[6] In Alsace there were "primitive weaving sheds" in which the entrepreneurs kept many people working at hand looms.[7]

Peter the Great, of Russia, established large central workshops in which cloth was made for his soldiers' uniforms. At Meissen in Germany, where fine porcelain (Dresden ware) comparable to the work of the Chinese was made, about 700 workmen were employed in the middle of the eighteenth century. At various other centers within the Empire there were erected other large potteries of more or less distinction. A workshop at Sèvres, in Paris, was established to make fine porcelain similar to that of Meissen. Even in its earliest years (about 1750) we find that it had considerable division of labor, with its chiefs of departments, 2 molders, 5 throwers, 2 potters, 27 repairers (adding flowers, handles, and reliefs), 2 chemists, 17 painters, and 2 burnishers.[8] Although at a later date power machinery was used in this establishment,[9] at first it was only a central workshop, and a good illustration of that type of industry.

In modern England much was done to improve ceramic art by Josiah Wedgwood (1730–95). This remarkable man was potter, artist, chemist, philosopher, and business organizer. In one of his early plants there were three sheds, housing eight workmen. These men commonly went from one task to another with little or no thought of specialization. Later Wedgwood established division of labor against the wishes of his workmen. He imported his clays through Liverpool and maintained an agent in London for the sale of his products. He made a great variety of goods: tea services, plates, vases, pitchers, candlesticks, snuff boxes, and tiles for fireplaces. In early days wooden trenchers had been used as plates, and indeed are still in a few places. Then pewter became the common ware. Wedgwood helped to displace both of these with his products.[10] Another pottery was established near London, employing about 300 workers.[11]

One of the most interesting instances is partly historical and partly legendary. John Winchcombe, of Newbury, had a very large establishment in the early sixteenth century for the making of woolen cloth, from the preparation of the wool to the finishing of the cloth. He is said to have employed children sorting wool, 100 women carding it, 200 maidens spinning yarn, 200 men with the same number of boys weaving it, 20 fullers, 40 dyers, 80 rowers (they raised the nap), and 50 shearmen. Another workshop, established in a former monastery, is said to have employed 2,000 workers.[12]

In the United States, central workshops existed as they did in Europe. Particularly was this true in the eighteenth century. Many of these central workshops were called factories, while in reality they were just large workshops with a great number of workers, some division of labor, and considerable capital. From 1753 onwards, intermittently for several years, there was a Manufacturing House in Boston where linen was spun and woven, and where, at least for a while at first, young people were taught to spin at the government's expense. There is no indication of the existence of power machinery. And around both Boston and Philadelphia there were set up during the Revolutionary War and shortly afterwards numerous establishments for making textiles. Until the plan of Samuel Slater came into existence, these were probably all central workshops. The larger establishments that made metal wares, however, have some genuine claims to be regarded as incipient factories.

In Porto Rico, before the coming of the Americans, practically every woman could make her own clothes and even the adornments of her own trousseau.[13] Americans provided a market for what had been purely usufactory production. The lower-class women and girls soon learned to go to the residences of Americans to sell their lace and drawn-work, and upper-class women sent their servants. The wares offered were often very cheap, but the sizes were impracticable and the designs badly placed. Such faults led American women to give definite orders for certain kinds of goods, raw materials often being supplied. But other troubles arose. The Porto Rican women made mistakes, sometimes due to their own stupidity, sometimes to the poor command of Spanish on the part of the American women. The goods would sometimes be torn in stretching on the frames. Materials sometimes never came back. There was, moreover, a good deal of petty annoyance caused by the Porto Ricans coming back ever so often for small advances of wages, saying that they needed some money to buy candles for their saint. In order to avoid the evils connected with this system, some American women undertook to make it their business to organize the workers, regularly putting out the material and supervising the work. To the consumer in Porto Rico and to the rising class of exporters this was a very satisfactory development. But this wholesale handicraft system soon had the central workshop as its rival. For instance, one American woman who had gone into partnership with a firm in New York City rented a large house and insisted on all her helpers going there to work. She gave them morning coffee and noon dinner, thinking to make the work more attractive and to provide more nourishing food. But she had great difficulty in keeping her workers. They did not like to arrive at a certain hour nor did they want to work every day. Talking could not be prevented and downright hair-pullings sometimes occurred. The American woman stuck to her central workshop, nevertheless, and during the Great War, when handwork from Europe was not forthcoming, she found a very favorable market for her output in the United States.

Along with these examples should be placed such public workshops as the parish workhouses and the national workshops. The former were for setting to work the able-bodied poor who, if left to their own guidance, would beg for a living. Such workhouses have existed in England since 1576. The second type of workshop is illustrated by the ephemeral experiment made in France in 1848 to provide the unemployed with work.

From the standpoint of the way in which work was done, there have been at least two kinds of central workshops. In one type only handwork was performed. In the other, hand machines were used, among them the potter's wheel, the stocking frame, the spinning jenny, and the sewing machine (Howe's and Singer's). The hand machine was promising and helpful, but had been used, and continued to be used, in the older types of industry. It contained no such potentiality for large-scale production as did the power machinery which made the factory system possible.

The central workshop has been regarded as a moral danger. Strawplaiting was done in a central workshop in Kirkwall, Scotland, but, because of the bad effect on the morals of the girls and women employed, the workshop was discontinued in 1841 and the plaiting was henceforth done in the homes.[14] Probably the danger to health was greater than to morals, for the early workshops were in old monastic buildings and rough barracks—in the days before sanitary engineering. Probably the workers themselves feared the loss of personal freedom more than the loss of either good morals or good health.

The loss of personal freedom, though a private misfortune, was a public gain. The central workshop in the modern period did for discipline what slavery had accomplished in ancient times. Untamed man likes to hunt, fish, play, and idle, as well as work. He rebels at regularity. In the wholesale handicraft stage no merchant or industrial entrepreneur, as has been noted, could be certain either of quality or quantity of goods supplied him. The demand might be brisk, while the supply was scant. Consumers might stand shivering for cloth and clothing while the artisans were making hay or going fishing. Golden opportunities might arise in Europe for selling staple wares in large quantities—in India or America, great trading companies might be anxious to pay high prices for the goods, and whole fleets might be ready to carry them to their destination. With the workers right under the eyes of foremen all day long, there was now little chance of neglect of industrial labors. Coming together to work was a sure step toward organization. Unquestionably it aided, without creating, the modern trade-union movement. From our present-day point of view we must write down as one of the merits of the central workshop the fact that it brought industry one step nearer to the factory system.

Some primitive peoples have no word for time. Indeed man has taken a long while in arriving at any fine conception of time and in developing effective instruments for its measurement.[15] Industrial workers preceding the central workshop had been slow in work and deliberate in effort. This had its rich rewarding aspects, but it also meant waste. Artisans worked long hours but without economizing in the use of time. The central workshop with its strict discipline speeded up the work and put a limit to the amount of time spent. In other words there was introduced into the world a real time thrift, an effective utilization of the worker's energies. Under this system the twelve-hour day has been cut almost in half. Time became a measure of value like money. A commodity took so much time to make. That was exactly known and could be used to reckon the total cost. This is no place for an exegesis or a panegyric on the use of time. The importance of time measurement is evident when we recall that it is the basis of our great unorganized co-operation of intercourse in work and in play, in worship and in social concourse. Over three generations of men have been catching railroad trains according to schedule. Thousands arrive at 10 A.M. for the ocean steamer; more thousands are at the theater at 8 P.M., or at 9 P.M. listen to the president's message. The central workshop was the first large organization that enforced a regular attendance upon duties. If a woman missed early mass, she could attend a later one. If the family could not go to morning service, it could go at night. In the central workshop, however, there was one hour and there was a strong necessity for arriving on time. The present-day method of having the employees punch a ticket by means of a clock is the most exact way of bringing about the desired result. Of course, like so many beneficial innovations the emphasis upon doing things on time and quickly has had its unfortunate results. Business men extend the idea to many of their intellectual and artistic workers in an absurd fashion. Many of such workers rebel and leave. Keeping office hours clearly has no place in producing results in the realms of higher effort. The same idea of saving a minute has entered into the whole make-up of modern industrial nations. It has helped kill reflection and has been the death of real leisure.

It is probably true that centralization made more labor available for industry, partly by driving individuals to greater effort. In many cases this was all to good. For women and children, however, industrial gain involved social loss. While both women and children had labored in industry under the earlier forms, they had worked at home with periods of rest and variation. In a central workshop, however, and later in a factory, women and children like other workers were forced to labor long hours and without adequate rest or change of occupation.

We have come a long distance on the industrial road and yet we have had no near view of that form of industrial organization best known to us, the factory. This is the real and historic situation. That giant, clothed with the power of good and evil, came very late. It was the creation of the eighteenth century and the climax of thousands of years of evolution. Little need be said about it at this point, except that it was the central workshop with power machinery added. The power might be provided by horses, or derived from waterfalls, or generated by coal, gas, or electricity. A sequence of events, material and cultural, made the inventions possible. The accumulations of capital in successful commerce, partly in goods manufactured in the stages of industry just described, were turned into factory production and came sufficiently early to give the movement a revolutionary career.

The question of continuity arises in the midst of our scattered illustrations. There are at least three ways in which industrial evolution may have been continuous: in individual establishments, in particular kinds of industries, and in just the general flow of industrial effort.

Within the individual plant there was doubtless some continuity. Peasants making wares for their own use would often develop into retail handicraftsmen; and the same family of retail handicraftsmen might enter the wholesale handicraft system either as masters or men. But probably in most cases there was no continuity within establishments. The reason for this is that it is in the very nature of competition that those who held to the old type or stage of manufacture should go down to defeat, while those who took on the new and promising form should succeed.

Continuity is to be expected, and is found, more within industries than within firms or individuals. The boot and shoe industry, the manufacture of textiles, and the making of clothing have all gone through the four stages here outlined. On the other hand, the mill industries have generally skipped the central workshop, as have the newest industries. Some of the newest manufactures have never experienced the central workshop, because when introduced they could be more appropriately carried on in factory form. Others, however, could never have been established if the central workshop had been the prevalent form. We need only two illustrations of this—the automobile and the airplane industries.

But there is another continuity of greater importance. There is a general evolution of industry which, while working through individual firms and particular industries, is larger than either. There are ways of doing things that are bigger than any individual effort or the habits of any particular industry. Experience teaches that opportunity lies in selling, and selling directly, to a consumer. Or, it shows the advantage of indirect or wholesale dealing. Middlemen see an advantage in buying up goods from small masters. Then they find that they can profit more—and society can gain more—if they become industrial entrepreneurs. Accordingly they reduce the independent small masters to a class of dependent workers. Then these entrepreneurs find it better to drive the workers into a central workshop. Finally they produce more and better goods by using power machinery. Such becomes the lore of industry, the accepted or improved method of doing things. Existing conditions have put the new stage to a test and the new stage has answered the test successfully, whilst the old form of industry has not.

NOTES TO CHAPTER VII

1. M. Rostovtzeff, *A large Estate in Egypt in the Third Century* B.C.: *A Study in Economic History* (1922), pp. 115–116. There is at least reasonable doubt whether the workers in question were working in their homes or in a central workshop, though the author inclines to the latter (so-called "factory").

2. *The Orations of Demosthenes* (Bohn's Classical Library, trans. by C. R. Kennedy, 1901), pp. 95, 98–99, 101; H. Francotte, *L'industrie dans la Grèce ancienne*, vol. i (1900), p. 227; G. Glotz, *Le travail dans la Grèce ancienne* (1920), p. 319.

3. See T. Frank, *An Economic History of Rome* (1920), p. 168.

4. *Ibid.*, p. 181.

5. J. P. Waltzing, *Les Corporations professionelles chez les Romains*, vol. ii (1896), p. 233.

6. E. Levasseur, *Histoire des classes ouvrières et de l'industrie en France avant 1789*, vol. ii (1859, 1901), p. 766.

7. J. H. Clapham, *Economic Development of France and Germany, 1815–1914* (1921), p. 65.

8. E. S. Auscher, *A History and Description of French Porcelain* (trans. by W. Burton, London, 1905), p. 44.

9. Taxile Doat, *Grand feu ceramics* (1903, trans. by S. E. Robineau, 1905), p. 51.

10. E. Meteyard, *The Life of Josiah Wedgwood*, vol. i (1865), pp. 80–81, 99, 259–261, 370, 470.

11. Article on Ceramics in the *Encyclopædia Britannica* (11th ed.).

12. E. Lipson, *The History of the English Woollen and Worsted Industries* (1921), pp. 46–48.

13. The details of the situation here described were supplied by a mature American woman in 1919.

14. W. R. Scott, *Report . . . on Home Industries in the Highlands and Islands* (1914), pp. 23, 179.

15. After the sundial came the hourglass and then the water clock. The mechanical clock was built for the larger churches and royal palaces in the early fourteenth century. Clocks became fairly common for household use in the eighteenth and early nineteenth centuries and watches only in the nineteenth century. The development of centralized industry not only established a popular demand for clock and watch but it made their cheapening possible. On the subject of clocks, see A. P. Usher, *A History of Mechanical Inventions* (1929), chs. vi and x.

CHAPTER VIII

THE INDUSTRIAL REVOLUTION IN ENGLAND
THE FACTORY IN THE TEXTILE INDUSTRY

IN THE whole recorded part of industrial history there has apparently occurred but one great break in evolutionary development. That break is called the Industrial Revolution,[1] which every school boy is taught should be placed in importance alongside of the Fall of Rome, the Reformation, and the French Revolution. The phrase Industrial Revolution means primarily the sharp industrial change that occurred about 1770–1825 in England. During this period power machinery came to be applied to manufacturing on a large scale. Whereas in times past it had been sporadic and ephemeral, or very limited in application as in the case of the mill, it now became the paramount factor in manufacture. The term Industrial Revolution is sometimes used to include the whole congeries of changes that came about in the period in question.[2] By some it is taken to be a great change in industrial organization which has continued down to the war of 1914–18.[3] Occasionally the term is applied to the struggles and attainments of the laboring class.[4] There is virtue in the chaster use of the phrase which arose not later than 1827[5] as an adequate summary of the rapid, far-reaching changes taking place. Later the term was used by Engels, Marx, Toynbee, and others.

Before considering the inventions that were made or developed and applied in the period 1770–1825, we must note the earlier mechanical improvements and discoveries. A mill for the throwing of silk was set up on the Derwent River at Derby in 1719. The ideas and designs for the machines had been surreptitiously secured in Italy; but the capital was English, provided by Thomas Lombe, a London mercer. Later both wealth and knighthood came to the sponsor of the new undertaking. In 1729 it was said that there was but "one Water Engine for throwing Silk in the Kingdom."[6] In 1777 this factory and an adjoining one were said to employ about 200 persons, male and female, adults and children.[7] This silk mill has been called the first factory in England;[8] almost certainly it was the first textile factory in England. Of course this instance throws us back to Italy as the possible fatherland of the silk factory; certainly as early as 1607 Italy had elaborate power machinery for the twisting and winding of silk thread.[9] In 1341 a silk manufacturer in Bologna, whose family had migrated from Lucca about 1272, received permission to set up a silk mill in a house on a canal in Bologna. This looks like a water mill for throwing silk. In 1330 and 1335 there seem to have been machines in Lucca that were so elaborate that they could have been driven only by horse or water power.[10] As far as England is concerned, however, silk was not nearly so important as cotton in the development of the factory system.

The rôle of effective pioneer in the Industrial Revolution has rightly been assigned to the spinning of cotton. About this there seems to be no disagreement. There are at least four divergent explanations, however, as to why this should have been the case. First, we might think that it was merely a logical step to take from the throwing of silk to the spinning of cotton. Indeed the silk industry was long prized as the touchstone of industrial progress. All aspiring nations sought to develop it. Although this was true in a general way, there is no clear evidence that the mechanical improvements in silk manufacture suggested similar developments in the other textiles. Indeed the cotton-spinning mechanisms seem to have been pure effusions, fresh upwellings from the experiences of sundry scattered workers. Secondly, it is commonly held that weavers were demanding more yarn than they could get. The invention of the flying shuttle by John Kay—of the gentle feminine countenance—not only made possible the more economical manufacture of wide cloth but accentuated the demand for yarn.[11] There can be little question that both parts of this statement are correct; but doubt has been rightly thrown upon the efficacy of the new influence.[12] Kay's invention was made in 1733 and must have taken some time to make itself felt. In that same year John Wyatt probably invented his promising, but imperfect, spinning machine. Accordingly we may conclude that while the demand for more cotton thread lay at the bottom of the impetus to invent, Kay's flying shuttle had little or no effect upon the early stages of invention. The third view is that the spinning of ordinary cotton yarn, much in demand, was obviously a simple thing to do mechanically.[13] Untrained weavers and other artisans undertook to invent an apparatus without any instruction and without prizes being offered for spinning machines. A fourth explanation is here suggested that it was the conjunction of the growing demand for yarn and the developing knowledge of, and faith in, mechanics. The latter had been slowly making headway since the twelfth century but in the seventeenth gained an unprecedented impetus.

The demand for cotton yarn and cotton cloth needs some explanation. The ancient western European textiles were woolens and linens. To be sure, during the twelfth and following centuries, silk had probably come through Italy from the East. In the period about 1300–1600 some cotton cloth was probably made from cotton fiber imported from the Near East. According to one view, some workers in cotton cloth left Flanders for England after the capture of Antwerp (1585) by the Spaniards.[14] But it is more likely that England at least got its suggestion for the making of cottons from the importations of calicoes by the East India Company which had been chartered in 1600. Just why the industry became localized in and around Manchester in northern England is not easy to explain, unless it be that in those parts gild monopoly and vested rights were not lodged in the hands of the makers of linens and woolens. Of course the moist climate of Lancashire is a standing invitation for the development of a textile industry.

When the cotton cloth of India began to threaten the native industries of England, protests were made. Pamphlets were printed and a petition was presented to parliament in 1680 against cottons made in India. In 1700 importation was forbidden by statute and in 1721 even the purchase and sale as well as the general use of Indian cottons were prohibited. The effect of these laws was not so much the exclusion of Indian calicoes as the encouragement of the manufacture of similar wares in England. At first these were made of cotton and linen yarn combined, later of cotton only. Some of the cotton thread was imported from India and some was made in England out of cotton fiber from the Near East. Here then we have the demand for cotton yarn that lay behind the demand for spinning machines. At first the cotton industry in England was developed in the independent form of the wholesale handicraft system, but by about 1740 it had passed on to the dependent form.[15]

There is a whole chapter relating to the invention of Wyatt's spinning machine, its improvements and straggling existence during the period about 1740–64. Both the machine itself and the business men behind its use were inefficient. The historic and effective beginning of spinning by power machinery centers in Arkwright's water-frame invented about 1767 and patented two years later. This spinning machine, driven by water power, was not very much better than Wyatt's, but Arkwright knew how to make a business success of his venture. Not an inventor himself, he had the ability to use inventors. Not a capitalist himself, he knew how to enlist the interest of capitalists. In other words this gross-lipped, pot-bellied barber, wigmaker, and horse-dealer was a man of business of rare parts. It would not be very extravagant to hold that he was one of the world's greatest manufacturers in his ability to solve all the problems of business policy as they arose. Although he was not the father of the first factory he was the father of the factory system.

Arkwright's own first factory, which was set up in Nottingham, apparently in 1770, used horse power. This factory was small and not very promising. In 1771 Arkwright established his second factory near Derby, after he had entered partnership with two successful hosiers, one of them Jedediah Strutt whose apprentice, Samuel Slater, was later to carry the cotton industry to the United States. At first the output of the factory, run by water power, was used for the manufacture of hosiery, but in 1773 Arkwright used the yarn for the manufacture of cotton cloth. This was the first purely cotton cloth made in England at least on a large scale and from cotton yarn spun in England.

Arkwright's water-frame spun cotton yarn very successfully but the yarn was coarse. Samuel Crompton, who invented the mule spinning machine about 1779, enabled English manufacturers to spin a strong fine yarn

A CRAFTSMAN PRINTING CALICO BY HAND,
EARLY NINETEENTH CENTURY

that could be used to make the finest calicoes. This machine was the result of four and a half years' work by a man who had had little or no experience as an inventor. Clearly his portrait shows him to have had a serious as well as a delicately chiselled face. The son of a yeoman and weaver, he knew the spinning jenny of Hargreaves at first hand. Indeed he indicated in calling his machine a mule that it was a cross between the spinning jenny and the water-frame. Hargreaves' spinning jenny had been invented in 1765 and patented in 1770. Being propelled by hand, it was used alike in the homes of workers in the wholesale handicraft system and in the central workshop. At last England was well on the road not only to spinning by power but to the spinning of the finest yarns by power. Invention followed invention until the industry reached an approximation to perfection. Unfortunately there came a time, and it is clearly seen today, when it was difficult to find a market for the whole of the output of the specialized spinning factories of northern England.

The cloth that was made out of machine-spun yarn was woven by hand until Edmund Cartwright's power loom was made available. Cartwright was a classical scholar and clergyman who had a keen interest in the material world about him. He saw clearly that the hand weavers could not use the whole supply of the developing spinning industry. In 1785 he had patented his own answer to the industry's needs, and soon he set up a small power weaving factory at Doncaster, in which animal power was used at first, then steam in 1789. Later he started a factory, in Manchester, which was burned by the mob. It seems that power looms had been invented in the seventeenth century, notably one at Danzig, for the making of ribbons, but had never come into wide use, at least partly because of the opposition of weavers.[16]

Power looms had now come to stay. By 1803 a power loom was made in England wholly of iron, to take the place of the wooden and iron machines in use heretofore. But the power loom did not take root so rapidly as the power spinning machines, particularly in the woolen industry. The woolen weavers clung tenaciously to their trade, accepting lower and lower wages under the wholesale handicraft system, until in the 1830's and 1840's the power loom won an all-but-complete victory. Of course, for the making of individual, or special, pieces of cloth and ribbon the hand loom is still used, but the amount of cloth woven in this way for sale in Europe is relatively slight.

When the factory came upon the scene, the workers divided, some entering it, some opposing it. And so with the masters who had operated under the systems of the wholesale handicraft and the central workshop. Those who entered the factory system such as Strutt, the hosier of Nottingham, and Gott, the clothier of Leeds,[17] transferred both business ability and commercial capital sorely needed by inventors such as Crompton and Cartwright. Soon there was greater production,[18] a lowering of prices, and increased exportation. At times not all the output of the factories could be sold. Crises came and went, killing off the badly managed factories.

One of the labor-saving inventions of the time was the cylindrical press for printing calicoes. In the year 1783, Thomas Bell, a Scotsman, succeeded in working out the new process, whilst others who were aiming at the same kind of device failed. Two years later the cylindrical press was put into operation in Lancashire, where specialized printing mills arose devoted solely to the printing of cottons. A man and a boy could print as much cotton with this machine (which was, of course, driven by power)

CALICO PRINTING BY POWER MACHINERY, EARLY NINETEENTH CENTURY as one hundred times their number using hand blocks.

The first power machines were commonly run by horses, but the chief general reliance in the late eighteenth century was upon water power. In water power the North of England was rich, as it also was in coal for steam engines. Steam engines had been commonly used for the pumping of water out of deep mines. The Newcomen engine of 1705 was fairly successful in this work in spite of the fact that it was a low-pressure engine, and was both wasteful and somewhat dangerous. It was while repairing a Newcomen engine belonging to the University of Glasgow that James Watt became interested in the possibilities of steam power. Watt was a maker and repairer of scientific instruments, who had gained some theoretical knowledge of physics from scientists at the University which he served. Indeed he was an engineer, a man whose beautiful eyes and magnificent forehead were offset by a pale skin and joyless mouth. While the first generation of inventors such as Wyatt, Hargreaves, Arkwright, Crompton, and Cartwright had been untrained in mechanics, Watt and his generation, which included Smeaton, Rennie, and Wilkinson, had considerable engineering knowledge and experience. Watt's original purpose was to make an engine which would be more economical in the use of steam. His first patent, taken out in 1769, was stated to be for that purpose. It was not until 1781 and 1782 that his patents of a rotative engine meant anything for industry. Even then, in 1782, Watt thought that his engine had little chance in competition with the powerful streams of northern England.[19] Indeed one of the early uses of the steam engine was to pump water which had fallen over the dam, back into the pond above the waterfall. This was as true of Newcomen's engine,[20] the predecessor of Watt's, as of Watt's own engine. Watt's partner,

Matthew Boulton, however, was too farsighted a business man to accept Watt's point of view.

The firm of Boulton and Watt, established in 1775 for twenty-five years, illustrates that happy form of partnership in which one man trusts the other and in which one supplements the other. Watt brought the inventor's ideas and zeal, while Boulton was the manager and capitalist. Boulton mortgaged his own lands, borrowed from friends, and negotiated loans from bankers. He marketed engines first in the copper mines of Cornwall and then in industrial plants. When he was not making much headway with the mine operators, he bought his way into the ownership of the mines. He built a flour mill at Southwark (London) to help demonstrate the use of the steam engine. The Boulton and Watt works, located in Soho, Birmingham, manufactured sundry metal products such as buttons, spurs, candlesticks, bells, and coffee pots. For a time the firm made only a few parts for the steam engine, notably valves and nozzles. The other parts were made at other similar works of which there were at least four in Britain, or they were made by the mechanics setting up the engine. In the period 1792–95 Boulton and Watt came to manufacture the whole engine and to install it complete. At first their income had been derived from their royalty on the patent and their profits from supplying the parts. In 1795, however, they abandoned the royalty charge in favor of one lump sum for the completed engine.

The Boulton and Watt works at Soho contained a forge, hearths, and foundry, as well as a machine shop and a carpenter shop. Perhaps the greatest difficulty was to find men of sufficient sobriety and skill to make their products. All the various difficulties were gradually overcome and the enterprise made a financial success.

It should be noted that the steam engine introduced a later phase in the Industrial Revolution. Factories got their start and carried on without steam. Indeed in the first 10 years of Boulton and Watt's existence only 66 engines were installed with a total horsepower of 1,238. Of these 66 engines, about 22 were for copper mines and 5 for collieries; 17 for foundries and forges and 7 for water works; while 2 were for flour mills and 2 for cotton factories. But in the next decade few, if any, were erected in copper mines and 47 were set up in cotton factories. By 1800 there had been 84 Boulton and Watt engines installed in Britain,[21] and a few other machines by imitators who had violated Watt's patent.

Although it is true that the steam engine played no part in the first phase of the Industrial Revolution, it is an outstanding fact that in the second phase its influence was tremendous. The steam engine provided a continuous supply of power, whilst the old water wheel had worked well only when the water was high in the river or in the mill pond. It enabled the manufacturer to set up his plant in cities where there was a labor supply or a market for the products, or in fact anywhere that promised opportunities quite apart from water power. Moreover, in providing a greater amount of power, the steam engine aided in the centralization of manufacture in a single plant, in the increase in the size of the plant, and ultimately in the integration of processes.

The Industrial Revolution was a hard fact by 1800 in the cotton and iron industries. Later, the changes it stood for were adopted in the woolen and linen industries, and later still in the manufacture of boots and shoes, the making of clothing, and even the manufacture of silverware, to say nothing of such very recent conquests as cigarettes and cigars.

The Industrial Revolution extended not only to other products but to other countries. To America, to Switzerland, to Belgium, and elsewhere went English ideas and English workmen. In 1833 a Glasgow cotton spinner and power-loom weaver said that "we find now in all the foreign markets a competition in our stouter fabrics, particularly from the American manufacturers." Continental countries, he pointed out, were beginning to supply their own markets but not the overseas market.[22] The rest of the story is detailed, how the tide of machinery driven by power gradually covered all the favorable spots of the earth as far as Japan and eastern China.

The immediate outstanding result of the Industrial Revolution was to enable Britain to wage, almost single handed, a long and bitter war against France and most of the rest of Europe fighting for the dominance of Napoleon and also against America which thought it was fighting for freedom of the seas. In this great struggle there were many factors, but hardly any more important than the Industrial Revolution, which gave to Britain a greater command over her own resources and over the resources of the western and southern seas. If France had experienced an industrial revolution in the eighteenth century, it might never have had a political and social revolution. Or, if it had had both, and with them the ambitions of a Napoleon, it would possibly have conquered the whole world of civilized peoples. Such a vitally important difference between the industrial developments of the two countries is a fit subject for reflection.

France probably had more men working in central workshops, notably in silk works and potteries, than England had. France probably was almost as inventive in hand looms as England was. The French had a finer technique in toolmaking than the English possessed.

In spite of all this, France did not experience the revolutionary changes in industry that came to England, though a fair promise of such was finally to come in the period 1825–60. This failure to become industrial was not because the French were less inventive. It was not because the French lacked coal and usable iron. The explanation lies rather in the fact that the French genius lay, and still lies, in the direction of luxury goods which do not lend themselves to power machinery so readily as do the staple wares of England. The loss of Canada in 1763 and other dominions at other times merely accentuated this one tendency. Whether France is endowed by nature with a feeling for form and color and an aversion to repetition and standardization is difficult to state. Certainly the development of the silk industry, especially at Lyon from the fifteenth century onward, has tended to increase the flair for fine workmanship. There are some who, forgetting the Frankish and Celtic parts, maintain that France is Latin and therefore artistic by inheritance. These hold that France is not only far from experiencing an industrial revolution now—following the Great War with its acquisitions of raw materials—but never will experience such a revolution. Whether France's predisposition to high craftsmanship and individual workmanship is due to biological or social inheritances is not easy to determine. The fact is clear enough; and, if the source is biological, it will hardly ever be changed.

NOTES TO CHAPTER VIII

1. On this subject, see the following works: T. S. Ashton, *Iron and Steel in the Industrial Revolution* (1924); S. Chapman, *The Lancashire Cotton Industry, a Study in Economic Development* (1904); W. Cunningham, *Growth of English Industry and Commerce*, vol. ii, pt. i (1903); G. W. Daniels, *The Early English Cotton Industry, with some unpublished Letters of Samuel Crompton* (1920); W. Felkin, *History of the Machine Wrought Hosiery and Lace Manufactures* (1867); H. Heaton, *The Yorkshire Woollen and Worsted Industries from the Earliest Times up to the Industrial Revolution* (1920); R. H. Thurston, *History of the Growth of the Steam Engine* (1878); G. Unwin, "Transition to the Factory System," *English Historical Review*, vol. xxxvi (1922), pp. 206–218 and 383–397.

Professor Edwin F. Gay is engaged in the preparation of a volume dealing with the background and essentials of the Industrial Revolution. Among the contributions he will make is a statistical comparison of English and French trade in the eighteenth century and the elucidation of the factor of demand in the Revolution. He will emphasize, in the progress from one stage of industry to another, the part played by the need for the production of goods on time.

2. See A. Jones, *The Industrial Revolution* (n. d.).

3. A. P. Usher, *An Industrial History of England* (1920), p. 275.

4. See, for example, *The New Industrial Revolution and Wages* (1929) by W. Jett Lauck.

5. See Anna Bezanson, "The Early Use of the Term Industrial Revolution," *Quarterly Journal of Economics*, vol. xxxvi (1922), pp. 343–349.

6. Joshua Gee, *The Trade and Navigation of Great Britain* (1729), p. 92.

7. W. Bray, "Sketch of a Tour into Derbyshire and Yorkshire," in *Voyages and Travels* (1777, ed. by J. Pinkerton, 1810), vol. ii, p. 371.

8. R. W. Cooke-Taylor, *Introduction to a History of the Factory System* (1886), p. 363.

9. See Vittorio Zonca, *Novo Teatro di Machine et Edificii* (Padua, 1607), pp. 68–75.

10. See Florence Edler, The Silk Trade of Lucca during the Thirteenth and Fourteenth Centuries (Ph. D. thesis, University of Chicago, 1930), p. 178, quoting Giovanni Livi in *Archivio storico Italiano*, series 4, vol. vii (1881), pp. 51–52. See also *Atti della R. Academia Lucchese*, vol. xv (1854), p. 54.

11. See Paul Mantoux, *The Industrial Revolution in the Eighteenth Century* (1906, 1928), p. 211.

12. See A. P. Usher, *A History of Mechanical Inventions* (1929), p. 262.

13. *Ibid.*

14. This is the view of Schulze-Gävernitz as referred to in Paul Mantoux, *op. cit.*, p. 202.

15. See Paul Mantoux, *op. cit.*, pp. 208–209.

16. *Ibid.*, p. 245.

17. See Herbert Heaton, "Benjamin Gott and the Anglo-American Cloth Trade," *Journal of Economic and Business History*, vol. ii (1929–30), p. 148.

18. Manufacture of printed cottons in England (by yards):

1796	21 millions
1800	33 "
1814	125 "
1830	347 "

G. R. Porter, *Progress of the Nation* (ed. by F. W. Hirst, 1912), p. 305.

19. See Samuel Smiles, *Lives of the Engineers*, vol. iv (1865), p. 327.

20. See T. S. Ashton, *Iron and Steel in the Industrial Revolution* (1924), p. 99.

21. See John Lord, *Capital and Steam-Power*, 1750–1800 (1923), p. 175.

22. *Minutes of Evidence before Select Committee on Manufactures, Commerce, and Shipping*, vol. vi (London, 1833), p. 321.

CHAPTER IX

THE INDUSTRIAL REVOLUTION IN NEW ENGLAND: THE MANUFACTURE OF COTTONS

THE textile industry, particularly the woolen branch, went through the same stages in the United States as in Britain; but, as has so generally happened in the development of European economic institutions and habits in America, the middle stages were not so well developed as the first and last. Usufacture lasted long, particularly in isolated parts, and the centralized industry soon became overtowering, once it got a start. It was in the manufacture of cotton, however, that centralized industry made its most dramatic conquests and assumed factory leadership.

There is considerable uncertainty about the nature of the industrial establishments in the period 1775–89. In Philadelphia a manufactory was set up in 1775 for making cotton and other yarn. Hand jennies were used for spinning, but horse power is thought to have been used to run some machines. The building was burned in 1790. In Beverly, Massachusetts, a more pretentious plant was started in 1787 for the carding, spinning, and weaving of cotton. It employed one carding machine, four jennies, and eleven looms. Two large horses are said to have supplied some of the power used. This business succumbed before 1813.[1]

Ambitious American merchants in Atlantic coast towns were anxious to organize the cotton industry at home along the lines developed in England. Particularly was this the case after independence had been secured. Almy and Brown were prosperous partners in the coast and foreign trade centering in Providence, Rhode Island. They had behind them the rich Quaker, Moses Brown, kinsman of the second partner, who was himself particularly interested in manufacture. The firm of Almy and Brown had a central workshop, apparently in Pawtucket, a village near Providence, in which cotton was carded and spun by hand machines.[2] These did not work well, but they did produce yarn. Out of this yarn cloth was woven by artisans working in their homes. Without good yarn there could be no satisfactory cloth. Under the leadership of Moses Brown the firm of Almy and Brown sought to establish a plant in which spinning would be done by the water-frame, that is, by power machinery. Advertisements were placed in American newspapers, to enlist the aid of mechanics who knew the art of water spinning. No promising person appeared until Samuel Slater arrived.

Slater had learned a great deal about the different branches of work in a spinning factory while apprenticed to the partner of Sir Richard Arkwright. Reading of the offers of American merchants and being ambitious of becoming something more than a factory operative, he left home for America in 1789. Because of the strict laws of England against the export of machinery, he could carry only plans; and doubtless they were in his head and there only. In order to ensure getting away safely, he dressed as a farm laborer. In this guise the young Prometheus stole the sacred fire of England's Industrial Revolution.

Once in America Samuel Slater soon came into contact with Moses Brown towards the close of 1789. Next year a partnership was formed under the name of Almy, Brown, and Slater. William Almy, Smith Brown, and Samuel Slater were to spin cotton by means of water power. Slater was to supply the technical knowledge of manufacture, supervise the construction of the necessary machinery, superintend the work, possess one half the assets, and receive one half of the net profits. Almy and Brown were to provide the necessary capital on their account and were to advance the half needed on Slater's account. Slater was to repay with interest his share of the advances made toward the construction and operation of the factory. Almy and Brown were to have the sole right of marketing the yarn made.[3]

The general plan was a good one. All depended upon the ability of Slater to construct the machines and supervise their operation. He employed a local carpenter and a blacksmith (later to be his father-in-law) to make the machines under his direction. Both of these were Quakers, as indeed was a third man who made the cards.[4] Clearly the stolen fire had come into the midst of Friends.

Soon roving and spinning were being done by power machinery. At first, however, the power was furnished by an old Negro, later by the waters of a river. Both of these deserve to have their names recorded. The Negro was Samuel Brunius Jenks, the father of power spinning in America. The river was the Blackstone, mother of many mills. The first workers were children who were taught by Slater himself for a while and then by another (in a Sunday School, said to have been the first in America). How typical the whole procedure was of the new régime! Knowledge was required, not skill. The expert was essential to construct and repair the machine; the operative could be quickly instructed in his part. The factory was soon in operation but it did not do quite all of the work connected with spinning, since the yarn had to be cleaned and whipped by outworkers laboring in their homes.

By at least June, 1791, the yarn from this first cotton factory, located at Pawtucket, was on sale in nearby towns in New England. It was at this point that the

MACHINERY FOR CARDING, DRAWING, ROVING, AND SPINNING, AS INTRODUCED BY SAMUEL SLATER IN RHODE ISLAND, 1790

commercial knowledge and connections of Almy and Brown played a vital part. This firm pushed the sale by methods which they knew to be effective. They offered credit for a period of about six months, but expected prompt payment when the time was up. Soon the yarn was being sold in the towns even on the Hudson. Offers of yarn to be sold on a commission of five per cent were made to facilitate marketing. By 1801 both storekeepers and industrial entrepreneurs from Portland to Philadelphia were buying the yarn. The industrial entrepreneurs were putting out the yarn to weavers under the dependent form of the wholesa'e handicraft system. The success attained was due not simply to good salesmanship but also to the excellence of the yarn that was spun. The reputation of the output soon became a vital factor in the situation. As it was the basis of the success of the Almy, Brown, and Slater partnership, so did it become the hope of an additional partnership.

In 1800 Slater entered into partnership with his father-in-law, Oziel Wilkinson, and two brothers-in-law to start a second factory, the White Mill, in competition with the original plant set up ten years before. Doubtless Slater had gained most of his capital from the first factory. Thus do we see the effusion of cap tal within the industry itself. Slater was superintendent of the factory, Wilkinson was doubtless the maker of the machinery, and the brothers-in-law probably managed the distribution of the products.

Confident in himself as Samuel Slater was, he knew that he had keen competitors. Anxious to keep ahead in technological processes, he persuaded his brother John to migrate in 1803. But first his brother was asked to visit Oldham and Manchester so as to be able to bring the latest information about cotton spinning. A new partnership was formed, Almy, Brown, and Slaters, the Slaters being

Samuel and John. Apparently each partner had one-fourth share. A third factory was established, this time at Slaterville, Rhode Island. It seems that John managed the mill, while Almy and Brown sold the output. Almy and Brown gave out some of the yarn to be woven under the dependent form of the wholesale handicraft system. As we learn from a letter of 1808, they much preferred to sell the yarn itself, however, and accordingly gave favorable terms of credit to weavers. The result would be to change the position of the weavers from the dependent to the independent form. Nevertheless, it is not to be implied that such weavers were the small single-handed loomsmen, but rather the independent masters who were ambitious of setting up many looms and employing a number of journeymen.

The Green Mill was started in Webster, Massachusetts, to spin cotton yarn, with Bela Tiffany as partner and manager, Samuel Slater being the innovator and capitalist. The same year a mill was set up nearby to spin woolen yarn. Later Slater bought shares in other mills, notably at Amoskeag Village, New Hampshire. In 1827 he and his partners erected his first steam mill—at Providence. In this port, coal could be secured by tidewater at low rates. Herein lay a suggestion that was later to bear fruit in the development of the textile industry at Fall River and New Bedford. The future really lay with steam rather than with water power.

We are much inclined to admire the technical abilities of Samuel Slater and to accept him as a business man of great ability. We cannot find so much to praise in his management of labor.[5] From 1790 to about 1831 the workmen and work children were largely old American stock, as we gather from the recurrence of such names as Green, Chase, and Learned. But beginning in 1831 such

Irish names appear in the Slater records as Ryan, Corcoran, and Callaghan. Not long afterwards French or French-Canadian names begin to appear. The labor seems to have been almost on a family basis. In 1813 we find four Reynolds, four Bensons, and five Howlands working for Slater. Frequently Jr. and Sr. appear after the names. The day was the sun's full allowance of twelve hours. The pay about 1817–19 was approximately one dollar a day for men and as little as fifty cents a week for children. Women often worked at a piece wage. To be sure, the cost of living was low, board and room being only two dollars a week for men.

So far, we have observed Samuel Slater at work spinning cotton yarn. It was his preference to specialize in spinning and allied processes. He put out yarn to weavers in town and county for manufacture into cloth. About half of the spinners in his factories also did some weaving for him. Finding many of the workmen of little skill and less inclination toward punctuality, he employed a subcontractor or agent to accept all responsibilities for outwork. Such a system seems to have been at its height about 1820–25. At this time scores of families were getting their living from Slater's industry, commonly receiving in payment orders for goods in his own stores. Such a system prevailed in England where Slater had learned his trade. Slater took the obvious next step and introduced the power loom in 1829, at about the same time as that loom was making headway in England. Indeed in Slater we see a bit of Old England transplanted to New England.

The extension of cotton growing in the South and the use of Whitney's cotton gin, invented in 1793, provided Slater's mills with plenty of cotton. The fame of his yarn and the financial success of his ventures led to the establishment of many other plants such as his, in Rhode Island

and in that part of Massachusetts just to the north. A very different sort of competition, however, came into being through the activities of certain Boston capitalists who had made their fortunes very largely in foreign trade. Among these were P. J. Jackson, Nathan Appleton, Israel Thorndike, Jr., and Francis C. Lowell. They formed the Boston Manufacturing Company which in 1814 set up a mill in Waltham on the Charles River. The basis of their plans was the water loom invented by Lowell.[6] How much Lowell owed to Crompton's loom is hard to learn. Certainly Lowell had been in Britain in 1811.[7] Apparently his loom was a distinct improvement over the English machines. Besides weaving its own cloth, the Company found it profitable to spin its own yarn. In fact, the Boston Manufacturing Company should be remembered for the combination of all processes in one establishment.

It soon became clear that the future of the Boston Manufacturing Company was limited by the small amount of water power available on the Charles. Accordingly, some of the shareholders and directors formed a new concern called the Merrimack Manufacturing Company, which set up its factory at what is now Lowell, where power was abundant as the Merrimac tumbled with its load of waters toward the sea. On the payment of $15,000 the new Company received from the Boston Manufacturing Company in 1822 permission to use the same type of machinery, patented or unpatented, present or future, as was used on the Charles, the right to use patterns, and the privilege of inspecting the Waltham plant and calling upon the engineer of the Boston Company when needed.[8] Just as Manchester (England) probably contributed to Waltham (Massachusetts), so did Waltham aid in the foundation of the industry of Lowell.

The Merrimac River was to become the rival of the Blackstone. In 1823 the first factory, the one just mentioned, was put into operation. Later Lawrence, below, and Manchester, above, were to become rival textile centers. The prosperity of these industrial towns was to become phenomenal and typically American.

We are more interested in the contrast between the two industrial systems than in the details of the development of the one which was to become so prevalent in America. On the Blackstone the water power was relatively slight and the mills accordingly were small, while on the Merrimac there was an enormous amount of power capable of driving mills of unprecedented requirements. On the Blackstone capital was not so important as skill, while on the Merrimac capital came first and skill followed. Such capital as was originally required on the Blackstone came from Providence, while that needed on the Merrimac came from Boston. On the Blackstone a fine grade of yarn and cloth was made, while on the Merrimac the work was of coarser quality. On the Blackstone there was specialization, on the Merrimac integration of spinning, weaving, dyeing, and finishing. On the Blackstone the form of company organization was the partnership, though Slater did turn somewhat toward the corporation at the close of his career. But on the Merrimac the joint-stock corporation, closely held by Boston capitalists, to be sure, was the prevailing form of organization. On the Blackstone the unit of labor seemed to be the family; on the Merrimac it was the individual worker. Contemporaries had little to admire in the labor system on the Blackstone, while at home and abroad the labor conditions on the Merrimac were praised. It was to the latter river that girls came to work for a few years in order to buy their own trousseaux or to provide financial assistance to their parents on the farm. Their living quarters were admirable, and their social and literary activities often praised. Beginning in 1840 there was published a literary journal called the *Lowell Offering.*[9] As a rival the *Operatives' Magazine* was begun in 1841 with the aid of a clergyman in another congregation of the same City of Lowell. These and other such journals, written by the girl workers themselves, were much noted at home and abroad. Clearly they reflected the attitudes of the middle-class homes from which the girls had come and to which they hoped to return. It seems to have been those girls who were not looking forward to a farm in the valley, that set up rival journals in which their more literary sisters and the employers themselves were both attacked. Such a journal as the *Factory Girl,* which appeared in 1842, reflected the point of view of the permanent laboring class. It might have been read with avidity in the Blackstone Valley.

On the whole such a picture is much fairer than that of Slater with his children spinning, before whom there was little hope except the chance to weave, to weave at home. Of course, in respect to labor, it was a matter of degree, for neither set of employers had the enlightened notions of today in the management of labor. And there came a time on the Merrimac, when the Anglo-Saxon workers were supplanted by the Irish, and later they by the French-Canadians who in their turn gave way to Greeks. Before the Great War I saw in Lawrence Greeks living in bunks tier upon tier, with no cleanliness and no family life. In some of the bakeries catering to these people there was filth as dangerous to the health as noxious to the senses. But on the whole the contrast between the Blackstone and the Merrimac stands, at least for the period before the Civil War.

NOTES TO CHAPTER IX

1. See W. R. Bagnall, *The Textile Industries of the United States*, vol. i, *1639–1810* (1893), pp. 64–79, 88–99.

2. See G. S. White, *Memoir of Samuel Slater* (1836), pp. 64–65.

3. *Ibid.*, pp. 74–75.

4. I am following the case, Samuel Slater and the American Textile Industry, prepared by Mr. K. W. Porter and based on printed sources, a doctoral dissertation by Miss Caroline F. Ware, and the Slater Papers in the Baker Library, Harvard University.

5. On this subject, the thesis of Caroline F. Ware (Radcliffe College) is particularly valuable.

6. See the Director's Records, Oct. 20, 1813, to Oct. 4, 1825, Boston Manufacturing Company, a manuscript volume in the Baker Library.

7. See Nathan Appleton, *Introduction of the Power Loom, and Origin of Lowell* (Lowell, 1858), p. 7.

8. See above, note 6.

9. See Bertha M. Stearns, "Early Factory Magazines in New England," *Journal of Economic and Business History*, vol. ii (1929–30), pp. 685–705.

CHAPTER X

REVOLUTIONS IN THE IRON AND STEEL INDUSTRY IN EUROPE AND AMERICA[1]

THE textiles with which we have just been concerned and the metals to which we now turn have been two of man's prime utilities in life. The chief metal has long been and still is iron. Part of man's material civilization has gone hand in hand with the use of metals. The first practical metallurgist was the bearded smith, Hephaestus, who limped as he labored on Mt. Olympus—to the amusement of his fellow gods. The theft of fire for man's use was the contribution of Prometheus. Soon there were human workers in the metals everywhere. Tubal Cain was but one of the earliest of such craftsmen.

Just when iron was first used by man is not recorded in sober history. Archaeology points to the prior use of bronze (copper and tin). But it may be that, while early bronze has been preserved, early iron has disappeared. Certainly bronze was easier to work than iron. But iron was more useful and indeed without it some of the more difficult work, such as the carving of diorite, could hardly have been performed. Although the use of iron has not generally been held to antedate 1000 B.C. in Egypt, it has been recently pushed back to about 2900 B.C.[2] It is very likely that iron or steel, the alloy being nickel, was chipped from meteorites, where available, by quite primitive peoples. But these occasional sources of supply, important even for the modern Esquimaux of Greenland, could have led to no important industry. It is likely that iron and steel were first regularly made in Asia Minor. The Greeks seem to have obtained their name for steel (chalybs) from an Asia Minor people, the Chalybes, famed for their work in iron and steel. The Egyptians probably obtained a more or less regular supply of iron from the district of Mt. Sinai, not earlier than the eleventh century B.C.

The earliest stage in the history of the iron industry is typified by the Catalan forge, which was really long used in Asia Minor before it was in Catalonia. This was a simple oven-like forge either built in the hillside in order to secure a draft or blown by a hand bellows. Iron ore and charcoal were mixed and burned together. As was to be expected, such a forge would necessarily be located near both forest and ore supply. The ore would frequently be dug from bogs. The product was sometimes good, sometimes bad. Much depended upon the untutored skill of the forgeman and upon the quality of the ore. In the Middle Ages the excellent Swedish and Spanish iron was as high in fame as today. The Germans had great skill in iron-working as had the Arabs and the distant peoples of India.

The same forge that smelted the ore might heat and reheat the molten mass for hammering on a rock or an anvil until the impurities were removed. It might be used even to fashion the iron into tools and weapons. As progress went on, distinction was made between the bloomery which produced the blooms or pigs of raw iron and the blacksmith's shop which manufactured the finished articles.

An English village blacksmith's shop in 1448 possessed besides the forge a pair of bellows, a hearthstave or puddler's rabble, a great anvil with a pike-horn or beak, two forehammers, one handhammer, two pairs of tongs, one pair of pincers, a washtub, a butteris, and a calker.[3] The raw material was probably in the form of gads and the chief finished products were horseshoes, parts of plows and carts, and hinges and straps for doors. Such was the workshop of Vulcan before the machine shop and farrier's shop were differentiated.

After the Catalan forge, came the power furnace, beginning at the close of the Middle Ages. The old hand bellows, often propelled by a boy, was unable to make the ore sufficiently hot to expell the impurities. The hitching of a larger bellows to water power made possible both the production of a better iron and the use of a higher and larger furnace. When a hammer propelled by water was also used, more impurities could be forced out.[4] The new furnace produced enough heat to melt iron so as to make cast iron, that is, iron containing a large amount of carbon. This cast iron was either used for casting, such as the making of iron fences, bells, and even cannon, or it was remelted and hammered into wrought iron which contained much less carbon and was therefore tougher. This remelting completed the indirect process which is taken to characterize the whole system. On the Continent books were being written on metallurgy, for instance, by Vanuccio Biringuccio in 1540, by Georg Agricola in 1546, and by Andrea Cesalpino in 1602. At about the same time the relatively advanced methods of the Germans were introduced into England. Dudley's *Metallum Martis* was published in London in 1665. The seriousness with which the science of metals was studied at the time is indicated by the attention given to alchemy, the high point of which was the transmutation of the baser metals into gold.

In the indirect system, just described, the typical plant probably contained a charcoal burner's kiln, a bloomery, and a forge. Obviously the plant would be located near iron ore and near a forest, and of course on a river or stream. Often it was managed in conjunction with agricul-

LANDSCAPE WITH BLAST FURNACE, LATE SIXTEENTH CENTURY

ture. It is doubtful whether such a mill normally employed more than a score or two of workmen.

First the Catalan forge, then the power furnace, and now, thirdly, the making of iron by coke. This third stage was the great modern industrial revolution in iron manufacture that took place in England chiefly in the period 1760–1800 and thereafter spread to other countries. It involved the making of iron, not steel, but it included both cast iron and wrought iron, and was closely connected with the use of the improved steam engine manufactured by Boulton and Watt.

In the seventeenth century Dud Dudley (1599–1684) had invented and used in his own works a method of smelting iron by means of coal,[5] probably in the form of coke. He encountered a good deal of local opposition in his work which seems to have led to no permanent practices. It was a Quaker, Abraham Darby, who not only invented or reinvented the high-powered blast furnace using coke instead of charcoal, but started the process on its career of continuous and practical success. Wherever the iron industry had gone, forests had been decimated or destroyed. In England even the supply of timbers for ships was first threatened and then all but depleted.[6] A substitute for charcoal had to be found, if the iron industry was to remain in England and thrive. At the same time there was a demand for iron so completely fused that it would run into the most intricate molds to make the more delicate castings. It was the needs of the molder or founder that were at stake.

At Coalbrookdale, in Shropshire, Abraham Darby succeeded in using coke to make cast iron. The picturesque tale, apparently referring to the year 1709, is that after six days and six nights of ceaseless effort, Darby succeeded in getting an iron that would run freely and one that was relatively pure. Like a hero of the industrial strife, after six days of battle, he was borne to his much needed rest by his workmen.[7] Darby also learned how to cast his iron in sand instead of in loam. This was a great saving in both time and expense. While the casting in sand seems to have spread rather widely, the smelting by coke was not adopted in the North of England and Scotland until after 1760.[8]

The fame of Abraham Darby has not run high, in spite of the magnitude of his discovery. It is true that he produced good cast iron at low price, that he used a larger furnace, and that he turned from charcoal to coke. But his ways were not widely known at the time, and his furnace needed a powerful blast, for which he was compelled to rely upon the inventions of other men. At first their pumps were run by water power, but later by steam. Indeed the iron cast by Darby's process was used in Boulton and Watt engines which in turn made the working of Darby's furnace more smooth and effective. The new cast iron was also used for the making of pots, stoves, cannon, bridges, and rails. In providing cheap iron for such uses, Darby's processes were more than playing their part in the general revolution in industrial methods.

One of the results of the new high-powered blast furnace using coke as fuel and driven by a steam engine was the increase in the size of the individual plant. Perhaps we may say that the mill had become the factory.[9] In 1715 Darby's mill was worth £5,000, while in 1794 the company was valued at over £62,000 and operated several plants. It worked coal and iron mines, possessed furnaces, water and steam engines for forcing blasts of air through the furnaces, several forges, a foundry, and more than twenty miles of iron railroad. Hundreds of workmen were employed.[10]

Abraham Darby and the other iron-masters and engineers who worked and planned along the same lines gave us just one part of the revolution in iron-making. They produced cast iron, leaving wrought iron to be imported from Sweden or Russia or to be smelted out of English ore and by use of charcoal from the vanishing English forests. For work which required iron that could withstand knocks and blows, the product of Darby's furnace was of little use. A wrought iron, cheaply manufactured, was now in demand. Moreover, only half the job had been done by Darby and others when wrought iron was left to be made with charcoal, for the refining process used in making the wrought iron required much more charcoal per ton than had the old-time smelting.

The double need of saving charcoal and of making good cheap wrought iron was met by Henry Cort. Both Cort and Darby are but little known to history, while the corresponding heroes of the Protestant Revolution, Luther and Calvin, occupy about as high pedestals as they deserve. The fires of protesting souls made the new irons of religion, Luther's a brittle cast iron, not unlike the old steel of Catholicism, while Calvin's was a tough fiber that bent but little—neither did it break. Moreover, both Darby and Cort on the one hand and Luther and Calvin on the other have been singled out partly for the sake of emphasis, not because each stood alone in his sphere of work. Others whose deeds are recorded, worked with our heroes of the iron revolution in friendly or in hostile rivalry, but we shall leave them unnamed.

Henry Cort had been a naval agent in London from 1765 to 1775. He entered the iron business as an experimenter rather than as a practical iron-master. His background was administration rather than engineering. He seems to have been led to experiment in the smelting of iron by the high price of Russian iron, of which he as a naval agent was deeply conscious. He was probably the first to carry on the manufacture of high quality pig iron by a single process; certainly he was the first to take out a patent (1784) and to follow it up. It was the simple boast of this simple man that he could make ordinary tough iron "by a short and simple process."[11] After 1789 he received no royalties because of a misadventure, but he was pensioned by the government, 1794–1800.

Cort's process was to smelt ore in a reverberatory furnace and then to fashion the iron, while still hot, into half-blooms. The fashioning was done by means of a hammer, worked at first by water power and later by a steam engine. After the half-bloom had been hammered, it was put through rollers. Such dross as escaped the hammers was eliminated by the rolling process. Here we have great economy of operation and a high quality of iron, comparable with the Swedish product.

The reverberatory furnace needs a word of explanation. In the old type of Catalan forge and power furnace, the ore and the fuel had been mixed together. The charcoal had helped expel impurities in the form of gases and it had added carbon to the content of the iron. In the new furnace of Cort the fuel was kept apart from the ore. The flames from the fuel were forced upward onto the ore, melting it without contaminating it. Through a door, just above the level of the molten iron, a workman stirred or puddled the seething mass, in fact separating the iron from the dross. In this way the pure iron and the dross, "mixed together but not incorporated," could readily be eliminated by the subsequent hammering and rolling.

Moreover, the fuel used in this furnace was not charcoal but pit coal, refined into coke. In order to heat the ore sufficiently, especially in the high furnaces, a powerful blast of air had to be supplied from an engine. This was just as in the case of Darby's process of making cast iron.

It is a commonplace in industrial history that many processes and developments are very closely integrated. Darby's cast iron went into the parts of Watt's steam engine, as we have seen. Then this engine helped drive the blast through both Darby's and Cort's furnaces. Moreover, it was used to crush the ore and to hammer and roll the iron in the refining process. And, in turn, some of the tough iron from Cort's furnace was used on the engine itself as it was being improved.

As before, the new advances in technique led to a larger business unit. Not only were ore and coal being mined but smelting, refining, rolling into plates, and slitting into rods were all being done by the one firm.[12] A dispersion took place within the industry which moved into the district where it was to have its greatest success—the Midlands, North England, and South Wales.

With Henry Cort we link together the reverberatory furnace, the use of coke to make wrought iron, and the unification of smelting and refining. Where possible, wrought iron came to compete keenly with cast iron. England was freed from foreign dependence for ordinary iron. The reduction in the cost of the process—by about forty per cent—gave rise to a demand on the Continent. Soon England became an iron-exporting country. But, as generally happens, with the product went the producers. After 1815 iron-masters, engineers, and workmen were enticed to Belgium, France, and other countries on the Continent. In this way the process was dispersed to confer direct blessings upon those who had not aided in its creation. As the Hebrews have given us our religion, the Phoenicians probably our alphabet, the Greeks much of our art and science, and the Romans something of our law and agriculture, so the English have been our industrial benefactors.

In America the Catalan forges and the power furnaces were in operation shortly after the various settlements had been made along the Atlantic Coast. The first efforts were made in Virginia. Massachusetts experienced considerable success in its many scattered works using bog iron with lime, in the form of stones or oyster shells, as flux. The puddling and rolling of iron began to be used about 1817. Coal began to supplant charcoal in the 1830's, but it was anthracite rather than coke made from soft coal.[13] America was slow in adopting the methods of Darby and Cort because of the backwardness of metallurgy and engineering, because of the abundance of charcoal, and because of the lack of a brisk demand for iron products other than for hand tools and agricultural implements. During the period 1830–60, however, considerable progress was made in the introduction of the revolutionary processes of iron manufacture. Among the chief influences were the railroads and the factories.

The revolution in the manufacture of iron was followed in Europe and America by a revolution in the making of steel. It is customary and tolerably accurate to say that wrought iron contains less than one per cent carbon and that cast iron contains over two per cent carbon. Steel comes in between with from one to two per cent. The strength of the iron varies according to the carbon content. The wrought iron is malleable but tough, the cast iron is hard but brittle. The steel is both hard and strong.

Steel had been procured in early times from meteorites and had been made in the Catalan and power furnaces. To make steel was easy but to make dependable steel economically was impossible. In England, about 1740, Huntsman had learned to make a high grade of steel in small crucibles, but that steel was very expensive. No steel age could be built upon Huntsman's costly product.

As the modern iron age was introduced by Darby and Cort, so the modern age of steel was brought about by Bessemer and Siemens. But it was not by them alone. In order to make the chief elements of the age of steel stand out clearly, we shall have to combine the contributions of our inventors. Instead of Darby we have Bessemer and Thomas, and instead of Cort we have Siemens and Martin. This is like combining Luther and Melanchthon on the one hand and Calvin and Knox on the other.

The Bessemer-Thomas process of making steel out of cast iron in a converter was started in England about 1856.[14] In that year Henry Bessemer, an inventor and business man in one, took out his patent for making steel by decarbonizing cast iron. He used a large metal converter, somewhat the shape of an egg. This was heated to a very high temperature by the burning of coke inside it. Then the cast iron, preferably in a molten condition, taken from a blast furnace, was poured into the converter which swung on a swivel either to receive supplies or to emit the product. A blast of air was then blown from beneath, the oxygen uniting with the impurites and producing a pyrotechnic display that makes a deep impression upon the beholder. Within ten or twenty minutes the effervescence dies down and the cast iron has become steel.

Bessemer lined his converter with acid material, such as quartz and clay. The result was that he could not get rid of the phosphorus in the iron.[15] So far as England and the United States were concerned, this was not a serious matter. But it was otherwise in France, Belgium, and Germany which have ores of high phosphorus content. It was the contribution of Thomas, an Englishman, to point out in the year 1878 how the shortcoming of the Bessemer converter could be remedied. He simply added a basic lining, such as lime and magnesia, and, when necessary, threw in some lime as flux. In this way the Continent was able to make steel almost as cheaply as England could.

The second great invention is the Siemens-Martin process. In 1861 Siemens, a native German domiciled in England, a scientist as well as an inventor, put into operation a process of making steel in a reverberatory furnace. On the open hearth of this furnace the cast iron and wrought iron were heated by the flames coming either from coal or gas. But in either case the gases which were generated by the heating of the iron were themselves heated and then brought into the fire box to help raise the temperature. The Siemens process came to be used by Pierre Martin at his plant in Sireuil, France. Martin is said to have made a valuable addition in 1864: by manipulating the materials put onto the hearth, he could help control the carbon content. Thus to iron he added iron ore[16] which contained in each lump a good deal of oxygen which united with impurities and went off as gas. Martin also used scrap iron and scrap steel. In view of the growing amount of this second-hand iron and steel, any process which can use them is bound to play an important part. When phosphorus ores or iron were to be made into steel by the open-hearth process, a basic lining was used and lime was thrown in as flux—as in the Bessemer-Thomas process. This latter is called the basic open-hearth process.

The Bessemer-Thomas converter swung on a swivel

EXTERIOR OF THE WYANDOTTE MILL, 1870's

OPEN-HEARTH FURNACE, SWIVEL TYPE, ABOUT 1928

while the Siemens-Martin furnace was until recently stationary. The former was quick acting, the latter slow. The former used an air blast, the latter relied upon the great heat it could engender and upon the proper mixture of ingredients to get the quality of steel needed. The rivalry between the two processes has been keen since the 1880's.

Although the essentials of the acid process of Bessemer were independently discovered, and at a slightly earlier date, by William Kelly, a Kentucky iron-master, nothing at first actually came from the invention, apart from the patent. Although Kelly claimed that Bessemer copied his methods, this seems to be just one of the many instances of almost simultaneous independent inventions that lead to misunderstandings and lawsuits. The Kelly process, under Kelly's direction, was used near Detroit, Michigan, in the Wyandotte Rolling Mill Company in 1864 and beginning in 1872 in Chicago. Apparently the Bessemer acid process was used for the making of steel rails in America about 1867, while the basic process of Bessemer and Thomas was used not later than 1888. In the former case it was the Cambria Iron Company of Johnstown and in the latter Carnegie's plant in Homestead, in both cases in Pennsylvania. For long, the Bessemer process led in the race with the Siemens-Martin open-hearth process. In the period 1905–09, however, the open hearth obtained the lead in America. At the present about six times as much steel is made by the Siemens-Martin open-hearth process as by the Bessemer-Thomas.[17]

And so the age of steel has come, on the whole rather rapidly. Low-grade as well as high-grade ores can be used. The furnaces have become very large and the price of the product very cheap. Steel of all shapes and sizes is made for railroads, steamships, factory machinery, and skyscrapers. It is dependable and strong. But we should note that the age of steel really entered by the back door. It came in partly by changing the definition of steel. The steel made by the two processes just described would not have passed the test of the old-time hammered steel or the crucible steel of Huntsman. It was really just uncommonly good iron—iron with practically no impurities.

But as the age of steel has come, so is it about to go, as some think. In its place comes the age of alloys. There are at least four advantages in the use of alloys. The alloys are lighter than the iron or steel necessary to provide the same strength and toughness, a valuable asset for automobiles and airplanes. Alloys are temperature resistant, a quality indispensable for certain engine parts which, if made of iron or steel, would be twisted out of shape. By the addition of nickel, chromium, manganese, tungsten, molybdenum, and vanadium, alloy steel can be made hard enough to cut ordinary steel and to stand the hardest kind of wear and tension. By combining steel and chromium in a special way a stainless steel can be produced, one that will not rust under ordinary circumstances. But the cost of manufacture is prohibitive for ordinary purposes. In the meantime iron and steel are made and used up in enormous quantities. Rust plays its silent, insidious part. Just as we say "dust to dust" of the body, so we can say "rust to rust" of iron and steel. The industrial world awaits a means of combating the hitherto inevitable process of decay. In the meantime an alloy of aluminum and such other metals as copper and tungsten is being made that is taking the place of iron and steel and other commodities for many uses. The resultant compound is light, strong, and durable.

The battle of alloys is on. The witches' caldron seethes with anxious effort. Aluminum alloy and steel alloy play a great part. It has been estimated that in 1929 automobiles used over 61 per cent of alloy steel, machine tools over 6 per cent, the oil industry and agriculture each over 4 per cent, and construction almost 4 per cent.[18] Aluminum alloys go into airplanes and the electrical industry. The future seems to belong to alloys, especially alloys of the lighter metals such as aluminum, magnesium, and beryllium. Perhaps the next age is really an aluminum-alloy age. If so, we shall have run through the whole gamut of iron and steel possibilities, arriving at something like the bronze age of old. Instead of tin and copper for making the alloy (bronze), it may be aluminum and copper. Certainly aluminum has the advantage of being much more plentiful (physically but not commercially) than tin or even iron, and some day its production may be as cheap as that of iron and steel.

America's part in metallurgy has been important on the practical rather than on the theoretical side. The business unit in America has become large like the furnace that smelts the metal. The American consumption has come to a place where the individual uses about six times his weight of steel each year. It has been estimated that the relative consumption in pounds of steel per person is as follows:[19]

United States	999	Great Britain	581
Belgium and Luxemburg	937	Germany	438
		France	299

In a sense this accomplishment is retrospective—a summary of the past. What points more to the future is the discovery and use of alloys—for ships in the air and some day for ships at sea, for tools in the machine shop and some day for machines in the factory.

NOTES TO CHAPTER X

1. On this subject see T. S. Ashton, *Iron and Steel in the Industrial Revolution* (1924); W. T. Jeans, *The Creators of the Age of Steel* (1884); V. S. Clark, *History of Manufactures in the United States*, 3 vols. (1929 ed.); M. Keir, *Manufacturing Industries in America, Fundamental Economic Factors* (1920); L. Beck, *Die Geschichte des Eisens in technischen und kulturgeschichtlichen Beziehung*, 5 vols. (1884–1903).

2. H. Garland, *Ancient Egyptian Metallurgy* (1927), p. 89.

3. See N. S. B. and Ethel C. Gras, *The Economic and Social History of an English Village* (1930), p. 485.

4. An example of such a hammer in use in Sussex, England, is given by L. F. Salzmann, *English Industries of the Middle Ages* (1913), p. 30.

5. See Dud Dudley, *Metallum Martis: or, Iron made with Pit-coale, Sea-coale, etc., and with the same Fuell to Melt and Fine Imperfect Mettals, and Refine perfect Mettals* (London, 1665, 1851).

6. Cf. R. G. Albion, *Forests and Sea Power, the Timber Problem of the Royal Navy 1652–1862* (Cambridge, Mass., 1926), pp. 116–119.

7. T. S. Ashton, *Iron and Steel in the Industrial Revolution* (1924), p. 32.

8. See *ibid.*, pp. 31 ff., 249 ff.

9. See above, ch. vi, p. 74.

10. T. S. Ashton, *op. cit.*, pp. 40–43.

11. See Cort's letter of 1783, T. S. Ashton, *op. cit.*, p. 91, n. 1.

12. T. S. Ashton, *op. cit.*, p. 100.

13. See V. S. Clark, *History of Manufactures in the United States, 1607–1860*, vol. i (1916, 1929), pp. 412–415.

14. On Bessemer, see W. T. Jeans, *The Creators of the Age of Steel* (1884), chs. i–v.

15. See the article on "Iron and Steel" by H. M. Howe in the *Encyclopædia Britannica* (11th ed.).

16. See T. Laurent, "Le developpement économique de la France: L'industrie metallurgique," *Le Musée Social, Memoirs et documents supplement aux annales* (1912), p. 120.

17. See the *Statistical Abstract of the United States, 1929* (1929), p. 752.

18. *Iron Trade Review*, Jan. 2, 1930, p. 14.

19. *Ibid.*, p. 11.

CHAPTER XI

THE SHOE INDUSTRY IN THE UNITED STATES, ESPECIALLY IN MASSACHUSETTS

THERE was once a feeling on the part of shoemakers that they were better than their fellow artisans. They had Hans Sachs, Gabriel Cappelini, and Simon Eyre of the late Middle Ages and early Modern Period to look back to and they had Samuel Drew of the eighteenth century and Henry Wilson of the nineteenth. The last was distinguished, in popular notice, by his having been vice-president of the United States, and Simon Eyre was notable for having become mayor of London, whilst the others were men of considerable personal abilities. Apparently shoemakers half believed their trade song which enrolled kings and saints in their profession. And then there was the obvious fact that in the shoemaker's shop more news was to be obtained and more serious talk to be heard than in any other spot in the town. Shoemakers had two pairs of eyes, one for their needle and last, another for the printed page before them. Occasionally, indeed, they employed a reader. Whilst their hours of work were long, their minds had time to ponder the problems of life. They educated themselves and helped uplift their neighbors.

The shoe industry in the United States[1] illustrates some of the chief developments in American economic history. It is the one industry which can be called supremely American. It typifies the genius of the American people. Not least among its merits, for the student of industrial history, is the fact that it has compressed into its 300 years of existence all the changes that Europe experienced in twice that time; and in the period beginning about 1860 the mechanical technique in America outdistanced all that had gone before. The industry in the United States alone produces over 300,000,000 pairs of shoes, slippers, and the like annually. For about three generations in the nineteenth and twentieth centuries, American shoes have been the most attractive to look at, the most comfortable to wear, and the best value for the price paid. Americans have during that time been the best shod people in the world. It is maintained, however, that a great many of the cheaper American shoes are unable to stand rain and snow as well as the corresponding shoes in Europe. It is thought that this is due to the inferior tanning of the leather—inferior chemicals and haste in the work. But in America it is now assumed that both men and women will wear rubbers whenever their shoes are in danger of being put to the severe test of very wet weather.

The long history of this industry has been studied particularly in Massachusetts[2] which has been and still is the leader. The earliest stage was the familiar usufacture. The first settlers, and to some extent the frontiersmen as settlement has rolled westward, made shoes for themselves and families out of leather tanned from the hides of animals of their own raising. A few of these settlers who developed some special skill undertook to help their neighbors. They became itinerant workers, introducing the second phase of usufacture. Probably the early period 1620–50 was almost wholly a usufacture period. But it is to be noted that this type of industry has persisted in primitive parts for a much longer period, particularly for coarser footwear. Among the Indians the usufacture of moccasins was an art as well as a craft.

Perhaps as early as 1650 along the Atlantic Coast and

later in other parts—whenever towns came into being, it was found advantageous to let the worker give up his itinerant habits and to let him select the hides, thread, cloth, and nails required to make the shoes. Accordingly in the small towns the retail handicraft system came into existence. This system was to have a much longer life than usufacture in the shoe industry. Generally speaking, we may say that it has shod at least the first two generations of settlers back from the Coast. The workmanship was good and the stock well selected. Since the shoe was commonly made for the customer, it came pretty near fitting him. One of the specialities, which I can remember from boyhood, was the custom-made high-top boot which the farmer wore, a coarse type for working, and one of fine leather for Sunday use. One pair for Sunday display was known to have done yeoman service for seventeen years without appearing shabby!

In Europe the shoemakers' craft had a gild which regulated the industry and inspected the product. At Boston in 1648 the shoemakers were given permission by the Massachusetts Bay Colony to form an association.[3] They were empowered to elect the usual master and wardens, the sealer and searcher, and other officials. This gild was to have the right to make rules and to enforce them by fines up to 40s. Any shoemaker found to be without skill might be suppressed. This permission, like a similar one to the coopers, was to last for only three years. It was not destined to be of long life or great importance. One reason for this was that the shoe industry no sooner got started in the Atlantic Coast towns than it developed the wholesale handicraft stage. This stage was not one that insisted strongly upon quality: it catered rather to the demands of the market.

In America as in Europe the retail handicraftsmen

made shoes for chance sale, shoes which could be traded in along the coast or sent abroad. But if this practice went far, if surplus stock for sale to distant consumers became an important part of their work, we may speak of a transition to the wholesale handicraft system rather than the system itself. In Philadelphia there are illustrations of this transition in the period 1792–1806.[4] Retail handicraftsmen who had been doing bespoke or customer's work, that is, manufacture for the use of local customers, turned to advertising shoes and selling them in large quantities in the coast towns from Alexandria to New Orleans. Prosperity came to the masters, at least one of whom, John Bedford, had twenty-four workmen and another, William Montgomery, twenty. The workmen struck for higher wages and the employers formed an association to resist their demands. Clearly the workshop, though large, was of the old type in which each journeyman made a whole shoe. For this he received a piece wage. The only division of labor lay in the practice of one man's making one kind of boot or shoe while another made a second kind. But this division did not proceed far.

As early as 1650 it was said that even though the shoes made in New England were of high price, they could be sold in foreign parts.[5] The surplus for export was said to be 5,938 pairs in 1771. Increase was slow, for in 1791 the amount had risen to only 7,046 pairs. By 1796, however, 212,774 pairs of shoes and slippers were exported. This was an industrial activity that could not be maintained, though 163,430 pairs were exported in 1806.[6]

It seems likely that we can place the period of the growing dominance of the wholesale handicraft system at about 1650–1830. During this same time, usufacture lingered in the back country, and the retail handicraft held its own in purely local trade. It is a matter of common observation that, as has been said, the long-drawn-out stages of European industrial development were compressed in America.

Evidence for the independent form of the wholesale handicraft system is apparently not so plentiful as for the dependent form. Indeed the two forms probably grew up together, partly to meet existing conditions and partly in imitation of what the settlers had known in Europe. One of the most interesting cases which I have seen belongs to such an early period that I am led to believe it was largely an Old World method transplanted to new soil. This is the case of John Meges, of New Haven, Connecticut.[7]

In the year 1647 New Haven was much disturbed by the bad shoes it was getting. Several witnesses gave evidence of the fact that these shoes fell to pieces on their feet within a week or a fortnight. A certain Mr. Evans, apparently a merchant of New Haven, had bargained with John Meges for £30 worth of shoes which he wanted in a hurry. Meges, as the industrial entrepreneur, turned to an old man in Stratford, called Henry Gregory, to make the shoes. Fourteen dozen pairs were to be made at one shilling a pair. Meges supplied to Gregory the leather, welts, and last. He failed to provide the hemp for thread. Accordingly Gregory himself provided flax thread. Meges was found by the court to be at fault in furnishing bad leather and in encouraging Gregory to do bad work. It was established that Meges had said to Gregory: "Flap them up, they are to go far enough." In other words these shoes were to be sold in other towns, to persons who were far away. Meges was fined £10. Gregory, old and with defective eyesight, was fined £5 and ordered to pay the court charges. His offence was defective workmanship. The shoes were ordered to be sold as faulty, but they were not to be sent elsewhere to disgrace New Haven. Gregory had suffered at the hands of Meges by the latter's failure to provide him with fifteen weeks' work as promised. Here we have the well-known system of dependent wholesale handicraft with the evils that were incident thereto. If the shoes in question had all been sent to the West Indies or to southern plantations, nothing might have been heard of the fraud. There would have been no legal case.

About 1830 in Massachusetts the centralized form of industry was introduced in the making of boots and shoes, and for thirty years it was the characteristically new form of manufacture. Such a form had existed in England, for instance, in the business of Brunel, the engineer, in London about 1812–15. Brunel had invented a machine, run by a treadle, to fasten soles to uppers by means of metallic pegs.[8] After the war, in which he had played a part by supplying a better quality of shoes at a low price, his industry apparently came to an end. In Massachusetts the central workshop arose, in Lynn and elsewhere, quite apart from English or other experiences.

The central workshop[9] for shoes was an old house or store, sometimes with a room or two built onto it, in which there was division of labor and discipline. Some of the artisans were asked to leave their little ten-footers (or workshops) to work in the central shop. And their ten-footers are said to have been henceforth used as henhouses, coal bins, or kitchens. In the new central workshop different kinds of work were done, such as cutting, treeing, and varnishing. The leather was cut out for uppers and for soles. The uppers with the necessary additional fittings were put out to artisans who still remained in the wholesale handicraft stage. When finished by the outworkers, the uppers were returned to the central workshop. Then uppers and soles were assorted and put out to other outworkers to be stitched together by hand. One advantage in the central workshop was clearly the elimination or reduction of theft. When the parts were cut out of the leather under the eye of the owner or his foreman there could be no filching of material. It is said that the wholesale handicraftsman commonly had a cabbage box into which he put not vegetables but parts of the leather that had been entrusted to him. In this way did he "cabbage" his employer's goods, but, of course, the shoemaker was no more at fault than other such dependent small masters, for example, the tailors.

In the period about 1836–46 Henry Wilson was active in a central workshop in Natick. Some of his accounts are still extant. In 1838 he employed 18 workmen, turning out 18,000 pairs of shoes; in 1845, 52 workers, producing 58,000 pairs; and in 1847, 109 workers, making 122,000 pairs.[10] Eddy and Leach had a central workshop in Middleboro, also in Massachusetts. Eddy had been the postmaster and general storekeeper. He had $10,000 to invest. Leach had been a farmer and shoemaker, apparently under the wholesale handicraft system. He had only $200 in cash to contribute, but his knowledge of the business was a great asset. The new business was started in 1852 in the old store building of Eddy, where each story was used for a special purpose. Later workmen were brought in to stitch the uppers and to fasten the soles to the uppers, that is, to make a complete shoe.[11]

As before in the wholesale handicraft stage, so now in the central workshop, the marketing was centralized in Boston. In 1859 Boston sent 5,078 cases of shoes abroad. It also sent 714,981 cases to other parts of the

United States, New York receiving the greatest number—182,027, and San Francisco coming next with 63,887 cases.[12]

Although the central workshop soon outlived its general usefulness, it survived, or was freshly established, to serve some special purpose. In 1920 I visited a central workshop, the A. A. Cutter Co., in Eau Claire, Wisconsin. A large number of old men were at work making shoes. These shoemakers had been trained in their native lands—Norway, Sweden, and Germany. Some of them had been employed in usufacture on large landed estates in the Old World. They would tan a hide, whittle a last, and make a complete shoe. The foreman told the story of his effort to get one of them to make a cheaper shoe for a special purpose. This the worker would not do. He insisted on selecting only the finest parts of the leather. This plant had been established to make lumbermen's boots—for use in the neighboring forests of Michigan Wisconsin, and Minnesota. In days gone by, a lumberman went into the forest in the fall to remain until spring, with no contact with the outside world. He needed to have a pair of shoes that would last. At the time of the visit the market was changing, much of the output going to the State of Washington, to Siberia, even to West Africa. The threatening problems in 1920 seemed to be both market and labor. It was not clear where workmen could be found to replace these old men who could not live much longer. American youths would never stop to learn how to make a whole shoe by hand. In 1928 the plant was sold to a shoe manufacturing company of St. Paul, which installed power machinery and turned out a cheap work-shoe. Thus the new work-shoe, made by machinery, and the old handmade logging-shoe are now joint products. Certainly the new shoe is in greater demand than the old one, but it has to meet the keen competition of other plants.

Into the central workshop crept the sewing machine. Elias Howe had patented his machine in 1846 and I. M. Singer his in 1851. But, of course, these machines were run by foot power and not by steam. They were even more used in the shops of the outworkers for stitching the uppers. Other hand machines had been patented in the early nineteenth century, some entering the central workshop. Still there was no power machinery, only a preparation for it.

Just which was the first kind of power machinery introduced into a central workshop to transmute it into a factory is not likely to be discovered. It is said that William F. Trowbridge of Feltonville (town of Hudson, Massachusetts) used horse power in the boot and shoe industry as early as 1855, and that before that time the power had been supplied by two or three Irishmen.[13] In 1858 John Wooldridge, who had been one of the first to introduce sewing machines into the central workshop, was apparently the first in Lynn to introduce steam power. His machine was for the purpose of making heels.[14] Pegging has also been held to have been the first process to adopt power machinery. It was the McKay machine for stitching uppers directly onto the soles, however, that introduced the factory system on a large scale. The machine had been invented in 1857 and patented in 1858 by Lyman Reed Blake,[15] one of three partners operating a central workshop, and was exploited by Gordon McKay beginning in New England in 1860. It has been stated that William Porter and Sons of Lynn were the first (1861) to install the McKay machine. It was introduced slowly, improvements being made in 1864 and 1867. Blake is said to have claimed that in the period

1861–76 there had been sewed over 177,000,000 pairs of shoes by means of his machine and at a saving of $14,000,000.[16] By means of this machine the Union armies were supplied with good cheap shoes with which to march to victory. There have been so many explanations of why the North won in the Civil War that we shall not add a new one in contemplating the progress of the shoe industry.

The McKay machine stitched the uppers to the sole without the use of a welt. This meant that seams would be left on the sole and that at first at least there were few cobblers who could adequately repair such shoes. Of course, the machine could be used for the making of only coarser shoes.[17] The situation changed when the Goodyear welt machine was introduced. It had been patented in 1862 by Augustus Destouy, a mechanic of New York City,[18] but had not been perfected and widely used until 1876. At first it was used to sew turned shoes, especially for ladies. After improvements had been made by Christian Dancel, a superintendent in the Goodyear firm, it could sew a welt to the insole and upper while stretched on a last. This addition of 1874 was purchased by the Goodyear firm in 1885. Another machine was used to sew the welt to the outsole. Thus could the finest shoes be made by machinery, by power machinery driven at a rapid even rate of speed.

The history of the shoe industry offers several illustrations of profits going to the business organizer. It is true that McKay was partly responsible for later improvements of the Blake machine and that Blake did not miss either honor or profits. But the advantages of Destouy's machine went to Charles Goodyear, Jr., who was the son of the inventor of the process of vulcanizing rubber. It should be said, however, that Destouy's machine was

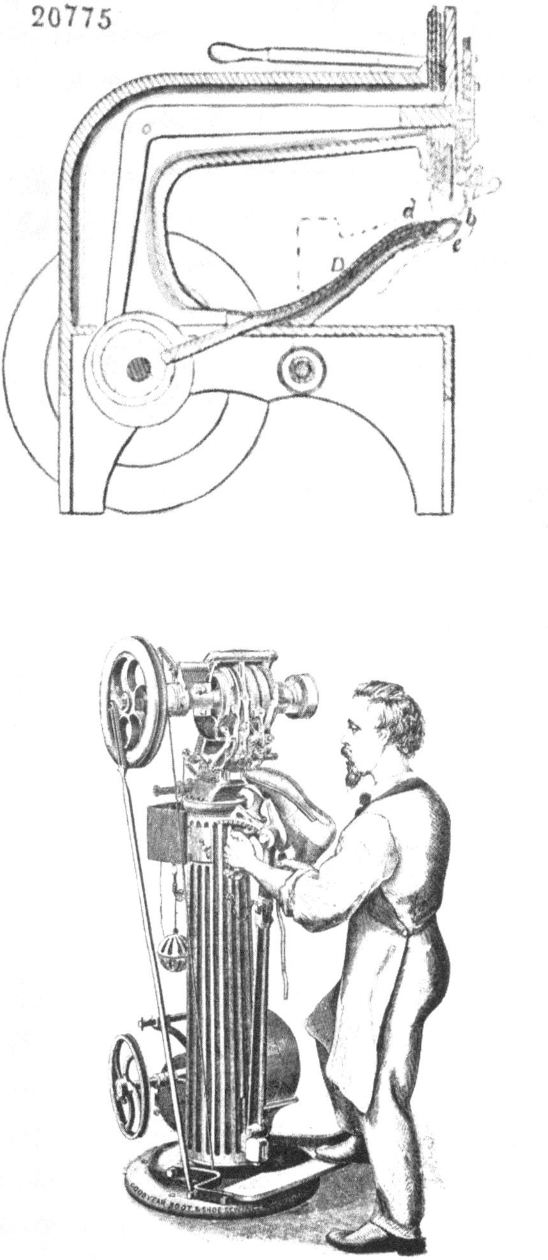

AN EARLY MODEL OF THE GOODYEAR WELT MACHINE

very imperfect and had no future unless it could be improved in some way.

An examination of the early patents, both the descriptive statements and the plates, fails to disclose any plans for hitching the shoe machinery to power. This was a later development. When the first factories, using the McKay and the Goodyear machinery driven by power, were set up, and where, is not easy to discover.

The application of power was relatively slow. The total horse power used in the shoe industry in the United States in the census of 1870 was 3,069. In the census of 1880 it was 11,574. Almost all the power came from steam, most of the available water power being used for textile mills or other purposes. In 1870 the chief machine driven by steam was the McKay. In 1880 the McKay and Goodyear machines, jointly, occupied the first place.

Many have been the inventions made in the shoe industry since the Goodyear welt machine was put into operation. The chief ones were for lasting and were made in the period 1880–1912. The increasing effectiveness of machine production is remarkable. The McKay sewing machine reduced the cost of sewing on soles from 75 cents to 3 cents a pair. By 1880, pegging by machine cost about 1 1/5 cents a pair, while by hand it was about 5 cents. Ten years later one worker could last by machine as many as 12 had formerly been able to do by hand. And one man with a Goodyear machine could do as much as 54 with an awl.[19]

Three machinery companies were developed: the Goodyear Shoe Machinery Company, the McKay Lasting Machine Company, and the McKay Shoe Machinery Company. The third made machines for attaching soles and heels by metallic fastenings. These three companies were consolidated in 1899 to form the United Shoe

Machinery Company, of Beverly, Massachusetts. It is the distinction of this company to manufacture over 350 different types of machines, some of almost unbelievable human qualities. Most of the machines, particularly those still covered by patents, are not sold but leased to manufacturers, payment being commonly made according to the number of shoes manufactured. The leasing system goes back to the days of the Blake-McKay machine which was leased because buyers could not be found. And, in order to keep the royalties coming in, a service man had to be sent out to keep the machines in repair. This method of leasing has proved of great assistance to small concerns which are thereby freed from the necessity of locking up their capital in mechanical equipment. Moreover the United Shoe Machinery Company (or Corporation since 1917) employs a corps of experts to keep these machines in good condition. It replaces old models by new ones as soon as it is economical to do so. Unfortunately, the machines cannot be made cheaply, because they cannot be made in large quantities. Six or a dozen of a type are commonly assembled at one time. If there were no other firms competing in the United States, and if it were not necessary to have separate factories abroad, then the output in the central plant at Beverly, being greater, would cost less per unit. Under such a condition of virtual monopoly, however, we should not assume that the lower costs would be passed on to the manufacturer of shoes or to the consumers of the shoes.

America's early strength in the shoe industry lay in its possession of abundance of hides and tanning material. As these have receded, she has developed her supreme position in power machinery. Many of the machines that America has made use of and even improved were invented abroad. Shoe machinery, however, is America's own product. And as America sends out these machines to the rest of the world, she helps to pay for the many good things which she has received from abroad. The United Shoe Machinery Corporation has plants in Canada, England, France, and Germany. It sends its output almost everywhere. Gradually this export of machinery is having its effect upon American exports. At present both Britain and Czechoslovakia have greater exports of shoes, and the latter country is invading the American market for women's shoes to such an extent that New England is crying out for a protective tariff.

In the museum of the United Shoe Machinery Corporation in Boston there are said to be about 1,300 shoes on exhibit, ranging in point of time from Egyptian sandals of 3,000 years ago to present-day shoes. Until the eighteenth century there seems to have been little or no distinction between the right and the left shoe; this was true of women's shoes until the 1880's. The early shoes were often elaborately decorated and the workmanship was at times most delicate. But the machine, the power-driven monster of the publicist's hate, has at last made a shoe that has beautiful lines. Let the stylists and designers conceive a beautiful shoe: the machine can make it. This shoe has an exquisite finish and follows the contour of the foot. The latest important labor-saving machine was put into operation in 1912. It came only after careful planning, enormous labor, and the expenditure of a fortune. It pulls the shoe tightly over the last in a way not possible for the handicraftsman.[20] No important process now remains to be machinized. Those hundreds of rather ugly machines have been invented by man and remain the instruments for the production of the beautiful.

NOTES TO CHAPTER XI

1. On this general subject, see M. Keir, *Manufacturing Industries in America* (1920), chs. viii and ix. In the writing of this present chapter I have had the benefit of the suggestions and criticisms of Major Charles T. Cahill, of the United Shoe Machinery Corporation.

2. By Blanche E. Hazard, *The Organization of the Boot and Shoe Industry in Massachusetts before 1875* (1921).

3. See Hazard, *op. cit.*, pp. 171–172.

4. *The Trial of the Boot & Shoemakers of Philadelphia, on an Indictment for a Combination and Conspiracy to raise their Wages, taken in short-hand by Thomas Lloyd* (Philadelphia, 1806), pp. 34–59.

5. See Hazard, *op. cit.*, p. 171.

6. Timothy Pitkin, *A Statistical View of the Commerce of the United States of America* (1816), pp. 68–70.

7. See the *Records of the Colony and Plantation of New Haven from 1638 to 1649* (ed. by C. J. Hoadly, 1857), pp. 345–353.

8. See R. Beamish, *Life of Sir Marc Isambard Brunel* (1862), pp. 128–132.

9. See Hazard, *op. cit.*, pp. 42 ff.

10. Hazard, *op. cit.*, p. 69.

11. Hazard, *op. cit.*, pp. 71–72.

12. E. L. Bogart and C. M. Thompson, *Readings in the Economic History of the United States* (1916), pp. 302–303.

13. See the United States Census, 1900, *Manufactures*, vol. ix (1902), p. 756.

14. Hazard, *op. cit.*, p. 120.

15. See *Report of the Commissioner of Patents for the Year 1859, Arts and Manufactures*, vol. i (1859), p. 632 and vol. iii (1859), p. 198.

16. See the *Dictionary of American Biography*, vol. ii (1929), p. 344.

17. See *Report of the Commissioner of Patents for the Year 1862, Arts and Manufactures*, vol. i (1864), p. 187, and vol. ii (1865), p. 55.

18. See V. S. Clark, *History of Manufactures in the United States, 1860–1914* (1928), pp. 469–470.

19. *Ibid.*, pp. 469, 471.

20. M. A. Green, "How Shoes are made by Machines," in *A Popular History of American Invention* (ed. by Waldemar Kaempffert, 1924), vol. ii, p. 431.

CHAPTER XII

THE CHEMICAL INDUSTRIES

THE shoe industry with which we have just been concerned is bound up with the chemical industries. The leather is, of course, tanned by vegetable or mineral material. The glues and cements are specially prepared by chemists for the shoe industry. The dyes used in women's shoes are coal-tar products. The new composition soles are the results of chemical laboratory experiments.

The two groups of industries—the chemical in this chapter and the electrical in the one following—are but two in a considerable list. The wooden, leather, and stone industries seem to be losing relatively, while the iron and steel, non-ferrous metals, chemical, and electrical industries are gaining. The chemical and electrical industries have reached unprecedented heights in the period since about 1870. They have both become key industries. That is, they occupy strategic positions in the manufacturing world because of the fact that, without them, other industries could not be carried on with their present efficiency, and some not at all. The two—chemical and electrical—meet in one new field—electro-chemistry or the electrolytic process of the chemical and metallurgical industries.

Although we think of chemistry as a new science and a new industry, it is really very old as an empirical science and as an art. Primitive peoples have known how to make and to mix vegetable dyes for coloring their bodies and their utensils. They have compounded herbs as medicines, some harmless and without effect, others useful as purgatives or stimulants. Empirical metallurgy followed long after the discovery of fire. It is supposed to have been concerned with copper, lead, and tin before the more difficult metal, iron, was attempted. In both the ancient and the medieval periods efforts were made to understand chemical combinations and affinities. Medieval alchemy at its best marked considerable progress on the way to a chemical science.

The second stage may be called the stage of the individual scientist, working in his badly equipped laboratory but using his imagination and looking sharply to the results of his experiments. In England there were Boyle, Priestly, Dalton, Darby, and Faraday; in France, Lavoisier and Berthollet; and in Germany, Liebig. To the last named is given the credit of combining experimentation and instruction. His influence went out to other towns to establish fresh laboratories. So far did this go that there came a time when England, the land of inspired lone chemists, turned to Germany for well-trained men to teach the developing science. In 1840 it was admitted that Germany was ahead of Britain[1] and in 1845 A. W. von Hofmann was brought to Britain to occupy the chair of chemistry in the College of Chemistry. When he went back to Germany, it is almost true to say, he took the science with him, as far as educational institutions were concerned. Certainly Oxford and Cambridge were not ready to dilute Greek and Latin with chemistry. And what was equally serious is that the British firms were unwilling or unable to employ many trained chemists.[2] This was all the more serious in a land that had flourishing textile and metallic industries which use so many chemicals in the ordinary course of production. English specialization was at once a strength and a weakness. It was a strength in so far as it developed skill—for instance in the textile and iron and steel industries, but a weakness in so far as it left the chemical industry to Germany.

The third stage developed in Germany. It is the organized scientific experimentation of well-equipped laboratories in schools but more especially in industrial plants. The Farbwerk at Hoechst am Main was established in 1863; by the year 1912 it had 7,680 workmen. The Badische Anilin und Soda Fabrik in Ludwigshafen am Rhein began in 1865; by 1914 it had 11,000 workmen. Bayer and Company of Leverkusen is doubtless the best known in America of the larger firms in Germany because of its discovery and manufacture of aspirin, a priceless gift to suffering humanity. These firms and many others employed a great number of trained chemists, many holding the doctor's degree in chemistry. By patient experimentation, involving tens of thousands of efforts and millions of marks, a single medicine or a single dye was discovered. It is interesting to note that while the first coal-tar dye, mauve, was discovered by Perkin, an Englishman, practically all the rest have been of German origin. Discovery has been followed by patents in Germany and abroad. Soon the home market was glutted. Then the industrial countries of the world were supplied, and wherever a local effort was made to establish dye works, in Britain or in America, the prices of German dyes were reduced until the upstart firm had been discouraged. Occasionally subsidiary companies were established in foreign lands, for example, to use German processes for the manufacture of chemicals too heavy to transport long distances. Cartels were formed at home to maintain prices and to effect economies.[3] The total result was that Germany came to possess the most skilled chemists and the best organized chemical businesses. For dyes and pharmaceutical chemicals the world did her homage.

While Germany established and maintained her supremacy in the manufacture of expensive chemicals, she could never hope to develop a monopoly in the production of the heavy chemicals. These constitute the staple articles in the industry, and they enter into the very vitals of other industries. Sulphuric acid, cheap and bulky, is used in the iron and steel industry. Nitric acid is indispensable for making explosives and alloys. Muriatic acid is used in dyeing and tanning. Phosphoric acid goes into the making of fertilizers and is used to clarify sugar. Acetic acid is required for the making of white lead. Alcohol is indispensable in the artificial silk industry. These are, of course, only a few examples out of hundreds of instances.

The relation between the chemical industry and other industries is illustrated by textiles. In 1785 Berthollet used chlorine in the bleaching of vegetable fibers (cotton and linen), thereby greatly shortening the time required in the process. This method was adopted almost at once in both France and England. In 1844 a Lancashire textile printer, named John Mercer, discovered the effect of caustic soda on cotton cloth. He found that the soda strengthened the cloth and made it take dyes much better. But nothing came of the discovery because of the fact that the cloth was shrunk by one-fifth. In 1889 H. A. Low, also an Englishman, observed that if the soda was put onto the cotton fiber while taut, the fiber became roundish and therefore lustrous. This became the basis of the subsequent mercerized cotton industry. In 1884 Chardonnet discovered the first method (one of three) of making artificial silk. By 1891 the industry had been put on a commercial basis, but it has been only since 1920 that it has made much progress. It is not the cellulose nitrate silk of Chardonnet but a viscose silk, discovered in England in 1892, that is most in use at present.[4] Since about 1924 this has been called rayon in America where, as in England,

France, Belgium, and Germany, it has become the basis of a growing industry.

The chemical aspects of meat packing, paper making, and the petroleum industry are significant and typical.[5] The development of the coal-tar industry, however, is the stock example of the triumph of organic chemistry. By means of the distillation of coal various products are obtained. From these are produced aniline dyes, perfumes, medicines, and so on. The indigo producers of India have been forced to turn to other crops, as synthetic indigo has come upon the market in abundance and relatively cheap. This has been fortunate for India because now the cultivators grow more foodstuffs, thereby helping to obviate famines. The madder fields of France have been hard hit, and now the logwood industry of Jamaica is beginning to feel the competition of coal-tar dyes. This vegetable dye, logwood, has been one of the last to hold out, but is now losing to artificial products made in France and America.[6] The coal-tar industry has enabled districts possessing coal to develop chemical industries which they had not known before. Germany had already put the extraction of chemicals from lignite on a commercial basis and France is making experiments of its own looking toward the same goal.[7]

American industrial history has a streak of chemistry running all through it. In 1608 the Virginia Company sent Poles and Germans to make pitch, tar, glass, and soap. But no great amount of skill was developed. As is to be expected, the dependence upon foreign skill, especially German, has been very great. Perhaps the potash industry was the most widespread, though it flourished better in the North. But as the forests were cut down and substitutes discovered, it gradually lost in the nineteenth century. The Pennsylvania Society for the

Encouragement of Manufactures and the Useful Arts offered its highest prize for the discovery of chemical processes in 1787. These were for the production of potash, pearlash, and printers' colors.[8] In 1816 Howard Sims and Isaac Tyson, incorporated in 1822, began the manufacture of chemicals, paints, and medicines in Baltimore. It is notable that they established a laboratory of their own.[9] In the period 1879–83, it is said, nine American firms began to make dyes, but five shut down in 1883, four continuing until the Great War.[10] In 1884 the Solvay process of making soda ash was introduced in Syracuse in New York State. Both the process and the firm have been successful. But so little general progress had been made in America by 1892 that a specialist in the chemical industries could say that America had been least successful among the great nations and had made least effort.[11] Of course, this applied less to the heavy chemical industries than to dyes and medicines. The explanation of America's lack of progress in the manufacture of the lighter chemicals is partly a matter of comparative advantage. Germany had a better market in Europe for these chemicals and could afford to emphasize them. Until the War period there was no great commercial advantage in producing the lighter chemicals in the United States. Accordingly, American manufacturers did not go far in the direction of discovery or manufacture. Probably another factor in the situation is America's lack of progress in theoretical chemistry comparable to what was taking place in Germany.

The War called America's attention to her dependence upon Germany. That country was supplying about nine-tenths of the needs of the chief manufacturing countries of the world and, working at full speed, could probably have also accommodated the people of Mars—unless we are misled by statements about overproduction. The price of dyes suddenly rose when war broke out. The dramatic visits of the submarine *Deutschland* off the coast of America, supplying American customers with the distilled essence of German skill, called America's attention at once to its dependence in time of peace and its exposed position in time of war. Efforts were made by American manufacturers to do in a few years what it had taken Germany fifty years to accomplish. Some success was attained but most progress came after the German secrets had been appropriated by the American government. The ethics of this procedure may be judged by each one according to his light.

During the War the property of the German chemical works and agents in America was seized by the Alien Property Custodian. In 1919 he handed over the dye patents — 4,500 in all— to the Chemical Foundation Incorporated. This body had a capital stock of $500,000 owned largely, if not wholly, by chemical concerns in America. For the patents the Foundation paid the sum of $250,000, a price that was "necessarily determined somewhat arbitrarily," as the president of the Foundation stated. The patents are now leased to American firms and the returns, above six per cent dividends, are to be used in the interest of chemical science. How valuable the patents were is not to be easily determined. Salvarsan was said by the president above-mentioned to have been the most valuable because needed by 10,000,000 syphilitics in the United States.[12]

America became chemically minded during the War. In 1919 it was said that loyal Americans had invested $450,000,000 in the chemical business. In 1922 it was asserted that more than $40,000,000 were invested in buildings and equipment for chemical education in the United States.[13] During the same year an American senator said that "chemistry is what is governing the world today, both in war and in peace." In 1924 the capital invested in industries in America, more or less dependent upon chemistry, was said to amount to $60,000,000,000.[14] And in 1928 America was said to have the largest chemical industry in the world.[15]

In spite of this unquestioned fact of rapid advance, it should be noted that in 1928 the value of industrial chemicals imported almost equaled the value exported. In that year America imported a total value of the various chemical categories somewhat in excess of its exports of those same categories. America has attained success in making medicinal and pharmaceutical chemicals and the more obvious coal-tar dyes. European countries, even Germany, are fighting to hold their own. It is probably true that Germany has lost about one-half of its market for coal-tar products since 1914, but it has maintained great influence upon the production of these wares in various countries by market agreements through the agency of large combines. Since the different competing groups have their governments firmly behind them, we really have a silent contest of the greatest magnitude going on before our eyes.

America has seen the need of big business units in the chemical industry. In 1899 the General Chemical Company was formed out of twelve firms.[16] In 1920 it joined four others to form the Allied Chemical and Dye Corporation. In this concern the General Chemical Company specializes in acids, the Solvay Process Company in alkalies, the Semet-Solvay Company in coke and its by-products, and the Barrett Company and National Aniline and Chemical Company in dyes. With this American concern should be compared the German Interessen Gemeinschaft Farbenindustrie Aktiengesellschaft (or German dye trust) and the English Imperial Chemical Industries. The German dye trust is probably Germany's biggest industrial combination. With a capital of 1,100,-000,000 Reichsmarks in 1928, it produces one-third of Germany's output and employs one-fourth of the workmen in the industry.[17] The second great chemical concern in America is the E. I. du Pont de Nemours and Company which has been distinguished for its long service to society in the manufacture of explosives. It now has a giant laboratory with about 200 chemists, located at Wilmington, Delaware, and employs in all not less than 1,500 chemists. This Company has been diversifying its interests and activities especially since 1915. It owns or controls many plants scattered over the eastern part of the United States. It is truly a general chemical company. It makes not only explosives, heavy chemicals, and fertilizers but dyes, paints, varnishes, rayon, fabrikoid, cinematograph films, and non-shatterable glass.[18] Only such large concerns can afford to maintain well-equipped laboratories and only big units can economically operate the tank cars needed for the transportation of heavy chemicals.

Although electro-chemistry is a European science, America has made considerable progress in its practical application. Indeed some are inclined to see an important original contribution of applied science in America's application of electrolysis to the production of chemicals and metals. America's special position, if such it proves to be, is due partly to its possession of water power and partly to the development of the electrical industry. Of course America's position in electro-chemistry is rivaled by Germany's, the decision between the two being left to the future.

NOTES TO CHAPTER XII

1. Cf. J. H. Clapham, *Economic Development of France and Germany, 1815–1914* (1921), p. 303.

2. See E. E. Slosson, *Creative Chemistry* (1919, 1923), p. 80.

3. Cf. A. Mitchell Palmer and Francis P. Garvan, *The Chemical Foundation Incorporated* (1919), pp. 11 ff.

4. *Industrial Chemistry* (ed. by Allen Rogers, 1912, 1926), pp. 1078–1080.

5. For these and other industries, see *Chemistry in Industry* (ed. by H. E. Howe, 1924).

6. *The Chemical Trade Journal and Chemical Engineer*, vol. lxxxii (1928), p. 37.

7. *Ibid.*, p. 298.

8. J. Leander Bishop, *A History of American Manufactures from 1608 to 1860*, vol. i (1864), p. 407.

9. *Ibid.*, p. 231.

10. A. Mitchell Palmer and Francis P. Garvan, *op. cit.*, p. 16.

11. See V. S. Clark, *History of Manufactures in the United States*, vol. ii (1928), p. 524.

12. *Statement of Mr. Francis P. Garvan, Alien Property Custodian* (Dec. 13, 1919, printed in pamphlet form), p. 51.

13. Statement of a Committee of American Chemists, Aug. 16, 1922, printed in the *Way of Progress* (Synthetic Organic Chemical Manufacturers Association, New York, 1922), pp. 30–31.

14. *Chemistry Extending its Frontier* (Harvard University, March, 1924), p. 9.

15. V. S. Clark, *History of Manufactures in the Un ted States*, vol. iii (1929), p. 347.

16. See *The General Chemical Company after Twenty Years* (1899–1919, General Chemical Company, 1919).

17. See *German Chemical Developments in 1928*, Bureau of Foreign and Domestic Commerce, Trade Information Bulletin No. 605 (Washington, 1929), pp. 1–4, 35.

18. See *Du Pont Activities and the College and University Graduates* (E. I. du Pont de Nemours & Company, Wilmington, 1929 or 1930), pp. 3–17.

CHAPTER XIII

THE ELECTRICAL INDUSTRIES

BEFORE the history of the electrical industries began, there was a long period of preparation. The minds and imaginations of many generations reached out feebly to grasp the mysterious flow of energy which we now so easily control. Thales knew that amber when rubbed on other substances had some slight power of attraction. Aristotle had knowledge of the magnetic properties of the ore that we now call magnetite. In the Middle Ages the magnetic needle was used as a compass. In the seventeenth century the Leyden jar was invented and used. Franklin demonstrated experimentally that lightning and electricity were the same. About 1785 Galvani, an Italian professor, observed the phenomenon of animal electricity. In 1799 Volta, also an Italian professor, made what was apparently the first battery. He succeeded in generating electricity by chemical action. In 1831 Faraday made the first dynamo. In subsequent experimentations and formulations many European nations played a part, but England's was probably the most important. It would be hard to match Clerk Maxwell, Lord Kelvin, and Sir J. J. Thomson. And yet in Germany there were Hertz and Roentgen, so vital to recent electrical progress.

England was a pioneer in both chemistry and electricity. In the former it lost to Germany and in the latter to the United States. So notable has America's part been in the electrical industry that we are inclined to compare it with corresponding accomplishments in the boot and shoe industry and in the manufacture of agricultural machinery.

There seem to be three periods in the history of the electrical industries in the United States. The first introduces the telegraph, cable, telephone, arc light, and incandescent light. It covers the period 1844–80. It is the period during which America's chief competitor was England. Morse's telegraph, successfully used between Washington and Baltimore in 1844, though not the first telegraph, introduced its practical use. Its success was assured, however, only when the railroads took it over to facilitate the dispatching of trains. At first battery cells, later dynamos, supplied the electric current. The first practical cable of importance was laid between Dover and Calais in 1851. While many Englishmen and some Americans scoffed at the possibility of an Atlantic cable, one was actually laid in 1858 under the leadership of the American capitalist, Cyrus W. Field. The second came in 1865. It is notable that the English ultimately obtained their greatest success in electricity by the laying and operation of cables in various parts of the world. The need for imperial and commercial connections explains this development.

The telephone came in 1875–76. If it had not been introduced by the Scotsman, Bell, it might have been by the American, Elisha Gray, of Chicago, whose discoveries were made at about the same time as Bell's. It is hard to refrain, in passing, from dilating upon the vastness of connections, the magnitude of service, and the popular satisfaction with the Bell telephone companies. This has been under the leadership of the American Telephone and Telegraph Company. New York was connected with San Francisco by direct service in 1915, while transoceanic telephoning, through the aid of the radio, was made commercially possible only in the year 1927.

There was some success in introducing the arc light in Britain in 1862, and in Paris in 1876. In 1878 Charles F. Bush made a complete lighting system in America, using an arc light and dynamo. The same year the Thompson-Houston system of arc light and dynamo was introduced, a system that was successful for many years. It was also in 1878 that Edison made his incandescent lamp, the most practical up to that time. In 1879 he greatly improved the dynamo and in 1880 he introduced his system in a commercial way by installing it in a steamship.[1] A great electrical revolution was clearly under way.

In the second period of the electrical industry in the United States, from 1880 to 1920, England was out of the race, but Germany was a good second. During this period dynamos were greatly improved and the use of electric lights spread widely. The first central power station in America was established in Appleton, Wisconsin, in 1882. Soon thereafter another was set up in New York City. But the chief characteristic of the period is the use of the electric motor.

The electric motor was used for locomotion before it was adapted to stationary purposes. In the period 1882–84 it was used to drive an elevator. It is not too much to say that the electric elevator has made the skyscraper possible. In 1884 an electric tramway or street car was tried experimentally in Cleveland, Ohio.[2] The Westinghouse Electric and Manufacturing Company, formed in 1885, bought up and improved a number of patents. In 1886 it not only installed the first alternating-current generator in the United States but it manufactured a transformer invented by one of its engineers. In 1888 it acquired the patent rights to the Tesla motor which used the alternating current. Toward the close of the century it made a turbo-generator that rivalled the best of its day. By these and similar devices electricity was generated in large stations and distributed widely at low rates both for lighting and power purposes.[3] It is interesting to note that one of the chief opponents of the alternating current was Edison. In the period 1890–1920 the street car, both within the city and in urban districts, met a great need in providing cheap transportation for factory workers and others and indeed for the rank and file of people who had no other means of getting around. In 1891 the first electric automobile was built in Chicago. It is, of course, the automobile, but driven by a gasoline engine rather than by an electric motor, that is now driving out the street car. In 1895 the electric locomotive was used experimentally on a railroad and in 1904 the New York Central Railroad decided to use this power on a considerable scale. The most extensive use in America is now on the Chicago, Milwaukee, and St. Paul Railroad over 600 miles of its track through the Rocky Mountains, the engines used being capable on the down grade of generating electricity, thereby effecting a saving of 10 per cent or over in the cost of power.

The motor was used in a cotton factory in Connecticut in 1893 and gradually spread to all kinds of industries. Perhaps its most distinctive use in factory production is in iron- and steel-works, such as in the Gary plant of the United States Steel Corporation. In the Ford Motor Company there is a gigantic modern turbo-generator plant. It consumes 2,200 tons of coal a day, generating 2,500,000 kilowatts in the same period.[4] This electricity is put to a variety of uses, in driving the endless chains that carry the parts to their various destinations, in lighting the plant, in feeding the great magnets that lift the scrap iron, and in driving the hundreds or thousands of motors hitched to as many machines. The Ford Motor Company may be used as an example of many developments, for instance, of integration in industry, of standardization, of large-scale enterprise, of economy in the use of materials, of factory training of employees, and of the payment of high wages to employees who are worked hard but well looked after during the period of labor. But it is also notable for the use of machines driven each by its individual motor. For steadiness of operation and for economy in factory production, leadership has passed from the steam to the electric engine. During the decade 1920–30 England has made some progress along this line through the introduction of American motors.

Not only in factories but on farms and in the homes has the electric motor been introduced. It milks the farmer's cows and does many jobs for the housewife in country and in town, such as cleaning and polishing floors, washing dishes and clothes, ironing clothes, toasting bread, cooling food, and warming human beings in bed and out.

The extent to which the people of America have adopted electrical devices is indicated in the following table. The figures are only approximations and refer to the beginning of the year 1930.[5]

Estimate of Electrical Devices in Domestic Use in the United States, 1930

Total number of households	28,000,000
Households receiving electric service	20,000,000
Flatirons (worked by hand)	18,800,000
Vacuum cleaners	8,720,000
Toasters	7,420,000
Radio sets	7,100,000
Clothes washers	6,680,000
Fans	5,880,000
Coffee percolators	5,500,000
Heaters	3,200,000
Sewing machines (with motor)	3,000,000
Refrigerators	1,880,000
Ranges (for cooking)	880,000
Ironers (for large flat work)	580,000
Oil burners (electric ignition)	500,000
Dishwashers	75,000

Though very rough approximations, these figures are fraught with significance. They tell a story of brightness, convenience, cleanliness, and enjoyment. But as usual the story needs elucidation. In the first place, we should note that many parts of America have no electric service whatever. On the other hand, in large cities and towns as well as in some specially favored country districts, electricity is cheap and widely used. While fewer than one-quarter of the homes in Mississippi, Arkansas, and Alabama in the aggregate are supplied with electricity, almost all of those in New York, California, and Massachusetts are provided with electric service. There are homes and apartments where every last mechanism has been installed, from electric lights to curling tongs and from vacuum cleaners to egg beaters. It is a serious thing for an Irish maid or an English butler to enter one of these homes for the first time. There are some who think that the desire for power machinery, like the desire for cleanliness, has become a fetish, a kind of American madness. I am personally more impressed with the service than the disservice of the two cults, which in due time will probably be accepted in other countries.

Important as these devices are at home, they are not much thought of abroad. The one American attainment in the electrical field, or at least partly in that field, that has attracted worldwide attention is the moving picture. The moving picture industry uses the camera, the arc light, and the film. The arc light goes back to the 1840's and the film to 1889. It is only by an electric lamp that enough light can be furnished to throw the picture upon a screen without burning up the film. It was towards the end of the period with which we are dealing that the American moving picture made headway, both at home and abroad. Technically it is an international invention, but commercially it is predominantly American. The talking picture is even more American and is likely to have more far-reaching results than the silent picture.

The third electric period, 1920-present, witnesses the practical introduction of radio. Wireless had been invented by Marconi in 1896 and put into practical use soon thereafter. Messages were sent across the Atlantic about 1902 and a news service supplied to ships in 1904. But far beyond this in importance has been the radio, which became a practical art in 1920 with the beginning of regular broadcasting by the KDKA station in Pittsburgh, a station owned by the Westinghouse Company. In America the radio inventions are to be numbered only in the thousands. Most of the work of devising new products is done by electrical engineers working in large well-organized laboratories.[6] On the horizon is the further development of television which was the subject of successful experiment in England and America in 1925 and of public demonstration in America in 1927. It has been estimated that it took the telephone 45 years, the electric light 37 years, and the radio only 8 years to reach 7,500,000 homes in America.[7] At what speed will television be introduced and what will be its effects?

In 1878 the Edison Electric Light Company was formed, and in 1887 seven companies were joined in one to constitute the Edison General Electric Company. It 1892 this became the General Electric Company, one of the largest concerns in the industry and one of the most forward looking. The other large firm is the Westinghouse Company with its chief factory at Pittsburgh and a plant at Niagara Falls. In 1899 it began to form subsidiary companies abroad. In 1896 the Westinghouse and General Electric Companies pooled their patents and in 1930 they secured joint control of the Radio Corporation of America. Thus did the rivals, Westinghouse championing the alternating current and Edison the direct current, come together, not in person but in commercial relations.

The Radio Corporation had been formed in 1919, partly to make America more independent of foreign wireless and cable companies. This corporation owns a broadcasting station in Washington and another in New York City. Its subsidiary, the National Broadcasting Company, owns the WEAF station in New York City and reaches radio listeners in all parts of the United States and Canada. In 1930 the American government instituted a suit to dissolve the monopoly possessed by the General Electric, the Westinghouse Company, the American Telephone and Telegraph Company, and others. In spite of all the progress made by these firms and the cheapening of instruments and service, there is fear of a monopoly. In England control is in the hands of the government; in America private initiative dominates. It remains to be seen which system will bring about the best results. Probably the English are getting more selective programs at present, but in the long run commercialized control will probably make for greater improvements.

America is clearly on the top of the electric ladder, if we consider both foreign exports and domestic use. There is no nation today that can be called a close second, except Germany. In exports abroad, however, the United States does not greatly surpass Germany or Great Britain.[8] In 1927 the estimated production of electrical equipment in the United States was $1,754,000,000. The chief items are insulated wires and cables, radio, incandescent lamps, storage batteries, and portable vacuum cleaners.[9] In 1928 America exported nearly $89,000,000 worth of electrical equipment, while it imported less than $3,000,000 worth.

Why the industry has developed in America and Germany and lost in England can only be inferred from general circumstances. It has been said that England lost partly because a law of 1882 gave to private companies only a short-term monopoly in the business of providing municipalities with light and power and no adequate compensation at the end of their period of monopoly.[10] I should weigh rather more heavily other factors, such as the fact that English manufacturers had their attention fixed upon the textile and steel industries. There was a lack of instruction in electricity in English universities. And also there was in England no water power comparable, for instance, to that in America.

When Germany and America girded their loins for industrial combat, they saw some difficult fields to conquer, some that were more easy. Iron and steel and the textiles were well developed in England and elsewhere. In the electrical industry there was practically an even start in the period 1870–80. The German banks greatly aided the German producers and at least by 1890 Germany was ahead of England. At the outbreak of the Great War Germany was independent of foreign nations in all important parts of the electrical industry. The Allgemeine Elektrizitäts-Gesellschaft has been a tower of strength in developing the electrical industry in Germany and in getting business abroad. It had developed in large part out of the same (or corresponding) firms as the General Electric Company in America. Both giant concerns had been founded upon the Edison and Thompson-Houston patents. In 1883 the Deutsche Edison-Gesellschaft had been formed; and in 1892 the Union-Elektrizitäts-Gesellschaft, using Thompson-Houston patents, especially for the building of electric street railways.[11] Indeed we can say that the influence of America on the electrical industry of Germany has been comparable to that of Germany on the chemical industry of America.

Just as there have been two great companies in the electrical industry in America—the General Electric and Westinghouse, so in Germany there have been two—the Allgemeine Elektrizitäts-Gesellschaft and the Siemens-Schuckert Company. The latter Company has been ahead recently but fresh amalgamations are reported. Just as the former German company had been closely associated with the General Electric Company, as we have seen, so has the latter German company had an agreement with the Westinghouse firm since 1925. We wonder whether the existence of two big concerns in an industry in the modern state does not approach something like the natural order, at least for the time being. In America there are the Ford Motor Company and the General Motors Corporation, the Allied Chemical and Dye Corporation and the Du Pont de Nemours and Company, and also the United States Steel Corporation and the Bethlehem Steel Corporation. To be sure, the tendency for two big concerns in an industry to join forces, even to amalgamate, is very strong, but there are reasons against such amalgamation. Public opinion is against it, of course, but an even more potent objection is the fact that amalgamation would be at once followed by the union of smaller rival firms. In this case, of course, there would be still two big combinations.

American progress has been due to a combination of circumstances. Labor-saving devices have been in demand in America from the first. Even consumers welcome mechanical tools and power machines, while in some countries, where labor is plentiful, there is a proud disdain of anything that aids the maidservant or the manservant. The home market in America is so large that even very special products are sufficiently in demand to enable manufacturers to produce in large quantities. There are waterfalls of great power, as at Niagara and Muscle Shoals. America has had many practical engineers without much mathematical training but with ingenuity and imagination. In spite of hampering legislation in America, particularly in the period 1877–1917, large business units have been formed and have flourished. The welding together of local power companies is at present one of the outstanding developments in American industrial history; it is not taking place without scrutiny and criticism, but it is actually going ahead rapidly.

NOTES TO CHAPTER XIII

1. Henry Schroeder, *History of Electric Light*, Smithsonian Miscellaneous Collections, vol. lxxvi, no. 2 (Washington, 1923), pp. 26–50.

2. V. S. Clark, *History of Manufactures in the United States*, vol. iii (1929), p. 379.

3. See H. C. Prout, *A Life of George Westinghouse* (1922), pp. 113 ff.

4. See *Ford Industries*, Ford Motor Company (1929), p. 19.

5. Electrical News Item for March 13, 1930, National Electric Light Association (New York). See the *Electrical World*, vol. xcv, no. i (Jan. 4, 1930), p. 10.

6. Cf. John T. Broderick, *Forty Years with the General Electric* (1929), pp. 89 ff.

7. See David Sarnoff, *The Development of the Radio Art and Radio Industry since 1920* (Harvard University, 1928).

8. See Thomas Butts, *Exports of Electrical Equipment from Germany, 1913–1927*, Bureau of Foreign and Domestic Commerce (Washington, 1928), pp. ii, 1 ff.

9. *Statistical Abstract of the United States for 1929* (Washington, 1929), pp. 833–834.

10. Emile Garcke in *Encyclopædia Britannica* (11th ed., 1910), vol, ix, p. 199a.

11. See Hermann Brinckmeyer, *Die Rathenaus* (1922), pp. 23, 44.

CHAPTER XIV

HISTORY OF A SINGLE AMERICAN FACTORY, 1844–1930

THE factory singled out for separate notice is the Dennison Manufacturing Company, Framingham, Massachusetts. It is engaged in neither chemical nor electrical production, but it has had a relatively long history, having taken its start in 1844, and has exhibited some of the most advanced policies adopted by manufacturers. A distinction of great significance from the standpoint of industrial history is the fact that the Company has recorded its own history which it keeps up to date. The industry in which it is engaged—the manufacture of jewelers' boxes, stationers' supplies, and the like—is highly specialized, with no tendency toward integration. It is not to be regarded as staple, it is not a key industry, and therefore may be taken to stand for those many businesses otherwise left unnoticed in this book.

The Dennison Manufacturing Company makes paper articles—boxes, crêpe, Christmas cards, gummed paper, and tags. It might be thought that it was no great step for such a firm to turn to record on paper the experiences through which it had passed. On his own initiative, one of the members of the managerial group, at present director of clerical activities and warehousing, began to collect material for the firm's history. Then official sanction was given to the enterprise in 1920 by the appointment of an historian, whose task it was to collect further records and to put them into shape for a narrative history. So far as I know, this is the first instance of the appointment of a business historian whose work is to record the history of a firm for the use of its directors. Up to date there have been three historians,[1] the second of whom has been drafted to assist in investigations of urgent policies of management and organization.

Over the History Room the historian with her assistant holds sway. Here the voluminous records are kept. For the period from 1844 to about 1871 the chief sources of information are family letters. For the period from 1871 to 1900 there are business records but they are incomplete. Since the year 1900 all essential material has been preserved. Besides the assortment of the original documents, there is a detailed history in thirty-two typewritten volumes up to and including the year 1923. Not only are the facts preserved but explanations are given. A consistent effort has been made to record the history of the firm from the standpoint of the business cycle. In this way the fortunes of the Company are correlated with general economic conditions.

The history of the Dennison Manufacturing Company has been compiled at considerable expense over a period of years, not as an advertising effort but as a guide to current business policy. It is an objective, highly critical history of successes and failures. Each new director is asked to study it and wherever possible excerpts are made for distribution to the directors whenever the experience of the past promises to throw any light upon the present. From time to time material pertinent to current problems is gathered from the history and distributed. The president of the Company, Mr. Henry S. Dennison, has made it clear that the history is no frill but a useful guide in the formulation of major as well as minor policies. The history is used to supply background for publication in little books of information, which are given to managers and employees. On at least one occasion the material collected was the basis of a victory in a lawsuit over patents.

So far in this volume we have been dealing with the economic history of manufactures. In this chapter, however, we turn away from the general treatment of marketing, technique, and general factors to business history. This latter subject is concerned with the way in which the factors of labor, management, and capital are made to yield profits and other satisfactions in a single business. There is really little in economic history that does not belong to business history, but the emphasis in business history is upon the way in which the different factors, public and private, have been woven together into the pattern of private business.

The Dennison firm had its start in Brunswick, a small inland town in Maine. The first Dennison concerned in the business had been a jeweler.[2] He undertook to make jewelers' boxes. He secured the assistance of other members of his family and soon the enterprise was moderately successful. Other articles were added, notably tags, gummed labels, and crêpe paper. A patent, taken out in 1863 for a tag with a re-enforced hole, may be said to have put the firm upon a secure foundation.

Soon after the beginning of manufacture, a sales office was opened in Boston, then one in New York City in 1853, in Philadelphia in 1862, and in Chicago in 1868. Now there are five stores and twenty-two main sales offices in the United States and Canada, a store in London, sales offices in London, Manchester, Hamburg, and Copenhagen, and other offices in Mexico, Cuba, Argentina, Brazil, India, and Australia.[3]

Manufacture, beginning in 1844 in Brunswick, was also carried on in Boston from 1850 onwards and in Roxbury after the Boston fire of 1872. In 1894 the Brunswick plant was given up, and in 1897 and 1898 the manufacturing establishment was moved from Roxbury to Framingham, a small industrial satellite about twenty miles from Boston. In the Framingham plant there are about 2,500 employees, approximately half of them women. Nearby, in Marlboro, Massachusetts, boxes are made in a second plant and in London, England, some commodities are also manufactured. A factory is about to be established in the Province of Quebec, Canada, partly to enjoy the advantage of water power but chiefly to avoid paying the heavy Canadian duties.

Outside the chief plant or plants not a little work has been done for the Dennison firm by people—women and children—working in their own homes.[4] Such outwork is more common in the Old World than in the New. It is sometimes regarded as "un-American." In general, and notably in the case of the Dennison firm, it is clearly necessitated by the peculiar requirements of the work or by the shortage of factory labor. Beginning about 1872, paper boxes were made in the Brunswick district. From 1906 to 1924 some boxes were made in this way in the same district, but the percentage of the total number of boxes was never large. For the stringing of tags, outside labor in homes had to be drawn upon because of the lack of machinery to do this kind of work. The system was at its height 1890–1910. During the World War most of the stringing came to be done in the factory by machines. At present, less than 20 per cent of the Dennison tags are strung in homes. The cost of employing outworkers is at present higher than using machines. Control of working conditions—sanitation and the use of children—is difficult, though since 1913 a careful system of inspection has been adopted. But the system of outwork continues, tags being now delivered to the homes and called for by truck, essentially as had been done under the dependent phase of the wholesale handicraft system, hundreds of years ago.

Indeed this system has in many districts been an adjunct to the factory ever since the Industrial Revolution.

One of the keys to the history of this firm, as is to be expected, is the general condition of the country's business. From 1844 to 1898, except for the Civil War period, a buyers' market generally prevailed. It was a hard job to sell goods. Sales offices were multiplied to reach the trade.[5] From 1898 to 1906 a sellers' market prevailed and with the ease of marketing goods came an emphasis upon production. An effort was made to improve both machinery and organization. Then came a buyers' market again, in the years 1906–15, in which there was an increase of sales offices from five major offices to thirty in all, many of the latter number being quite small. At the same time, however, the management of sales was closely centralized, like production, at the factory in Framingham. The war period, 1915–20, saw a sellers' market, with a decline in the efficiency of the sales organization. Beginning in 1921 came the present buyers' market, with a gradually dawning fear that the centralization of sales had gone too far. During the year 1930 the control of sales was partly decentralized again by the establishment of general sales managers at Chicago, Philadelphia, and Cleveland, but all controlled by the director of sales at Framingham.[6] There is now such a consciousness of policy, such an awareness of dangers, that the old-time swings are not likely to be repeated, at least in their extremes. The pendulum will probably not swing so far.

When the firm began, it was owned and managed by an individual member of the Dennison family, though soon other members were taken in. A partnership with three employees was established in 1855, lasting until 1878. In that year a corporation was formed, the Dennison Manufacturing Company. This was done, at least in part, so that ownership and control could be shared with those persons in managerial posts who were actually making the business a success. The (common) stock was distributed by the directors, who were all large shareholders, during the period 1878–1911, and distributed according to their own will and pleasure.[7] There were two weaknesses involved in this plan. Discontent arose because of the arbitrary way in which the distribution took place, "office politics" being charged as the determining factor in the distribution. Moreover, there was also a danger that the stock going to the managerial group would in time be possessed by outsiders. Accordingly, Mr. Henry S. Dennison and his uncle, C. S. Dennison, then president, devised a system which went into effect in the year 1911.[8] This is called the managerial industrial partnership plan.

Under this new plan the managerial group shares in the profits according to the salary received. From 1911 to 1919 those who had been employed at least five years and who received not less than a stated minimum salary were included in the plan. From 1919 to 1926 distinction was made between those who used a high degree of imagination, tact, and judgment in their work and those who did not. Obviously this was hard to determine. From 1926 onward, a careful rating has been made of persons and jobs. This has been done by specialists and with great difficulty because of the fact that in the last analysis the basis of decision is human judgment. Some objective tests are possible, for example, whether a man selling to dealers does more business than the average of his class. If not, he would not ordinarily be included in the plan.[9] On January 31, 1930, there were approximately 175 in the managerial group (of a total of about 450) who were actually participating in profit sharing. In 1929 a change was instituted whereby no manager received any stock dividend on the first $1,500 of his salary. This was proposed by the president and accepted by the managerial group.

The method of bringing about the sharing of profits is significant. In the reorganization of 1911 two classes of primary stock were provided for. One was debenture stock to be held by the former owners of the business. The stock was made non-voting and transferable. The dividend was fixed at eight per cent. A second class of stock was created, the common stock, the holders of which alone possessed the voting power. The dividends were to vary according to earnings. It was this class of stock that was distributed among the members of the managerial group. If holders of this stock, that is, the managerial group, could not pay the fixed rate of eight per cent on the debenture stock, then control reverted to the debenture stockholders. And, if an owner of common stock left the Company, he exchanged his holdings for seven per cent preferred stock (a third category) which was non-voting but transferable.

Accordingly, the different persons regarded as managers, either in manufacture or sales, received each year so many shares as their portion of the profits. This would mean but little unless they could earn dividends over the eight per cent on the debenture stock and seven per cent on the preferred. Here is, of course, an incentive to further effort. It is the view of those entitled to know that the managerial industrial partnership plan is on the whole successful.

It is the managerial group of salaried people, which since 1911 has shared in the profits, that elects the directors and the president, in short, controls the business. But, to repeat, this is only so long as they pay the fixed charges on debenture stock.

The way that the profit-sharing scheme has actually worked out for two of the managers is shown in the following figures. I take only two out of ten instances supplied by the firm.[10]

Year	First Manager				Second Manager			
	Salary	Stock	Cash Div.	Total	Salary	Stock	Cash Div.	Total
1920	$2,520	$1,680		$4,200	$3,210	$2,140		$5,350
1921	2,640	530	$134	3,304	4,020	800	$171	4,991
1922	2,880	960	177	4,017	4,380	1,460	235	6,075
1923	3,120	1,250	317	4,687	4,730	1,890	440	7,060
1924	3,120	310	221	3,651	4,875	490	315	5,680
1925	3,120	780	378	4,278	5,100	1,270	542	6,912
1926	3,600	900	386	4,886	5,580	1,390	564	7,534
1927	3,600	540	449	4,589	6,000	900	661	7,561
1928	3,600	540	556	4,696	6,600	990	827	8,417
1929	3,600	420	599	4,619	7,200	1,140	906	9,246
Total	31,800	7,910	3,217	42,927	51,695	12,470	4,661	68,826

It is notable that the lower-salaried manager received less stock dividend in 1929 than in the preceding years, while the higher-salaried manager received more. This is in accordance with the new plan whereby no stock is distributed on the first $1,500 of salary.

In the year 1919 an employee industrial partnership plan was created.[11] It was actually conceived and worked out by the Company's union, or works committee. The directors of the Company accepted the plan as an experiment. To say the least, this plan is not now so universally regarded as a success as the one dealt with above. It is at least very doubtful whether it has led to increased effort on the part of the rank and file of the employees.

All employees who are not in the managerial system, who have served at least two years, participate in the employee partnership plan. In 1927 the two years of service were increased to five years. The amount that each employee receives is according to his length of service. Each year he receives so much stock as his share in the profits. In 1927 there were 2,363 employee partners who received $96,750 worth of stock. In 1929 there were 1,866 who received $102,350 worth of stock.

The profits are allotted each year as follows: cash dividends are paid, first, to the debenture and preferred stockholders and, secondly, to the managerial and employee groups holding common stock. Then a stock dividend is given to the two groups, two-thirds of the total amount available for distribution to the managers and one-third to the workmen. In 1928 and 1929 this worked out as follows:

	1928	1929
Debenture stock, at 8 per cent....	$ 333,070.00	$ 330,920.00
Preferred stock, at 7 per cent......	161,803.25	178,746.75
Common stock, at 8 per cent......	313,436.00	323,929.30
Stock dividends to the 2 classes....	356,505.69	333,859.14
Total profits divided	$1,164,815.94	$1,167,455.19

These payments came out of net earnings of $1,271,929.62 on net sales of $16,375,000 for the year 1928 and out of net earnings of $1,275,310.53 on net sales of $16,800,000 for the year 1929.[12]

In order to complete the outline of the organization, we should note the existence of an investors' advisory council, established in 1927 as an experiment but now accepted as permanent. The purpose was to get outside opinion concerning general policy. It was feared that there might be dangerous inbreeding of ideas and methods. The new council is made up of five men who are directors of banks, raliroads, and manufacturing concerns. They are holders of small amounts of preferred stock in the Dennison Manufacturing Company. Since the first year the remuneration for each councillor has been in the form of cash payments.

Even at this point we might feel that the Dennison Manufacturing Company is all organization. How could the individuals ever find time to manufacture and sell, if they had to master this elaborate system? A visit to the

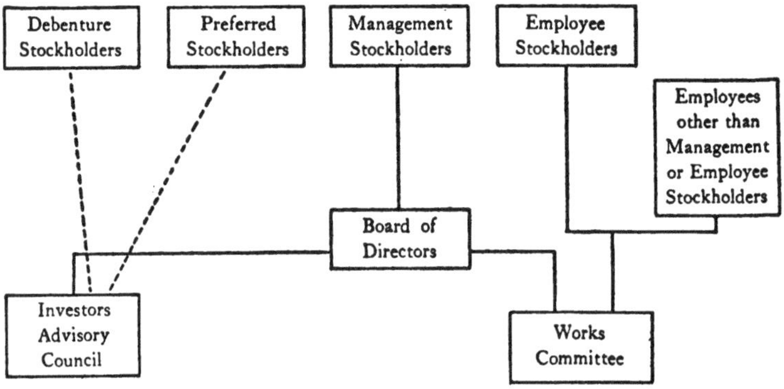

ORGANIZATION CONTROL CHART OF THE DENNISON MANUFACTURING COMPANY, 1930

plant, however, would show that it actually works with machine intensity. The capital structure, which we have been noting, is indeed a relatively simple part of the whole organization, as we are about to see.

The labor policy of the Company is enlightened. Trade unions are permitted but there is no closed shop. Besides the employee industrial partnership plan there is a company union, as already noted. This is known as the works committee plan or the employees' co-operative plan. The mass meeting that formulated it in 1919 was summoned by the War Industries Committee, apparently at the suggestion of Mr. Henry S. Dennison who presided on the occasion. In a general way the system that was adopted may be said to have had its prototype in an organization developed in the plant during the Great War. Certainly the purpose is to bring about co-operation and the forestalling of differences between employers and employees. Only the non-managerial group is concerned. Each of the employees, so understood, votes by secret ballot for one representative for his or her department. Some sixty of these departmental representatives constitute the general works committee, or congress of workmen, as we may call it. This general works committee chooses a central committee made up of one representative from each of the nine divisions of the Dennison plant. This we may regard as the cabinet.

Over each division there is a committee made up of the representatives of the various departments in the division, the chairman being the member of the central committee elected by the works committee. To this divisional committee or to the central committee go disputes or complaints made by individual employees or by groups of employees. If the employee wishes, his representative will be his advocate or adviser. There are four standing committees for looking after certain fields of activities: procedure and publicity; hours, wages, promotions, unemployment, classification, and suggestion; buildings, facilities, health, safety, and lunch room; and housing.[13] One half the members of each committee are appointed by the works committee, the other half by the management. Here we have a sharing of responsibility and the pooling of the experience of both groups.

At the close of 1929 inquiry was made among the employees as to the success of the works committee. Replies were made by means of unsigned questionnaires. Questions and answers have been tabulated as follows.[14]

	Yes	No	No Answer	Total
1. Has the works committee ever helped you personally?........	680	1,119	63	1,862
2. Do you think the works committee plan is working to the advantage of the employees as a whole?....................	1,466	286	111	1,866
3. Have you used your works committee representative?........	763	1,026	75	1,864
4. If any appropriate occasion should arise, would you consult with your works committee representative?	1,529	225	185	1,942
5. Do you think your foreman or chief clerk co-operates willingly with the works committee?...	1,187	382	288	1,864
6. Are you in favor of having the works committee plan continue?	1,485	210	138	1,833

There is a fund to assist in relieving distress in the case of unemployment. The fund has been supplied by the directors out of surplus Company earnings. If it is necessary to lay off an employee for a half day or longer, eighty per cent of the wages are paid if the employee has dependents and sixty per cent if no dependents. If an employee has to be transferred temporarily to a job where he receives less than his average rate of pay, the difference is made up from the fund. The payments from a fund amounting in the second year (1921) to $150,000 were less than $23,000, the following year only a little over $1,500. In 1928 the payments amounted to less than $8,000.

In addition, in this complex of organization, there is a men's mutual relief association, and one also for women. There is a savings fund and a credit union. There is a club for men. In 1909 a clinic was established, and also a lunch room. There is a reference library and a monthly magazine. Assistance is given in matters of getting a place to live, where to go for vacation, making a garden, and solving tax problems and legal difficulties. There is no pension fund, but pensions have been paid for almost forty years to individuals whose merits of long and faithful service clearly justified consideration. Employees are frequently recommended to insure their lives under the State insurance plan.

Under this strenuous régime of organization and assistance there has been a decline in labor turnover, as is seen in the following figures:

	Percentage		Percentage
1911	68	1921	28
1912	61	1922	23
1913	55	1923	22
1914	37	1924	18
1915	28	1925	27
1916	37	1926	25
1917	49	1927	18
1918	65	1928	18
1919	44	1929	28
1920	48		

Clearly the turnover is due in part to general conditions, but there has been a reduction to a healthful rate that is in part due to the Company's own efforts. Of course within these totals are many different situations in different groups. For instance, the older employees may be holding fast, while the younger ones may be changing a good deal.

For a long time a reward has been given for suggestions as to new products, improvements in the use of machinery, the reduction of waste, the prevention of accidents, and so on. In the year 1900 there were 267 suggestions made. In 1928 there were 4,023 received, of which 94 were awarded cash prizes, and 140 certificates. The plan has been to pay $25 for ten suggestions accepted. In 1929 certificates and cumulative awards were abolished and the minimum cash award was increased in order to secure a higher type of suggestion.

One wonders whether there is a single loose plate in the armor of the Dennison Manufacturing Company. Of course, it is possible that all the plates are sound but that the total weight is only such as the extinct dinosaur could bear. Many critics of modern conditions fear industrial regimentation as comparable to the medieval adscription to the soil. If profit sharing ties a man to a poorly paid job, there is no individual or social gain. But the individual in the Dennison Manufacturing Company can always leave and on leaving exchange his common stock, voting or non-voting, for seven per cent preferred stock. The danger of erecting too high a capital structure under the profit-sharing scheme will, of course, have to be watched. There is evidence that it is watched. Inbreeding is being avoided by the investors' advisory council. Overcentralization is feared and may be changed. The location in New England is one of the most serious of situations, but perhaps not yet considered a problem. Clearly the chief plant is not near the center of the national market, and it is located in a state which is no longer one of low costs. The struggle for western markets appears to be very keen and only partly successful. Some of the services provided by the firm have not really arisen out of the demands of the employees and have been abandoned, such as the circulating library and the dental clinic. The latter, however, had met a real need in helping to educate the workers to care for their teeth.

The week's work is forty-eight hours.[15] A week's vacation with pay is given to employees of ten years' service, and two weeks to those of fifteen years' service. Inside the factory gates there is no smoking allowed. But this is a measure of safety in the interest of all. Nor is there any tobacco chewing allowed—a sanitary rule of common benefit.

Although few, if any, of the institutions and practices here outlined are peculiar to the Dennison Manufacturing Company, it would seem that the aggregate is unusual. Indeed in America as a whole the old system of strenuous employer dominance may be said to prevail. The general system is one of autocracy; the Dennison system is management sharing. Ordinarily the owners of factories get all the profits, while the Dennison owners now share theirs. Ordinarily high salaries are paid to a few to drive the rank and file to harder effort, while the Dennison way is to pay rather lower salaries but to reward the many managers and other employees by stock dividends. Generally the sole aim of a manufacturer is profits; in the Dennison plant, however, it is profits combined with an intellectual interest in the ways of work. In America it is common for a manufacturing firm to belong to a great many associations and neglect almost all of them; the Dennison firm, however, takes its associations seriously, even though it belongs to about sixty-three of them, some trade, some local, and some scientific.

The influence of personalities runs throughout the history of the Dennison Manufacturing Company, but it has not been allowed to prevail apart from general business conditions. Among the several instances of outstanding individuals is Henry S. Dennison who was born in 1877, became a factor in the firm in 1906, and was elected president in 1917. He has been responsible for many changes, including the compilation of the business history. His practical idealism, his intellectual interest in business as a human and social problem, have made deep impressions upon the Company's organization and spirit.

Obviously the real test of the Dennison system is yet to come. When the master hand of the president is no longer at the helm, what will happen? At present he is elected by the managers and accepted by all. And, then, there are the hard times that may come some day when no dividends are available for debenture stock. In that case control reverts to the debenture stockholders. If there is no one among the debenture stockholders with the fine outlook of the present president, the whole scheme may be permanently scrapped and a notable experiment, a noble structure, thrown into the discard. But it would not have lived in vain, since it has established a precedent for getting the most out of human effort, for rewarding those who are able and willing to do the world's work, and for treating workers as individuals of dignity and feeling.

NOTES TO CHAPTER XIV

1. Dr. Thomas P. Martin, 1920–22; Mr. E. P. Hayes, 1922–26; and Miss Charlotte Heath, 1926–30. The first was a professional historian, the second had been a student of history and a teacher of English literature, and the third had specialized in English while in college.

2. See *Some Dennison Plans and Practices* (Dennison Manufacturing Co., Framingham, Mass., 1929) p. 3.

3. *Ibid.*, p. 5.

4. Information on this subject has been supplied by Miss Charlotte Heath, historian of the Dennison Manufacturing Company.

5. On this subject of fluctuating policy, see the "History of the Dennison Manufacturing Company" by E. P. Hayes in the *Journal of Economic and Business History*, vol. i (1928–29), pp. 467–502, and by Charlotte Heath *ibid.*, vol. ii (1929–30), pp. 163–202.

6. See the *Annual Report to Stockholders for the Year, 1929* (Dennison Manufacturing Co., Framingham, Mass., 1930).

7. See *Some Dennison Plans and Practices* (1929), p. 8.

8. Charlotte Heath, *op. cit.*, p. 176.

9. See "A Method of Determining Who Shall Participate Under a Managerial Profit-Sharing Plan," by J. S. Keir and E. P. Hayes, in *Proceedings of Institute of Management*, no. 10 (1929), p. 9. See Henry S. Dennison on "Who can hire Management," in *Profit Sharing and Stock Ownership for Employees* (1926), pp. 356–386, by Gorton James, Henry S. Dennison, Edwin F. Gay, Henry P. Kendall, and Arthur W. Burritt.

10. Provided by Miss Charlotte Heath at my request.

11. See *Dennison Employees' Co-operative Plan, Constitution and By-laws* (1928); *Dennison Employees' Co-operative Plan, Summary* (1928); *Employee Industrial Partnership Plan* (Dennison Manufacturing Co., Framingham, Mass., 1928).

12. See the *Annual Report to Stockholders for the Year, 1928* (Dennison Manufacturing Co., Framingham, Mass., 1929), and *ibid., 1929* (1930).

13. Recent changes in organization are found in a typed report entitled A Study of the Structure of the General Works Committee [early 1930].

14. Printed in *Round Robin*, vol. xxiv (Jan., 1930), p. 23. This is a monthly magazine for use of the employees.

15. See *Book of Information*, revised edition (Framingham, Mass., 1927), pp. 5–12.

CHAPTER XV

GENERAL DEVELOPMENTS IN RECENT INDUSTRIAL HISTORY

SO CONTINUOUS has been the progress in industry that some writers have regarded the Industrial Revolution which began in the eighteenth century as continuing throughout the nineteenth century[1] or even down to the present day. Others have suggested two new revolutions, the chemical and the electrical, for which there is not a little to be said. When we are farther away from the crowded industrial events of the last 150 years we may observe the incoming of a new stage. So far, however, all that has happened appears to be by way of the unfolding of what was begun in the eighteenth century.

The conquest of the joint-stock principle in industry has been slow but continuous. Although no special study seems to have been made of this subject, we can probably say that the development has occurred in textiles, iron and steel, oil refining, flour milling, lumber milling, and so on down to our day when even newspapers are ceasing to be owned by a single individual or by partners. Wherever greater capital or continuity of operations is at stake, the joint-stock form has the preference. Although the incorporation of a firm as a joint-stock company is sometimes a mere legal convenience, it generally means wider ownership and greater public confidence.

For a long time the single factory was sufficient for a single firm, though here and there during the Industrial Revolution one man might own two or more, notably in the case of John Wilkinson. But in recent years, as observed in America, it has been found profitable to combine several plants. One set of officials can manage certain aspects of the work of all together and make each supplement the others either in manufacturing process or in marketing. Moreover, the large corporation, which owns several factories, possessing greater credit than the small firm, can borrow money more easily and more cheaply. In this way economy and stability are effected. It can afford to employ engineers and others of special training. The Hood Rubber Company, manufacturing rubber shoes, tires, and other goods, had about nine manufacturing plants (located from Boston to Kansas City), with about forty branches and warehouses in various cities. In 1929 it was purchased by the B. F. Goodrich (Rubber) Company which has one big plant at Akron and several foreign subsidiaries. The new amalgamation is, of course, a very large and almost worldwide concern. The union points to the great advantage of having several factories under one management. Also, if the demand for one of the products lessens, there will still be others that can be marketed. Although some factories might have to close for a while, there would be less likelihood of bankruptcy. The United States Steel Corporation with its original eleven subordinate units, each with its own combination of factories, mines, railroads, and local companies, is another illustration, as is the International Harvester Company. We need only to look into *Moody's Manual of Investments* to discover how far amalgamation of factories has proceeded. In the period 1919–28 over 1,000 iron and steel concerns in the United States disappeared through merger, as did over 800 engaged in manufacturing foodstuffs and over 400 producing oil.[2] Only the least economical plants would be dismantled in the case of amalgamation or merger.

An outstanding instance of amalgamation is the General Motors Corporation, made up of a number of individual motor-car companies and other units, all welded together for purposes of financial stability and economy of sales. This corporation has for sale, directly or through its subsidiary companies, a variety of products of recent invention and manufacture—several makes and grades of pleasure automobiles, automobile trucks, electric refrigerators, radio sets, and talking machines. It is one of the outstanding business units in the United States. In the boom culminating in the panic of 1929 its shares were the object of a good deal of speculative dealing.

In certain favorably located districts, factories and other plants have arisen, quite apart from integration and combination. Commonly those districts had an advantage in raw materials, labor supply, transportation facilities, or demand for the finished product. Sometimes there has been a combination of all these favoring circumstances. In and around Boston, New York, Philadelphia, Pittsburgh, Cleveland, Detroit, Chicago, the Twin Cities, St. Louis, Kansas City, San Francisco, and Los Angeles conditions have been most favorable. But already there has set in a pronounced dispersion of factories from the East to the West and South and from larger cities to smaller towns. Much printing has moved away from New York City. The textile firms of New England have gone South for cheap labor and for relief from high taxes, and new shoe factories have sprung up in St. Louis and Milwaukee to be near the source of supply and a consuming market. The flour-milling firms of Minneapolis, however, have gone both eastward and westward, establishing new mills or buying up old ones in Buffalo, New York, as well as in Kansas and Utah. Both the Washburn Crosby Company and the Pillsbury Flour Milling Company have been anxious to secure the far-western supply of good wheat and to get the advantages of transportation rates which Buffalo offers.[3]

It has been the business side of factory production that has brought about these changes—concentration of ownership, localization, and dispersion. It is a reasonable expectation that many far-reaching changes are yet to take place along these lines.

On the technical as well as on the business side of factory production there has been improvement. Under the leadership of Taylor, Gantt, and others an effort has been made to make more effective use of the factors and forces at work.[4] It is true that many manufacturers have tried to follow the methods of these leaders without ever having heard of them or the system called Taylorism. Under the ægis of this scientific management, about which many books have been written, labor is economized and speeded up, machinery is used for longer hours and with less loss of working periods, and the number of movements involving lost motion has been reduced. The whole factory has been carefully planned, as have the various steps in the process of manufacture. In most cases the plant has been made into a splendid autocracy or plutocracy, with an hierarchical gradation from the board of directors down to the least of the employees. Responsibility has been fixed to a nicety, and record is kept of mistakes and losses for the purpose of further improvement. It must be admitted that many factory owners have never seen the need or advantage of introducing such a system and some that have done so have more of the system than they have of good results.

The reduction of accidents and the prevention of disease has been a notable achievement of the factory régime. Fresh air has been provided, dust removed from the atmosphere, the lighting made adequate, and machines guarded so that the unwary workman cannot injure himself. Various automatic devices have been put upon the machinery, not only to do the work but in case of emergency to stop the machine itself. Some of these improvements are due to legislation, some to the initiative of enlightened factory owners, and some to the working out of the insurance situation. Employers' liability insurance is a common imposition upon factories, and it has worked out very well. Insurance companies have varying rates for different grades of factories. The factory in which there is danger of accident has to pay a high rate, the well-ordered factory a lower one.

The introduction of schools into factories or co-ordination of the work in the factory with teaching in the school has proved to be at least a partial solution for the lack of an effective apprenticeship in America. The United Shoe Machinery Corporation in Beverly, Massachusetts, admits two groups of thirty-five boys each from the high school, one group one week, the other the next week. Thus does practical instruction supplement and enliven theoretical education. The boys receive one-half the wages of men performing the same type of work. While in the factory the students discover the kind of machine that fits them best and are encouraged to master some special line of work connected therewith so that they may become skilled operators, repairers, or inventors. Of course, many other industrial concerns have such schools, that of the Ford Motor Company being the best known.

The counterpart of factory schools is the public trade school or the college which gives its students theoretical and cultural training within its own walls and also sends them out for practical experience in factories and other plants. Antioch College keeps its students at their books for five weeks and then sends them out for five. The College of Engineering at the University of Cincinnati has had a notable plan since 1906. Students of applied arts, engineering, and commerce are kept four weeks at their desks and in their laboratories and then they are sent out to practical work in widely scattered towns and cities. For this work the students are paid. It is claimed that in a five-year course under such a plan more can be accomplished than in the usual four-year course. In such ways, by sending the student into the factory, or by forcing the industrial novice into the school, does modern society meet the situation of training once solved by apprenticeship to a master. Many factory owners have seen that their most precious asset is healthy and contented employees. Accordingly, rest rooms, baths, surgical and dental attention, and restaurants are provided. There is nothing too good for good workers. This is enlightened selfishness. Of course it is no substitute for good wages. Moreover, the workman does not want a bath for himself, whilst his wife and children at home have none. In addition there are athletic and social clubs, with their field days, singing contests, and bands. To some of the workers this kind of thing is welcome, to others it is just a part of a noxious industrial regimentation.

There seem to be only six states in the United States that have old-age pension systems,[5] none of them except Wisconsin having much industry. Individual industrial plants, commonly large concerns, have found it advisable to establish their own pension systems. To cast off the old employees, particularly those of long service, is both inhuman and productive of bad feeling on the part of employees generally. Moreover, to keep workmen after they are aged and inefficient is wasteful and harmful to the morale of the plant. There are apparently very few firms in the United States that have developed satisfactory systems. Individual cases are handled according to individual needs, or in some instances a certain percentage of the salary at the time of retiring is multiplied by the number of years of service. Obviously this is unfair in many cases. Moreover, there are few concerns that have provided for their pension schemes financially, the pensions being often paid out of current earnings. Accordingly there is a lack of certainty for the workmen and there is mounting liability for the firm. The United States Steel Corporation spent $281,000 for pensions in 1911 and $3,488,000 in 1928. There is said to be a tendency to put pensions on a contributory basis. While this may increase the amount of the pension, it is likely to tie the workman to one firm unless the scheme is carefully safeguarded. But at least we have this one assurance that manufacturers have developed a feeling of responsibility in the matter. Smaller plants, however, appear hopeless. The ultimate solution would seem to be a general contributory insurance plan managed by the state, much as in England.

The sharing of the profits of the factory has been an idea dreamed of by theorists and now put into practice as an enlightened measure, benefiting all concerned. Just how far it is introduced simply to get more work and better results and how far as a bit of social justice, it is difficult to state. In almost all cases it is probably true that abstractions have no part in the situation. The profits are shared in various ways, consideration being given to length of service and wages received.

Industrial democracy, or the sharing of management with the workers, has made headway but is not yet a generally accepted practice.[6] It is looked upon with more favor in England than in America. Certainly there is a feeling in the breasts of most men that they would like to have some control over their own destinies, or more specifically to decide matters of factory routine and discipline. The recognition of such a feeling is a part of wisdom as many employers have experienced. Rewards have come to the factory in the form of better work arising from contentment and in the form of valuable suggestions through formal organization. All this is no alternative to a living wage, but it is a part of industrial enlightenment. Of course, sharing management does not appeal to all alike. The discontented employee cares nothing for it and the revolutionary socialist wants all or none.

The régime of trade unionism has been tried and on the whole has been found not without merits, both to the factory and to the public as well as to the workman. A new device, however, has been adopted, largely since the Great War, with promising results. This is the company union.[7] Such a union brings into one large association all of the men and women employed in the factory. No trade unionism prevails to discriminate against such unskilled workers as the gate keepers and the sweepers. Negroes as well as whites are admitted. Both foremen and workmen, superintendents and office helpers are included. Some kind of organization is brought about, wherein there is both a congress and a cabinet. The labor manager always works with both interests, the employing and employed, endeavoring to keep an even keel. If he cannot, his usefulness is gone. I have heard workmen discuss this new development as one of the most threatening to trade unionism in the United States. One of the labor leaders said in 1926, "Well, if it is a good thing, why don't we accept it?" It was argued that the men were well satisfied and that they saw that, as fast as they could increase earnings for the firm, they could increase their own. But there was developed the argument, strongly urged, that in due time, when the trade unions had disappeared, the friendly attitude, of the masters would disappear. Experience has taught the workman that, in the past, employers have been as a class enlightened only when forced to be so.

Optimists will have us believe that a new industrial revolution has been born in America.[8] Wise men come out of Europe to view the miraculous event. No new shafts or wheels, no new motors or dynamos bring about the change. It is a new spirit, a new vision of a different world. The manufacturer is reducing prices and selling more goods. He is raising the wages of his employees so that they may buy his motor cars, radios, and the like. By means of efficient management, large-scale production, and high wages the wheels of industry have been humming. Hours of work have been shorter and hours of pleasure longer. Whether this new condition has come to stay or is just an aftermath of the Great War is yet to be learned. Certainly the rate of wages has been kept high with but little objection on the part of the employer—in England by means of the dole and minimum-wage laws and in America through the fear on the part of employers that, if they pay low wages, they will kill the market for their wares. Here is a new circle of relationship. Whether it is a vicious circle will in due time appear. Ordinarily such a condition settles down to a lower level of result than original enthusiasts ascribed to it.

Prohibition, or enforced temperance, has come to America under circumstances that are complicated. One of the certain features of the régime is the excellent effect upon poor workers and upon factory production.[9] Mondays used to be only part days, the workmen either not appearing or not being entirely sober. At noontime beer or whiskey was drunk, small in amount but sufficient to take off the fine edge of labor. At home the worker spent more for strong drink than for milk. As a child he was undernourished, so that when he became a worker his hand was not deft nor his brain clear. The opinion has been expressed by one enlightened factory owner that one glass of beer is too much for the modern delicately machinized factory. There seems to be a growing feeling abroad that foreign peoples cannot compete with a sober America. It is just this recognition that makes the enemies of prohibition at home and abroad so bitter in its denunciation. There are strong arguments against prohibition, but they do not pertain to general industry.

Economy in human labor through prohibition and other measures finds its counterpart in economy in the use of materials. In a well-organized factory of any size there is almost no waste product. Iron filings, waste paper, sweepings, sawdust, and the like are all saved. In meat packing, the hair, bone, gristle, blood, and intestines are all used as well as the flesh, hides, and fat.[10] Valuable by-products have been developed out of formerly wasted materials. From bagasse, a waste product in the paper industry, insulating board is now made; from corncobs hitherto only refuse in the canning factories, furfurol is now obtained; and from copper refinery sludge, gold and silver are salvaged.[11] It is said that some firms have paid their dividends out of their waste material.

While chemists have been largely responsible for the utilization of waste product, engineers have led the way in mechanical improvements. The standardization of parts of machines has saved both labor and the capital invested in parts. The simplification of designs and equipment has meant a great deal to workmen and other users of manufactured products. Each firm used to develop its own size and shape and the user thereof often was hard put to it to renew any parts broken or lost. In electrical equipment, beginning with the Great War, simplification made considerable headway. In the brick industry it is said that out of sixty-six varieties and sizes of paving bricks, sixty-two have been eliminated.[12]

The moving of goods within the factory has been until recently largely a matter of hand labor. It is true that the elevating of grain by means of conveyors goes back at least to the time of Oliver Evans in flour milling, and to an earlier date in rice mills, and that elevators or lifts have long been a valuable auxiliary in factory production. But now by means of chutes, endless belts, chain conveyors, and trucmotors great economies are effected. Still, much remains to be done.

Changes in the use of power are notable in America. More power and less labor per unit of product is being used. The power is being produced more economically through improved engines or other equipment. More and more electricity is being introduced into factory production. In America in 1899 only five per cent of the primary horsepower used came from electric motors, while in 1927 it was probably over seventy-five per cent.[13] Of course for effectiveness and economy there is at present no power comparable to electric.

There has been, of course, a gradual extension of machine production. This extension has been not only by way of the integration of various processes to produce a complete article, as in the case of the giant presses which turn out our metropolitan papers for better or for worse, but there have been invented new machines to do work hitherto performed only by hand. This is illustrated by the machines making cigarettes. Power machines are now used for redrying tobacco, for packing leaves, for cutting the tobacco, for printing the names on the cigarette papers, for making the body of the cigarette, for putting on cork tips, and for wrapping cigarettes in foil. In 1916 it was said that one machine could make 400 cigarettes in a minute.[14] Even the manufacture of cigars is becoming machinized. In 1929 there were about 3,000 automatic

AN AUTOMATIC BOTTLE-MAKING MACHINE, MADE UNDER PATENTS ISSUED 1904-16

machines at work in the United States. The hand workers complain but the movement proceeds. In the making of such machines, the International Cigar Machinery Company, incorporated in 1901, has a position similar to that of the United Shoe Machinery Corporation in the shoe industry. Since the cost of a single machine is about $4,000, the bigger manufacturers have an enormous advantage over the smaller ones.

Another example of automatic machinery invented and manufactured in the United States is found in bottle making.[15] In 1899 M. J. Owens of Toledo, Ohio, applied for a patent, which was issued in 1904. Other patents followed. The result is the machine here illustrated—and a complete revolution in bottle manufacture. Previously one man would blow one bottle at a time, the glass being gathered by hand on blow pipes. This machine, diabolical in appearance but effective in operation, sucks up its charges from a revolving pot fed by a melting furnace, and blows from 15 to 45 bottles at each revolution. It discharges them into the annealing oven at the rate of from 50 to 200 a minute, in sizes ranging from 32 ounces down to one dram capacity. Other Owens machines carry the sizes up to 12 gallons. The product is more uniform and cheaper than the handmade articles. Skilled workmen are completely done away with. Only a single machine tender is needed to watch the machine. It displaces from 50 to 150 men and boys, according to the size of the bottles made. The smaller the bottle the more the advantage with the machine. As illustrated, it contains approximately 9,000 parts, and weighs over 100,000 pounds. It has never been on sale. It was originally placed with a limited number of licensees under royalty. Later, the Owens Bottle Machine Company (now known as Owens-Illinois Glass Company of Toledo) developed its own bottle manufacturing business by the use of the Owens machine. It designs its own machines, which are manufactured for it by the Kent-Owens Machine Company of Toledo.

The increase in the size of plants has been common in progressive countries as has the increase in the capacity to produce, at lower cost, more exact wares and larger commodities. As illustration of the last-named, we mention only cannon, steam engines, and steel girders. Almost every year we learn of the largest engine, building, bridge, or boat, all made possible by the development of machinery capable of manufacturing some bigger product than before. Of course this particular change is largely in the iron and steel industry.

In spite of all of these improvements, wonderful to behold, unprecedented in history, we find slackening in each industry as it grows old, at least in the invention of fundamental machines and processes. For a period it was the textile industry, then the iron and steel, then the boot and shoe, then the chemical, and now the electrical. The big inventions come early and refinements follow. At first there is great promise for business men and workmen in each new industry. Then some other industry comes along and capital and effort shift. We have not had quite enough experience to be sure of all this. We cannot help remembering that the steel industry has taken on new life through the development of steel alloys and the textile industry through artificial fibers. Generally, it seems to be as true of the individual industry, that there is a slowing up, as of individual countries that rise and decline. The serious question is whether there is to come a slackening of invention as a whole. If such a general slackening comes this side of the discovery of the use of free energy, then it is serious indeed. If a slackening does not come until then, it will probably be indefinitely postponed. It is notable and possibly significant that, while engineers are generally optimistic about the future of invention, many economists are inclined to be pessimistic.

One of the most promising aspects of recent industrial history is the work of researchers within the factory and outside. The results are necessarily restricted by the lack of well-trained workers, but still they are already considerable. Individual large factories and associations of smaller factories maintain laboratories for the discovery of new processes and the improvement of old ones, for the discovery of new products and the use of waste, and for the opening up of new fields of activity. Perhaps we might find after a full investigation that nearly forty per cent of the investment in industrial research in recent years in the United States has shown a profit.[16]

Following the effusion of new ways of doing things and of new machinery has come diffusion. Factories have discovered how to make razor blades or radios and then others have adopted the method with slight change or sometimes with improvement. Patents have been infringed. Workmen have been enticed away. Nations have likewise had the same experience. In fact, to maintain industrial leadership, a people, like a factory, must keep on inventing, must keep "one jump ahead." England taught the world how to carry on the textile and iron and steel industries. Germany is teaching others how to improve their chemical industries. America has been a teacher in the use of shoe machinery. The same British or American firm that makes automatic weaving machinery for British factories sells it for use in Germany or Japan. The same firm that makes lasting machines and Goodyear welting machines sells or leases them abroad. The peoples, buying or leasing machines, learn both to use and to reproduce. In this way do new competitors arise.

And it is the same within the individual state. From the eastern part of the United States have gone the ideas and the machinery to build up the West and the South. Many of these had originally, at least in fundamentals, come from England. Engineers from various countries have been recently attracted to Russia in large numbers in order to teach machine methods of production.

Great has been the progress in technological matters. Factories have learned how to produce well and cheaply by means of marvellously efficient machinery and the careful organization of all the factors. But now they are experiencing an old problem that promises greater difficulty, that is, how to dispose of the goods when made. Through scientific management and through continuous invention, the increase in manufactured goods has been enormous. There is a latent capacity in the world of consumers to use all the output of the present and for years to come. But to increase the sale, the cost must be lowered, the service improved, and ease of purchase by means of small payments must be established. And further, the income of the great consuming public must be increased. For the factory this means an increase in the wages of its own employees. So long as the effectiveness of organization and machinery continues to grow, there is promise of increased wages. Where the limit lies, is the problem. By means of education and advertising a greater demand for material goods can be brought about. But here again there are limits which are quite unknown. And beyond the horizon is the lurking figure of war in the shadow of the struggle for markets. America seems to have been a great contributor in getting prosperity through higher wages, but if this leads to excessive competition at home and with foreign peoples and ultimately to war, the blessing will prove a curse.

There is, also, the problem of the evenness of production. The factory should go continuously without any periodic closing through the dislocation of the economic mechanism. Governments and bankers are doing what they can to obviate the danger of unemployment, but it is a towering fact in industrial production that labor must bear the brunt of an economic crisis. The outstanding plant in the world today, the Ford Motor Company, closes its doors or opens them as demand for products dictates. High wages are paid when the demand exists, none when it does not. Today there are high wages and terrific pressure; tomorrow there is no pay and no work at all.

The road of industrial history is marked by the graves of firms that have tramped along for a time, only to fall exhausted. Generally the few long-surviving concerns are small and local in their business. There is a malting firm in Philadelphia that dates back to 1687, a coppersmith to 1788. In Boston a pottery (now in Cambridge) has lived on since 1765, a book publisher since 1784, an iron foundry since 1810, an oil manufacturer since 1812, and a tannery since 1814. It would be interesting to learn how, for instance, the oil manufacturer has survived the keen competition of the large national companies, especially since the 1880's. Its chief products have been successively whale-oil, camphene, and kerosene illuminants, and now gasolene. In this concern—the Jenney Manufacturing Company—the same family that started the business in 1812 is in complete control today. There is a distinct tendency, but not peculiar to industry, to die out partly because of decay within. Up to date it seems that the moderate death-rate of industrial firms has been a sign of social health. Whether the increase in the size of units will tend to lengthen the life of concerns remains to be seen. Certainly all signs point to greater stability and longevity.

NOTES TO CHAPTER XV

1. For example, Professor A. P. Usher, *An Introduction to the Industrial History of England* (1920), p. 275.
2. See *Recent Economic Changes*, vol. i (1929), p. 186.
3. C. B. Kuhlmann, *The Development of the Flour-Milling Industry in the United States* (1929), ch. vii.
4. See F. W. Taylor, *The Principles of Scientific Management* (1911, 1923).
5. On this subject, see M. B. Folsom, "Old Age on the Balance Sheet," *Atlantic Monthly* (Sept., 1929), pp. 399–406.; and Robert Howe, "Industry and the Aged," *Harvard Business Review*, vol. viii (July, 1930), pp. 435–442.
6. See above, ch. xiiii, pp. 170 ff.
7. See above, ch. xiiii, pp. 174–176.
8. See W. Jett Lauck, *The New Industrial Revolution and Wages, a Survey of the Radical Changes in American Theory and Practise which have come in since the World War and Created the Present Era of Prosperity* (New York and London, 1929).
9. See Irving Fisher, *Prohibition at its Worst* (1926), and *Prohibition Still at its Worst* (1928).
10. See Rudolf A. Clemen, *By-Products in the Packing Industry* (1927).
11. See *Recent Economic Changes*, vol. i (1929), pp. 123–125.
12. See *ibid.*, vol. i (1929), pp. 88–90.
13. See *ibid.*, vol. i (1929), p. 126.
14. See W. W. Young, *The Story of the Cigarette* (1916), pp. 44, 46, 66, 70, 74, 84, 94, 96.
15. Much of this information has been supplied by Henry W. Carter, vice-president of the Owens-Illinois Glass Company. See W. S. Walbridge, *American Bottles Old and New* (1920).
16. See *Recent Economic Changes*, vol. i (1929), pp. 106–111.

CHAPTER XVI

GOVERNMENT AID AND OTHER FACTORS IN INDUSTRIAL DEVELOPMENT

THE remarkable developments in industry, which we have noted, have not been evenly spread over the world. Indeed we may draw the lines demarking industrial progress over the earth's surface. There is a zone, largely temperate, extending east and west round the world in the northern hemisphere, within which lies the greatest progress. This industrial belt is determined as much by climate as are the wheat belt, the beef belt, and the ranching area. In the two cold polar regions raw materials are scarce and working accommodations too restricted for a prosperous industry—beyond the needs of the natives. In the tropics, especially in the humid parts such as the Amazon region, the heat and moisture make continuous effort impracticable. But in the temperate zone, work, and lots of it, is congenial to the healthy man and woman. In a damp, cool climate such as England's, people may work in order to get warm. In the great West, the northern Mississippi Valley, men work partly because the dry, electrically charged atmosphere impels them to action.

Except for the desert places and some mountain regions, the lands of the industrial belts have raw materials for manufacture. There was a time, indeed, when the only products available were those obtained right on the spot. In the use of such materials men have gained great skill. The Egyptians made their paper from the papyrus of the Nile Delta. Greek sculptors reached their greatest heights in their own Parian marble. Germans became the finest metallurgists in Europe, working the iron of their own fatherland or from nearby Sweden. English industrial skill was gained in the making of cloth from English wool, fine, soft, and of long fiber. On the other hand the possession of fine merino wool did not make Spaniards great manufacturers. Indeed it is thus with the long list of individual factors that enter into the creation of industry: not one factor but a combination of several elements makes industry.

Happy the people who have both a favorable climate and plenty of raw materials, and, in addition, plenty of power. For the attainment of factory industry power is, of course, necessary. Slave power could not be indefinitely used in driving machinery, for a social system that allowed slavery would soon destroy machinery. Water power and wind power were probably man's first experimental fields. Then came coal, oil, and gas. Scientists now dream of tapping nature's own laboratory, harnessing endless streams of energy, which would make man the creator of many new material things. Certainly we are now spending our coal and oil as if we had some certain alternative in the years to come. But in the meantime shrewd men of business, in both the Old and the New World, are laying hands on coal in China and oil in Venezuela, Rumania, and elsewhere.

In the reorganization of industry which is to come soon, involving a shifting to new points of vantage, it is an often mooted question as to whether the raw material is to go to the power as generally in the past or the power to the raw material as some think in the future. If such a change takes place, then we may expect to see great developments in such widely separated countries as Newfoundland and Siberia.

Factors other than natural situations are no less important because they are themselves derived from complicated and varying circumstances. A people hitherto engaged in agriculture will undertake manufacture in order to increase its income for the support of a growing population. Indeed in medieval Europe in the thirteenth and fourteenth centuries we find a great increase in urban population—partly the overflow of the countryside—which facilitated the development of many commercial towns into industrial communities. In modern American history we find that the shoe industry flourished in the fishing communities north of Boston partly because of surplus female labor. Watches came to be made in the homes of Swiss peasants in the eighteenth century because an additional occupation was necessary to support the population.

Some peoples develop a strong proclivity for manufacture. They produce partly because they like to do so. They work more or less continuously and get satisfaction in their work. Such persons commonly develop a strenuous religion like Swiss Calvinism.[1] Many French towns became Huguenot in the sixteenth century, as did some German communities. In England, and even more in Scotland and Wales, this religion of strict accountability and hard labor made progress. That it did not take firm root in Italy and Spain is due to the Latin temperament and the strongly entrenched position of the Catholic Church. In expelling the Huguenots from France in 1685 Louis XIV was striking a blow for Latin culture and at the same time presenting to rival countries, to which the Huguenots fled, a gift of immense material significance. Prussia, Holland, England, and the American colonies all gained an industrial impetus from their coming.

The subject of the economic significance of religion has been much pondered, but the conclusions reached so far have been uncertain. It has been pointed out that Judaism is much like Calvinism,[2] but Judaism did not arise out of an industrial situation nor has it led Jews into industrial pursuits. In Europe today, it is claimed, such Churches as the Russian Orthodox, the Roman Catholic, and the Anglican tend to favor capitalism, including large-scale industry. It is said that such religion is opium for the workers, keeping them at hard labor for the benefit of the employer. Certainly Marxian socialists are striking a telling blow at the old form of supernaturalism with its ignorance of natural phenomena and its neglect of social situations. Perhaps it is a safe conclusion that anything that makes for a more open-minded and intelligent group of producers—even (or especially) in a machine age—helps create a better soil for industrial growth.

Of unquestionably greater importance than religion in industrial activity is the condition of science, particularly of applied science. For the invention and improvement of machinery, engineers are necessary. This is much more the case today than during the early stages of the Industrial Revolution when artisans, barbers, and clergymen made contributions of first-rate importance. Today a corps of trained scientists is employed in many factories, as we have seen, for the discovery of new materials and machines and the improvement of old ones. In competition with England, Germany, and America in both mill and factory production we find that China, India, and Russia are mere infants. But infants do finally grow up. Japan has already made rapid strides, while China is getting ready to follow. Engineers from various European countries have gone to Russia to help, and American specialists in textile manufacture are there also. But it takes a people about a generation to learn how to operate machinery and to adapt it to their own use. After that, they can begin to invent new processes and mechanisms.

America has even yet invented but few fundamentally important machines, though its invention of useful little things and its adaptations of big ones have been phenomenal. To be sure, the reaper, sewing machine, rotary press, shoe machinery, telephone, phonograph, incandescent light, and linotype and adding machines are American contributions, and, of course, should not be forgotten as important beginnings. America's genius has been chiefly in making practical and available for widespread use what has been invented or started in Europe. The total amount of mechanical adaptation in America has been astounding, as every visitor to a factory using automatic machinery quickly observes. Of this, the Waltham Watch Company is an excellent illustration.

Industrial production, after the usufacture stage, has depended upon business organization. Mercifacture in its three stages of retail handicraft, wholesale handicraft, and centralized industry has reflected marketing changes and business opportunities. Britain had access to a great empire for the sale of its staple wares; Germany by peaceful penetration found little spots for profitable trade all over the world; and the United States has in almost unbroken availability a great area and a large population of relatively high standards of consumption for ordinary goods. All the regions which have successfully participated in factory production have been situated on the lines of world travel, using their own ships or those of other peoples. Australia and South Africa are handicapped by their geographical isolation.

Big factories require big business units. Generally speaking, the individual producer has given way to the partnership,[3] and the partnership in turn to the joint-stock corporation. By the sale of shares, capital can be secured from scattered sources and the risk spread both as between classes of persons and communities. By means of cartels, trusts, and amalgamations small units can grow large and more stable.[4] Big business has been concentrated in a relatively few metropolitan centers which dispose of the products of industry and provide the credit required.

Credit has come to industry, largely for operating purposes, from local or metropolitan banks. The local banks are generally small, being confined to a single center, but are loyal to local industries which are likewise usually small. The metropolitan banks, however, are large enough to take care of the needs of the biggest industrial concerns. In Britain and on the Continent of Europe generally, as well as in Canada, there are large branch-banking systems. The branch banks play a very cautious game in the smaller towns. An industry has to present a pretty clear case before it can get a considerable loan. The branch managers are not given much discretion and the central directors have no enthusiasm for small undertakings or doubtful ventures. It is not unlikely that the beginnings of industry in America, at least during the last hundred years, have been greatly aided by the local community getting behind the little local industry through its own banks.

These little local banks have commonly gone beyond their reserves in helping industry and trade, agriculture and transportation. Accordingly when hard times have come along and crises occurred, the banks have gone to the wall, and with them the industries. Sometimes it has been a single industry which started the crash, the others going down through the disastrous effect upon the bank. The history of industrial enterprise is strewn with the wrecks of considerable crises. In America such crises have occurred in 1792, 1815, 1837, 1857, 1873, and 1893, with minor ones since that time. The establishment of the Federal Reserve System in 1914 has lessened the dangers of purely monetary dislocations, but there are other possible sources of distress and disaster to both employers and employees in industry. The speculation in securities which dates from the sixteenth century in Europe and dramatically from 1720 in France and England proved once again in 1929 that excessive optimism is an abiding human weakness and also a constant danger to industry.

In the course of the life of an industry there are subtle forces that determine its fate. Local advantages built up the textile industry in New England; the development of relatively greater advantages in the South has caused part of that industry to migrate. New England was long expanding its boot and shoe industry so as to meet the requirements of the whole country. But proximity to raw materials and to the consuming market has caused the shoe industry to grow more rapidly in the West. Unplanned advantages, such as have been mentioned, are supplemented by regional efforts largely engineered by chambers of commerce operating under a more or less regionalistic mercantilism.

Mercantilism is a relatively new term for an old policy. It means the regulation of production for the benefit of what is conceived to be the interest of the producers. The medieval towns, directly through their urban councils and indirectly through their gilds, regulated industry in favor of the master craftsmen. These craftsmen were often given a monopoly of manufacture and commonly the right to make ordinances favorable to themselves. They paid lower town tolls than outsiders, or no tolls at all. Such towns put themselves and the interests of their citizens foremost—over against the interests of countrymen and the citizens of all other towns.

Such urban mercantilism which had grown up in the twelfth and thirteenth centuries was supplanted by a larger policy in the fifteenth and sixteenth centuries. In some cases the territory was the new unit of regulation, as in German lands; in other cases it was the nation or the state, as in France and England. There grew up gradually a policy of national mercantilism which has had considerable bearing upon the course of industry.

In England Lord Burghley, the right-hand statesman of Queen Elizabeth during the period 1558–98, created a practical régime for the national control of industry.[5] Elaborate laws were passed to regulate industry, many of them being taken over from some one town or city, for instance, the rule that an apprentice must serve for seven years, which had long prevailed in London. Patents of monopoly were given to aliens and denizens for the introduction of some new industry or the better management of an old one. Those industries which made for strength in time of war or which provided goods for export abroad were favored. It was becoming a settled idea that a nation should export more than it imported so that it might have an inflow of gold and silver. Men and women were expected and, in certain cases, required to work in industry, the theory being that a busy working class was not likely to disturb the government and that it should expect little else in life except hard labor. Burghley was sufficiently farsighted to observe that he should create a balanced economic system. He did not fail to give encouragement to mining and agriculture which produced the raw materials of industry nor to shipping and commerce which made trade in industrial products possible and safe.

In France it was Colbert, the superintendent of finance, who played the part of Lord Burghley. During the period 1661–83 he made the most careful plans, drew up the most elaborate instructions for his officials, and personally managed the system he created.[6] He was responsible for two high tariffs aimed chiefly at the Dutch. He sought to build up the French merchant marine to a point where it could carry practically all the exports and imports of France. He brought workers in tin from Germany, mining engineers from Sweden, and glass workers from Venice. In order to give French manufactures prestige abroad he drew up regulations to insure standard sizes and high quality. In other words, he took over the gild policy of the Middle Ages. This policy had worked well enough when trade was local, that is, when customers were near and their tastes well known. But it was an unfortunate policy for France to adopt at a time when France was seeking in competition with England and Holland to capture markets abroad, even among the more primitve peoples overseas. In addition, Colbert made the mistake of discouraging the export of grain, his idea being to keep French grain for French use, so that the country would not lack the necessities of life. But his prohibitions against exportation caused production to be reduced to a minimum. Accordingly, in times of dearth, there was not only no corn for export but not enough for local use. French industry was handicapped by this agricultural disability. And yet it is likely that peasant artisans, working under the wholesale handicraft system, were forced to rely more upon their industry than upon their agriculture.

The mercantile system of the Great Elector of Prussia (1640–88) was notable for its effort to develop not only shipping and trade but manufacture. By encouraging

Flemish and French artisans to migrate to Prussia, he helped to build up industrial skill in a country that had been predominately agricultural. Although he did something for the silk industry, much more was accomplished later under Frederick the Great.[7] It is a notable fact that mercantilists commonly regarded the silk industry as of special importance in any national economic system.

The mercantile system, largely industrial, but also agricultural, commercial, and financial, became deeply entrenched in the European world in the period 1700–50. But in the next fifty years the whole plan was challenged by both theorists and statesmen. And then in the period 1800–60 its abolition was demanded by business men. The system that was dawning was free trade. It had been adumbrated by the Tory Free Traders before 1700.[8] What came to be its pivot, the favorable balance of trade, was smashingly challenged by David Hume.[9] To Adam Smith, however, we are to give the credit for formulating arguments that were widely read and that were convincing. His declaration of economic independence, "the liberal system of free exportation and free importation," was published in 1776.[10] William Pitt the Younger, Huskisson, Peel, and Gladstone carried through the reforms necessary to lift the shackles from England's trade. England championed the new policy because, having been the first to develop the factory system, it needed no protection against the industries of other nations, whilst it did need their good will and their raw materials and foodstuffs. What was originally a bit of logic became a practical national need and finally a highly idealized policy, notably in the speeches of John Bright.

Although the American colonies of Britain had suffered under the old mercantilist régime which gave a preference to the industries of the Mother Country, still there were strong arguments for the establishing of a comparable system in America itself from 1789 onwards. But in view of the new enlightenment, embodied in free-trade theory, there were many arguments against the erection of any such "outworn" system. The result, was a compromise during the period 1789–1861, in which, with many ups and downs, there was enacted, and from time to time changed, a tariff policy which primarily provided revenue for the central government but also gave to certain industries some measure of protection against foreign competition.[11] Since 1860, however, a higher, ever higher, tariff has been built up. In the early years of this period it was primarily for the purpose of raising revenue for paying off the debts incurred by the North in the Civil War. But once the system had been established and the taste of protection fully enjoyed, there was no going backward, though under Democratic governments and at times during Republican administrations reductions in the tariff were made. Of all the sorry spectacles in the annals of peaceful government, the scrambling of industries for tariff protection has been and is the worst. It is the bull fight of American politics. Men have lost their sense of honesty to say nothing of dignity; arguments have been perverted and facts distorted. For a long time the protection of infant industries was a useful slogan. But when the industries were no longer infantile, the new argument was invented of safeguarding the American industry and particularly the American workman against the lower standard of living of European producers. To a growing but helpless minority it has appeared that the argument of maintaining the workman's standard of living has been largely throwing dust into the eyes of the voter. The folly of protecting the American iron and steel industry in this generation and the boot and shoe industry (perhaps with certain exceptions for the finer grades) since the Civil War is patent enough to the impartial observer. At last the logical absurdity of a general protective system has come home to a great many people, since farmers have begun to demand a government subsidy on the same scale as national protection of industries. Behind the scene is the grasping hand of other productive interests, such as the steamship and railroad, ready to seize upon an additional precedent as argument for aid.

It is difficult to appraise tariff protection in the history of any country. We have to consider the value to the industry and to the country as a whole. We have to distinguish between the industrial necessity of protection and the mere industrial advantage incurred. Barring the protection of some infant industries, such as the silk and tin-plate,[12] it is doubtful whether much advantage has accrued to the industry protected in the long run. The government has probably been of greater service in maintaining law and order, providing a patent system, and regulating industry with the help of the Federal Trade Commission.

What the Bureau of Foreign and Domestic Commerce is to American trade, the Bureau of Standards is to American industry. This Bureau of Standards, comparing very favorably in personnel and equipment with the corresponding bureaus in Germany and Great Britain, is constantly at the service of manufacturers in the field of technique. It makes tests of products from heavy girders to light wire. It tests the tools and instruments of measurement used by manufacturers. It makes experiments looking toward a solution of the difficulties which manufacturers encounter in their work. These difficulties may have to do with the drawing capacity of a smoke stack or the grinding of iron products. The Bureau also works

AN APPARATUS FOR TESTING THE STRENGTH OF STEEL GIRDERS, MADE ABOUT 1911, UNITED STATES BUREAU OF STANDARDS

out plans on its own initiative for the improvement of both methods and products. It has gone so far as to set up a miniature paper mill of its own. It has found by experiment how to make without cracking a reflector for a telescope as large as seventy inches in diameter and ten inches in thickness. Manufacturers appeal to it for help both individually and through their associations. Largely at the expense of the public, the Bureau brings together a considerable number of physicists, chemists, electricians, and others trained in universities. The advantages that arise from their labors go directly to the manufacturer and, of course, ultimately to all consumers.

NOTES TO CHAPTER XVI

1. Compare W. Sombart, *The Quintessence of Capitalism* (1913, 1915), pp. 252, 256–260, 269. Consider also Max Weber, *General Economic History* (trans. by Frank H. Knight, 1927), pp. 352–369.

2. See W. Sombart, *The Jews and Modern Capitalism* (1911, 1913), pp. 248–251.

3. Henry Ford is an exception to this. Ford's company is actually a corporation, but the stock is all, or almost all, owned by himself or family. Cf. also, above, ch. v, pp. 59–61.

4. For the advantages involved, see above, ch. xv, pp. 182–183.

5. See W. Cunningham, *Growth of English Industry and Commerce, Mercantile System* (1903), pp. 25–84.

6. A convenient summary of Colbert's work is found in A. J. Sargent's *Economic Policy of Colbert* (1899).

7. See G. Schmoller, *The Mercantile System* (1884, 1896), p. 83.

8. See Sir W. J. Ashley, "The Tory Origin of Free Trade Policy," first published in 1897, in *Surveys Historic and Economic* (1900), pp. 268–303.

9. See Hume's essay entitled "Of the Balance of Trade," *Three Essays* (1787).

10. *The Wealth of Nations* (London, 1776). See the "Digression concerning the Corn Trade and Corn Laws," bk. iv, ch. v.

11. See F. W. Taussig, *Tariff History of the United States* (1888 and fol.), pt. i; V. S. Clark, *History of Manufactures in the United States, 1607–1860* (ed. of 1929), pp. 270 ff., *et passim.*

12. See F. W. Taussig, *Some Aspects of Tariff History* (1915), pp. 176–177, 257.

CHAPTER XVII

ASSOCIATION IN MODERN INDUSTRY
EMPLOYERS AND WORKMEN

FROM government aid in industry, we turn to self-help. In the medieval towns, from which our commercial and industrial practices have come in unbroken descent, the gilds were given the power to regulate their own trades.[1] As the gilds themselves weakened—through internal dissension and through the decline of town economy—the national government took over the functions of control. In place of elaborate gild regulations concerning the manufacturing of goods we have long national statutes specifying in part how commodities should be manufactured. The statute rolls begin to grow bulky with economic matter.

As national regulation increased in amount and in scope, the gilds declined in power and influence. Indeed they remained only as shadows of their former selves in England where industrial progress was greatest. The period 1558–1785 showed a maximum of government regulation and a minimum of organized self-help in England. At the top of the structure was the government, at the bottom the individual man of business. Under this order of affairs both trade and manufacture greatly prospered.

While the British government was guiding business with a strong hand and while the old gilds and livery companies were nestled in a twilight sleep that was to know no wakening, a new movement started without heralding and without any general policy. The General Chamber of Manufacturers of Great Britain, established in 1785, was the first, or about the first, of a long line of associations that were to play an effective part in modern industry. The Chamber included three growing industries—pottery, cotton, and iron and steel. The outstanding centers supporting it were Manchester and Birmingham. Two of the leading manufacturers in this association were the versatile Josiah Wedgwood and the forward-looking Matthew Boulton. The three industries in question had come to realize that they must fight for their existence. Among the threatening circumstances were the excise tax on cotton and the Irish proposals of the prime minister, William Pitt. By the excise tax the cotton manufactures were threatened, and by the Irish proposals all were embarrassed, if not endangered. According to these proposals, Irish linen was to be given preferential treatment in the English market, while foreign linen was to be kept out. This would rob England of a chance to get favorable terms for other industries in the foreign markets. The final result of the activity of the Chamber was that the proposals were modified and the excise tax withdrawn.[2]

From such small beginnings the trade association has developed until hardly an industry is without its association.[3] At first local or regional, they have become truly national and even international. They have changed from one policy to another. In early times they were concerned, as in the example given above, with the securing of freer trade from a mercantilist government, or even with the overthrow of that government and the establishment of a liberal economic régime which was attained in England about 1860. Then, in a general way, they stood out against the aggressive action of trade unions until they saw (or some of them did) that cooperation was of greater service to industry than conflict. The result has been the promotion of collective bargaining.

And, finally perhaps we may say, they have come to a place where they are anxious to offset the evils of a free competitive system which they themselves had helped to create. It is sometimes said that the associations now aim at the creation of co-operative competition, which is perhaps to be regarded, along with tariff protection, as part of the new mercantilism.

Unquestionably the biggest British association ever formed is the Federation of British Industries, established in 1916. It represents directly or indirectly thousands of British firms, organized by trades or in local or national associations. Its aims are to simplify the processes of law, cheapen the cost of patents, protect trademarks, gather data, promote research, and extend foreign trade. For the purpose of more effective operation the Federation has divided England into a number of sections, so that an individual firm is commonly represented both in a district group and in its trade association. The Federation is a kind of industrial state within the body politic. An example of its solid accomplishment is the reduction of English railroad rates on goods.

Another type of development of modern associations, seen alike in England and on the Continent, is the cartel. A group or association of manufacturers in a single industry establish a selling agency which will uphold prices, reduce the cost of distribution, and, in general, enable the members to compete with rivals at home and abroad. How far such associations have been socially desirable, it is difficult to state. In a great many cases, however, bankruptcy has been avoided by such a device and probably only by this means.

The trade associations of the masters are matched by the trade unions of the men. In the Middle Ages the craft gild included both employer and employee, though the employing class dominated the association. As we have seen, the employees formed journeymen's associations, which had long life on the Continent but not in England. Now, it was in England that the modern trade union was started. There could be no simpler and at the same time no surer evidence of the lack of continuity between the medieval and modern association. Of course, the craft gild, being a masters' association, could not have been the progenitor of the trade union, though some have held to this view. And, for the reason given, the medieval journeymen's association, the German *Brudershaft*, or the French *compagnonnage* could also not have been the ancestor of the trade union.

The modern trade union was a fresh growth. It sprang out of conditions in seventeenth- and eighteenth-century England. Those conditions pertained to the exploitation of workmen by their masters. The exploitation was most prominent in the wholesale handicraft system, particularly in the dependent phase.

It has been said that the first modern trade union was formed by the journeymen hatters of London at the end of the seventeenth century. Not far behind were the wool workers, notably the combers and weavers of the West Country. To be coupled with these also were the silk weavers, stockingers, and cutlers.[4] All of these trades were definitely in the wholesale handicraft system. But there were other industries that had trade unions, notably the tailors and perhaps the printers. The tailoring trade in London exhibited both the retail and the wholesale handicraft systems. It seems that the journeymen, who formed a union and demanded higher wages, belonged to both systems of industry. In all probability the journeymen printers were wholly in the retail handicraft system. Their early efforts indeed were relatively feeble and their association not very prominent. It is all very clear that the modern trade union took its origin in industries that had not yet been centralized. In other words, the trade union is not only older than the factory but older than the central workshop.

The first trade unions in England were, of course, local. Robert Owen had recommended national unions in 1833. In the next decade national associations were formed. Many and long have been the struggles of trade unions in England. Difficulties arose both within the ranks and outside. In general, the trade union in England has been able to keep itself practical and moderate. Victory on the outside, that is, in attaining social and legal status, has been no less real than within the association. At first, that is, in the seventeenth and eighteenth centuries, the trade unions were secret and under cover. Held to constitute conspiracy, the trade unions were compelled to meet in cellars and lofts, and at times to lie so low as practically to be quiescent. But they arose time and time again to strike a blow for the cause of the workman. In the period about 1800–24 they were suppressed by law, then about 1824–71 tolerated, and from about 1875 onward recognized and even accorded a special position in the body politic.[5] So far, indeed, has this gone that complaint has sometimes been made, especially following the legislation of 1906, that the trade unions occupy a privileged position, comparable to that of the landed aristocracy in the Middle Ages.

But the story of trade unions as such is no part of our concern here. Their history has been progressively interesting and significant. We are more concerned, however, with the general fact that trade unions arose in manufacture and later spread to transportation, agriculture, and other kinds of production. And, as has already been said, the trade unions and trade associations have come to co-operate for mutual advantage in what is called collective bargaining.

The parallelism of the development of trade unions in the United States and England has been closer than we should expect, especially in view of the fact that one country is much older than the other. Actually the economic forces at work, however, were not so different, for example, in Philadelphia, from those operating in London. The parallelism we can explain partly on the ground that like conditions produce like results and partly on the ground that English laborers were constantly migrating to America where they carried out strikes and formed unions pretty much as in the homeland.

The first trade unions in America seem to have been set up in the 1790's, for example, the shoemakers in Philadelphia in 1792 and the printers in New York in 1794.[6] It is as clearly established in America as in England that the trade-union movement antedated the factory. In no sense could the printing shops be regarded as factories, and shoemaking did not enter the factory stage until the 1860's. But the incoming of the factory did have its effect, as seen in the first recorded strike in a factory in Paterson, New Jersey, in 1828. Beginning in a dispute over the change of the dinner hour from twelve to one o'clock, it turned into a demand for a ten-hour day, and led finally to the calling out of the militia. This seems to have been the first case of such drastic action.[7]

In the 1830's there were national trades' unions, or unions of several trades, and two genuine trade unions. These were the printers' and cordwainers' unions, both prematurely developed on a national basis. The craft-union movement, dominant up to the present, saw the formation of the International (American and Canadian) Typographical Union in 1850, the Machinists' and Blacksmiths' International Union and the Iron Molders' International Union, both in 1859, and the National Forge of the Sons of Vulcan in 1862. The Knights of St. Crispin date from 1867. At its height, this union of shoemakers is said to have numbered about 50,000 members. Starting in Milwaukee, it spread widely, stimulated both by the rise of prices and by the use of unskilled labor in the newly formed shoe factories. This union lingered on till 1874, but, following the crisis of 1873, in weakened condition. Starting in demands for higher wages, the Knights ended in an inglorious battle for consumers' co-operation.[8]

The history of trade unions in America begins in local and spreads to national associations. It starts in manufacturing and reaches out to transportation and ultimately to almost all forms of production. But, whereas in England the unions have found it most profitable to form a political organization, in America politics have proved to be a delusion and a snare. As elsewhere, there have been two wings, but the more conservative has prevailed. Up to date the American Federation of Labor has been unwilling to form a labor party.

In America trade associations are older than trade unions, but the oldest of them appear to have been much like the medieval and early modern gilds in England and on the Continent. In 1648 the shoemakers and the coopers of Boston were both chartered to examine workers and exclude the inefficient. The petition of the coopers to have their charter renewed in 1668 was denied.[9] In 1724 the carpenters of Philadelphia, probably the master carpenters, were formed into an association which sought incorporation in 1792. In 1790 a Stone Cutters' Company and in 1809 a Master Bricklayers' Society were formed in Philadelphia. Other associations arose here and there to meet purely local conditions, most of them lasting only a short period.

Both in the 1830's and again in the 1860's trade associations arose to combat the trade unions. In the earlier decade an employers' association was formed in the leather industry in New York City to oppose the newly established unions. In the latter decade and thereafter, both local and national employers' associations were formed to withstand the action of trade unions.

The great movement to form trade associations in America really began during the Civil War. In 1861 came the Writing Paper Manufacturers' Association, in 1862 the United States Brewers' Association, in 1864 the National Association of Wool Manufacturers and the New England Cotton Manufacturers' Association, and in 1872 the Carriage Builders' National Association, the National Association of Stove Manufacturers, the Silk Association of America, and the Manufacturing Chemists' Association of the United States.[10] The formation of trade associations has gone on unabated, in good times and in bad, until now they are to be numbered only by the thousands. Attempts at classification have been made[11] but without great success. There are probably hundreds of associations of only manufacturers and thousands, particularly local, in which manufacturers are enrolled and play a part along with traders, bankers, and professional people.[12]

In a sense the National Association of Manufacturers of the United States of America, formed in 1895, with a membership of about 3,000 in 1930, is the most representative association of industry in the country. Since 1901 it has published two journals, one *American In-*

dustries and the other *Export*, devoted largely to the promotion of the exportation of American manufactures. Besides its activities on behalf of trade abroad and favorable legislation at home, the Association is known for its individualism in the management of business and in the ownership of property. This principle is clearly set forth in its constitution. The Association is opposed to the interference of organized labor in the affairs of the individual factory and has declared emphatically and repeatedly for the open shop.[13] It objects to efforts on the part of workmen to place any limitations upon apprenticeship. It is easy to maintain that this Association smacks of the spirit of the eighteenth century, but it probably represents the opinions of most American manufacturers.

Trade associations have become so numerous and so active that they are to be regarded as a prominent part of American social organization. Of course they have little vigor apart from the ever-changing interests which they serve: they are the established mouthpieces of groups seeking personal and craft benefits. As we have seen, trade associations in the past commonly arose to counteract the activities of working men,[14] and some still adhere to that policy. But beginning with the Great War, conflict was supplanted by co-operation and a policy of low wages was gradually replaced by a policy of high wages. Under the leadership of Henry Ford, the emphasis on the highest wage possible has tended to become a maxim for big business in America. At present the labor policy seems to be unprecedently intelligent; and in open discussions of the best methods the trade associations are playing their part. The recent trend has been toward company unions, in which the individual plant has its own private collective bargaining organization of masters and men. The labor leaders conceded 814 of such unions in America at the end of 1924, with about one million workers involved.[15] It is of course too soon to say whether such company unions are really for the best interests of all concerned.

Trade associations in America at present have many functions apart from labor relations.[16] Some of them are deeply concerned with tariff protection and maintain lobbyists at Washington in order to secure what is considered necessary or advisable. Statistics of sales and prices are collected and disseminated among the members. Costs are determined, and uniform cost accounting systems are worked out. There is a tendency for this practice to lead to the determination of a price that is high enough to maintain the least efficient producer. Of course, on this basis the better managed firms reap a rich reward for their efficiency. The standardization of terms, types, sizes, and capacities of men and machines within an industry has led to the saving of enormous sums. In 1893 the National Brick Manufacturers' Association caused the sizes of bricks to be reduced to five and in 1918 to three. The diameters and threads of bolts have been standardized. Most progress along these lines has been made by the automobile industry. Co-operative advertising has been brought about by such associations. Research in technical methods has made rapid progress, being sponsored by such associations as the Institute of Meat Packers, the American Institute of Baking, and the American Iron and Steel Institute. Arbitration has been furthered as a substitute for legal action, which is found to be expensive and often inequitable.

Just as the medieval gilds were conspicuous for their part in the development of a business ethics, so are the trade associations of modern times thought by some to be playing a fundamental rôle in the improvement of trade practices. Certainly the codes of some American trade associations are both elaborate and praiseworthy. Rather long codes have been adopted by the clothing manufacturers, confectioners, and printers.[17] Partly because of its brevity and partly because of its practical idealism, I shall quote the standards of business practice of the National Boot and Shoe Manufacturers' Association, adopted in 1924.[18]

Standards of Business Practice

The National Boot & Shoe Manufacturers' Association of the United States, Inc., acknowledge a responsibility for the advancement of its members' interests and an equal responsibility for safeguarding the interests of the consuming public.

To further both of these objectives, we, the members of this Association, in convention assembled, adopt the following standards as the basis of our business dealings.

To endeavor to conduct our business according to a standard of business morality that will make the members of our Association worthy of the highest measure of confidence of those with whom they have business dealings.

To always stand for fair dealing, honest grading and proper fulfillment of contracts, avoiding and discouraging unfair competition.

To do our best to promote uniformity and certainty in the customs and usages of business, using every effort to reform any abuses now existing in our trade.

To represent with truthfulness at all times the product of our factories both in our advertising and in our selling methods.

To endeavor to promote the spirit of friendliness and co-operation among the trade, accepting the principle of arbitration for the settlement of any controversies which cannot be mutually adjusted between the contending parties.

To secure and diffuse accurate and reliable information as to the standing of merchants and other matters that we may be mutually safeguarded in our business dealings.

To encourage education in all branches of the industry to the highest standard and dissemination of proper and authentic knowledge of the problems of the industry to the consuming public.

To know accurately the cost of management, production and distribution of our product in order that a fair price, an adequate wage, and an honest profit may be assured.

To maintain a high standard of factory conditions and to provide proper safety devices and methods for the prevention of accidents.

To use our best efforts in promoting the physical and moral welfare of those in our employ.

To avoid and discountenance interference with employees of competitors by inducing them to violate their real or implied contract of employment or to otherwise cause demoralization in local labor conditions.

To be loyal to the Association and its members and active in its affairs, contributing our best efforts to make the Association an influential and trusted factor in the community at large as well as in the Industrial World.

To take an intelligent interest in public affairs and through our Association to represent and safeguard the interests of our industry when its common interests are involved.

To carefully comply with all laws and be ever ready in time of need to render aid to the local, State or National Government.

To some it appears that the chief value of trade associations, in the long run, is not the inculcation of ethical practices but the preservation of the smaller firm. Certainly the large business unit can supply its own improvements by the employment of experts and the use of laboratories. The big corporation can often afford to be liberal and can often appear to be generous. The small business has neither the brains nor the capital, the will nor the genius, to make rapid progress. The small firm is commonly a single individual or partners with a few workers and constitutes on the whole a large segment of middle-class society. It is often regarded as the backbone of the nation's strength in war and in peace—in shouldering arms and in paying taxes. Where the general interest lies, as between the big independent corporation of great capacity for good and evil on the one hand and the small business unit without capacity for economies or progress, it is really hard to determine. Certainly the small man loses some of his handicaps when he joins with his fellows to form a trade association. Whether the consumer should pay the higher price for goods in order to uphold the small entrepreneur or should turn to the big capitalistic unit with its tendency to lower costs and lower prices, remains a question. The Supreme Court of the United States was divided on an issue something like this in the case of the American Hardwood Manufacturers' Association in 1921. The court decided against the open-price association in this case, but the two dissenting and liberal justices asked this question: "May not these hardwood lumber concerns, frustrated in their efforts to nationalize competition, be led to enter the inviting field of consolidation? And if they do, may not another huge trust with highly centralized control over vast resources, natural, manufacturing and financial, become so powerful as to dominate competition, wholesalers, retailers, consumers, employees and, in large measure, the community?" And so, the issue is sharply enjoined. We are losing our prejudices against big business, that is true enough, but the economic and social issues are still undecided.

The advantages of trade associations and trade unions, whether direct or indirect, have either been made evident or are obvious, and hence need no urging. Both types of associations have their faults, recorded in a wide gamut of offenses against custom and law. Perhaps the commonest demerit of the trade association, already dealt with, is the establishment of a price sufficiently high to support the most inefficient member of the association. A comparable practice on the part of the trade union is the contest for a uniform wage for one type of work, regardless of the capacity, industry, or integrity of the workman. Aimed at preventing the exploitation of the laborer, this policy tends to demoralize the worker and to raise the cost of manufacture. It leads employers to welcome machines which will displace men. In America those areas, such as New England, which are highly unionized are having a hard time to compete with western regions which have more open shops which pay workers what they are worth and get rid of the unfit. Although it is difficult to obtain statistics that are reliable on such a subject, the general fact may be accepted as stated. One clear illustration is the printing trade much of which will logically move westward, especially as the airplane reduces the time of transportation of copy and proof sheets.

In the control of industry there seem to be three possibilities in America. The government may influence production in accordance with its laws and by means of bureaus, such as the Interstate Commerce, Federal Trade, and Tariff Commissions. Or, industrial plants, becoming ever bigger and wiser, may be allowed to pioneer up to the limit of their great capacities, so long as the welfare of society be kept uppermost. In this case a large measure of genuine economic liberalism would prevail. Thirdly, the rank and file of business units, notably the small ones, may work out their own salvation through associations on a basis of broad social service. Although there are champions for each of these systems, it may actually happen that all three may be employed simultaneously in a system of economic and social checks and balances. Up to date the history of business seems to indicate that the competitive interplay of the three systems leads to the best results.

NOTES TO CHAPTER XVII

1. See above, ch. v, p. 51.

2. Witt Bowden, *The Rise of the Great Manufacturers of England, 1760–1790* (1919), pp. 70–75.

3. See the *Directory of Industrial and other Associations concerned with Matters relating to Conditions of Employment*, His Majesty's Stationery Office, London, 1919.

4. See S. and B. Webb, *The History of Trade Unionism* (1894, 1920), pp. 28–39.

5. See A. V. Dicey, *Law and Public Opinion in England during the Nineteenth Century* (1905, 1914), lectures iv-viii.

6. J. R. Commons and others, *History of Labour in the United States*, vol. i, (1918), p. 109.

7. *Ibid.*, p. 418.

8. D. D. Lescohier, *The Knights of St. Crispin, 1867–1874*, in the Bulletin of the University of Wisconsin, Economics and Political Science Series, vol. vii (1910), p. 49.

9. J. R. Commons and others, *op. cit.*, pp. 46–48.

10. See *Trade Associations, their Economic Significance and Legal Status*, National Industrial Conference Board (1925), pp. 327 ff.

11. *Ibid.*, pp. 319 ff.

12. See the *Commercial and Industrial Organizations of the United States*, 1913, etc., 1929. United States Department of Commerce, Washington.

13. See the pamphlet put out by the National Association of Manufacturers of the United States of America, entitled *Evidence in the Case for the Open Shop* (New York, 1923).

14. See W. F. Willoughby, "Employers' Associations for Dealing with Labor in the United States," *Quarterly Journal of Economics*, vol. xx (1905–06), pp. 110–150.

15. *The American Labor Year Book, 1926*, vol. vii (New York, 1926), pp. 186–187.

16. On this subject there is a good deal of information in Franklin D. Jones, *Trade Association Activities and the Law* (1922).

17. For an analysis of the codes of the Chamber of Commerce of the United States and of the Rotarians, see Carl F. Taeusch, *Professional and Business Ethics* (1926), pp. 246–271. See also Edgar L. Heermance, *The Ethics of Business* (1926), pp. 17–31.

18. See Edgar L. Heermance, *Codes of Ethics, a Handbook* (1924), pp. 475–476.

CHAPTER XVIII

ART IN INDUSTRY

THE creation of a fine piece of craftsmanship is one of the satisfactions of life; to go beyond and put individuality and introduce one's own being into the work of his hand is the realization of the craftsman's destiny. To design a useful commodity and then to execute the plan is doing the world's work; to go beyond and create a thing of beauty, transcending the reasonable demand of our fellow beings, is to make the world our debtor. In the higher reaches of old-time industry there was no line dividing craft from art.

We have traditional fields for skill of craftsmanship, but in reality it is found spread widely through the industries of man. It is found in the molding and painting of clay; it occurs in the weaving and dyeing of textiles; it shows itself in the fashioning and carving of objects of wood; it is manifest in the forming and finishing of metal and leather wares; it rises to great heights in the cutting of stone; and in the preparation of food and drink it attains the heights of divine stimulus and the depths of bestial surfeiting.

The primitive peoples have done well in their manufactures; and when contemplating their lack of tools, we applaud their work. With a few notable exceptions, however, the results are artistically either crude or mediocre.[1] Egypt was, as far as our knowledge goes, the first to attain what is called civilization. The tomb pictures show the people of that land early at work in industrial pursuits.[2] And what remains of their creation indicates at least great skill in the weaving of linen fine as silk, the making of paper culturally more precious than gold, and the carving and inlaying of furniture as appealing to the eye as restful to the body. Something might be said of the skill of Babylonians, especially in the weaving of tapestries with their bright hues and varied designs.[3] It may be that this skill was transferred to the Persians and from the Persians it has spread to almost the whole Oriental world of our day. Cretans were masters of hammering and carving gold and bronze.[4] But it is to the Greeks that we look for supreme excellence in craft and art. Imagination guided their hands, while genius sat nearby. Their early builders became architects, their stonecutters sculptors, and their potters designers and painters of unique powers. At this point our study shades off into the history of art where we can pursue it no farther.

The medieval and modern periods have also had their victories in craftsmanship. Gothic builders and sculptors worked with an inspiration, for which there was no exact precedent. In the early Modern Period, Dutch delftware and English imitation were worthy of their Chinese models. The tapestry of Brussels, the woolens of Flanders, the brocades of Florence deserved the admiration they received. The violins of Cremona, soft in tone and graceful in form, seem to have reached the highest pinnacle of human endeavor, due largely to the excellent craftsmanship of Stradivari (1644–1737).

Most countries, indeed, have attained distinction in craftsmanship of some kind. They produce perhaps not the dainty trifles of France or of the Far East but the stout cloth of England or Scotland. And yet there are a few peoples who have little or nothing to put to their credit. Americans and Jews have not been skilful in the work of their hands. In explaining these differences we would have to take into account many factors of sky and mountain, wealth and natural resource, cultural development and national aptitude.

Some of the industrial skill unquestionably developed in the usufacture stage. Though most of it in this stage went into the production of staple commodities, stout and pure, some of it really attained artistic proportions. Trained hands plucked the finest wool from sheep and goat, deft fingers spun the yarn, genius mixed the dyes, and religious zeal wove the prayer mat of the devout Mohammedan. It is to the retail handicraft of the town, however, that we must look for the earliest attainment of varied industrial skill. To the different crafts, skilled men gave all their time. Between them there was rivalry. And in their success lay both profit and esteem. When skill was attained locally, fame spread the news abroad. The purple dye of Tyre, the iron wares of Puteoli, the blades of Toledo, and the glass of Venice were demanded almost everywhere. Those merchants who stepped in to meet and stimulate the demand, not only enriched themselves but introduced the wholesale handicraft system. In other words, it seems, industrial manual skill arose in the first two stages and was popularized in the third. Not only did the wholesale handicraft create little or no skill, it actually seems to have debased ideals, at least in the second phase, when employers, pressed for cheap wares, goods that would sell if not endure, urged their workers in turn to produce what was demanded. The goods would never come back to shame the hands that made them. Often they bore no mark of their origin. The maker and the user were irretrievably separated, and, with some exceptions, skill and quality went down together.

Centralized industry continued the evil of marketing pressure and added the danger of machine production.

The central workshop was an organization for putting pressure upon the workers. The pressure involved in the supervision and the division of labor was beneficial in so far as such an evil as misusing the material was concerned, but it tended to take away individuality and it tended to produce more cheaply. It was not inherent in the nature of a central workshop that there should be no individuality: unique creations came regularly from potteries in the Old World. But the general influence is actually toward supplying a demand for wares. If the demand is for cheap, badly colored, or excessively ornate wares, then production is adapted accordingly. It is a nice question as to whether art for art's sake should bow to, or compromise with, demand. But it is an historic fact that catering to the needs of primitive peoples, frontier society, and peasant communities has lowered the standards of production. The central workshop was one of the agencies for bringing this about. Of course, we need not weep over this situation: it had its good side in the supplying of wares at reasonable cost to human beings in need. But the effect upon art and craftsmanship was unfortunate.

The same kind of influence continues even to our day. The most conspicuous example is the novelty store which sells at low prices. Such a store, or chain of stores, demands goods to sell at such and such a price. If the manufacturer cannot meet the demand, then the chain of stores may set up a plant to do the work itself. In many instances, perhaps in most, the result has been to reduce very greatly the cost of commodities, albeit at the expense of quality. In fairness to the novelty store, however, we should not pass without noting that in some cases a finer article, at least one with better design than ever before, has been made available for popular consumption.

Still we may put down this novelty store as a modern representative of the prostituting influence of marketing mechanism.

Central workshops dealt art in industry no such blow as did the factory. In this case it was not only marketing pressure but also uniformity and standardization of product. There is a good deal of mere prejudice and some silliness expressed in the denunciation of factory products. Only factories could make the beautiful shoes, automobile parts, and many other wares so widely enjoyed in America. Still there is in many factory goods a sameness that does not make for the highest artistic effect. At first the factories put out goods that were not only uniform and relatively fine in execution (as compared with articles of usufacture), but were made without any adequate designs. The factory owner or the foreman was commonly the designer. For a low order of consumption this was all right. New England cottons were at first quite sufficient for southern negroes and frontier communities. Gradually with the increasing of designs which are the creation of the well trained or the highly gifted, the factory has remedied this particular situation. And yet there has also come with the better design a tyranny which is stifling. In one of the finest American factories producing silverware I sought hard to find some real handicraftsmanship. The designs used for chalices and bowls, coffee pots and pitchers were very beautiful, but the designs were transferred to dies made of hardened steel and very expensive. Here came the worship of the design. The die produced all things alike. It was costly and not lightly to be thrown aside. Slight improvements were ignored because the original was pretty good. And this tyranny was carried even into the departments where hand work prevailed. Ask a chaser in such a plant whether he is allowed to vary a design. The answer invariably is that he has no discretion: he is a copier and little more. He makes his little incisions, punches a hole here, and makes a dent there—exactly as the design indicates. But he is the one who has the practical feel of the thing. A flat design on paper may not turn the handle of a cup as it was intended to do. The workman knows that, but he must obey. If only the chaser of silver could be allowed to take the basin or platter in the rough, as formed or partly stamped by machine and then, following the design for a few times, improve on the plan as his experience and skill dictated, the finished product would have the touch of individuality that it lacks at present.

It is an unfortunate fact that much of the feeling of creative parentage is lost in factory production, even where hand work is allowed. The design, as has been said, has robbed the workman of his own feeling in the work. But, if possible, even more the fact that one worker does only one small part of the whole, drives out the pride of fatherhood, the satisfaction of creation.

With all its shortcomings the factory is a great achievement and has come to stay. We must take into account the machine and its ways and the big factory organization and its weaknesses. We may not stop with the power machine in any consideration of art in industry; we must start with it. Obviously the beginning of art in machine production must lie in the design, since the machine itself can have no artistic impulses. Too often design is repetition of something created in the past. Our furniture, silverware, and ceramics are largely the slaves of periods of past efforts. Unless we can create something new to represent our own attitudes, we can have only limited success in design. Unfortunately, creative artists of high ability shun commercial uses. Many capable artists will not enter a factory. The factories tend to develop a copying type of artist whose talent is stunted at the start. The schools, on the other hand, would be more helpful if they were better staffed and gave more attention to the technical aspects of production. Practical experience combined with art education and cultural background seems to be the ideal. Manufacturers have difficulty in finding, or developing, such persons. European soil is more productive of artists than is American. European art schools seems to be further advanced and more successful than American.[5]

Art schools for instruction should be supplemented by museums for suggestion. Above all, the designer should be capable of feeling life so that he may create forms. If there were a copyright law in America that would guarantee to the creator of a design such profits as his efforts were worth to society, there might be more inclination on the part of artists of ability to participate in commercial work. Perhaps at present the nearest that America gets to genius in this connection is in her posters and other advertisements.

Wherever the machine has been victorious, the skilled artisan retires without argument on his own behalf. And nowhere has the victory of machinery been more complete than in America. But it is slowly emerging that, supplementing the machine, there is a place for the handicraftsman. Let the machine cut, press, and fashion the parts of a piece of furniture; there is still plenty of work for a hand carver and finisher. But letting such a skilled worker take the design of the artist and vary it as his abilities indicate, actually produces the finest result. Here we have in combination the artist, the machine, and the handicraftsman, with none tyrannizing over the others.

Of course, quite apart from the work of the factory is the production of the lone handicraftsman creating as his training or native skill will permit. For America it is a great loss that among its German immigrants no toy-makers can be found, among its French no potters, among its English no hand cutlery workers, and among its Italians no carvers of fine statuary. Of course some are actually found, but the tendency is for Europeans to give up their craftsmanship on reaching American soil. More about this general subject of the small-scale industry is expressed in the last chapter.

But little art is to be expected in any land unless there is a taste for fine products. Americans like fine shoes and automobiles and launches with exquisite lines; and its architects have created cyclopean buildings which are the astonishment, if not the admiration, of the world. But the general accomplishments along the line of high taste are not great. Moving pictures have done something to help, as have printed pictures. Some of the big stores have offered wares of the finest craftsmanship and most beautiful design. Rodman Wanamaker went so far as almost to embarrass his stores in New York and especially Philadelphia. He attempted to bring Paris to America. Schools and colleges are having their influence. Museums are now visited by people who know what they want to see—Chinese porcelains or Greek vases, French furniture or English pottery. But craftsmanship commonly fares badly in museums in America, for while some museums are devoted to high creative art others are scientific and mechanical.[6] The house beautiful, however, is becoming an ideal. Interior decoration is fast taking on the proportions of an honored profession. Antiques are blindly grasped by the man who ignorantly feels the need of something better than he has.

Shortly after 1850 the feeling arose in England and then on the Continent that, while much had been gained in the Industrial Revolution, something had also been lost. In England Dante Gabriel Rossetti and William Morris pointed out the possibility of the beautiful in articles of ordinary use. To a considerable extent this emphasis on the unique and the artistic was part of a romantic revival, of which both Gothic architecture and medieval handicraft were sources of inspiration. From small beginnings in 1877 the Home Arts and Industries Association was formed in 1884 to further the handicrafts in both households and charitable institutions. It is still (1930) very active. In 1888 the Arts and Crafts Exhibition Society[7] was established to promote the exhibition of the work of more skilled craftsmen and artists who obtained no recognition from traditional sources.

The movement in America may be said to have made its effective beginning by the establishment of the Society of Arts and Crafts in Boston in 1897.[8] It has aimed at promoting handicraft where the machine cannot do the work successfully. Craftsmen, master craftsmen, and those interested in the promotion of practical arts have carried the gospel of beauty in industry to many parts of the nation. In the parent store in Boston (there used to be one in New York) there are on exhibit fine silver sets, porcelain vases, glassware, wrought iron, tapestries, and carved wooden objects. These articles have been sent on consignment by the members of the Society of Arts and Crafts. They stand for sale to the rich and for the admiration and despair of the rank and file. Although socially desirable these stores are not commercially prosperous.

I inquired in the Boston Arts and Crafts Shop whether any of the works of Mrs. Adelaide Alsop Robineau were

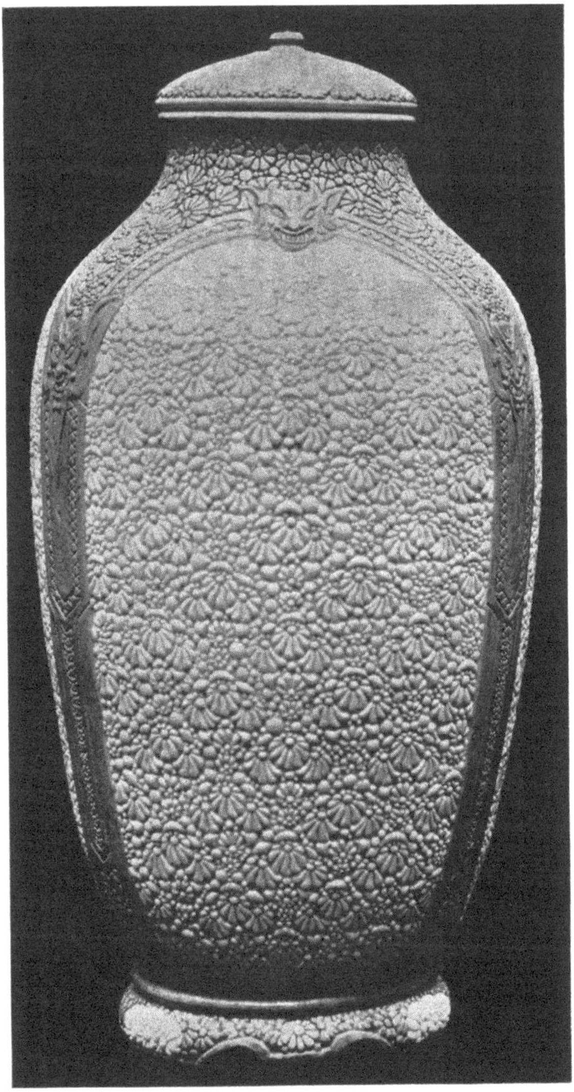

A PASTORAL VASE, MADE BY MRS. ADELAIDE ALSOP ROBINEAU IN 1910

on exhibit or for sale. The reply was that since her death in 1929 they had been withdrawn. This ceramist whose kiln was in Syracuse, New York, had consumate skill and a profound sense of beauty. Her work was recognized both at home and abroad. She belongs now to the history of art. Her delicate Egg-Shell Porcelain Bowl (1924) is in the Metropolitan Museum in New York; a photograph of her superb Pastoral Vase (1910) is reproduced here.

Before there can be any widespread attainment of the goal, such as all civilized peoples may reasonably expect, there must be a reduction in the cost of distributing art wares. At present it costs too much to buy fine pictures or wrought iron on Fifth Avenue in New York or on Boylston Street in Boston. Well-equipped stores offer us lamps and vases that are at once beautiful and unique. But these cost more than the average man of cultivated taste can afford. Only the rich can indulge their tastes, but I fear that often they give blanket orders for interior decorators to make the necessary selections. The solution to this problem is not to be separated from the general task of reducing the cost of marketing goods; and, of course, as such it does not specially concern us here. But we may note that American manufacturers have discovered that, if the price of automobiles, electric refrigerators, and radios is reduced, the sale thereby being greatly increased, the cost of manufacture can be lowered through the economies involved in large-scale production. Then, by means of direct selling agencies, the products may be put out to the consumer at low cost. Of course, the objection may be raised at this point that this plan of reducing prices depends upon standardization and mechanical production which, as we have seen, are inimicable to the finest artistic effects. And yet, with modifications and within limits, the general principle may be applied. It is indeed a reasonable assumption that we may see some measure of reorganization in business methods so as to meet the dawning, even developing, sense of the beautiful in house furnishings. In this reorganization there may be found a place for small-scale industries in America comparable to their position in Europe.

NOTES TO CHAPTER XVIII

1. For the manufactures of a fishing folk, North American Indians in the stage of collectional economy, see F. Boas, "Ethnology of the Kwakiutl," *Thirty-fifth Annual Report of the Bureau of American Ethnology, 1913–1914* (1921), pp. 57–172. More advanced, even skilled, work is described in C. Wissler, *The American Indian* (1917) chs. iii–viii.

2. See *Beni Hasan, Archæological Survey of Egypt* (ed. by P. E. Newberry), vol. ii, plate v; P. E. Newberry, *The Life of Rekhmara* (1900), pp. 336–337.

3. A. H. Sayce, *Babylonians and Assyrians* (1909), p. 107.

4. J. H. Breasted, *Ancient Times* (1916), p. 234.

5. See Charles R. Richards, *Art in Industry* (1922), pp. 487–488.

6. For foreign industrial museums, see the two books by Charles R. Richards, *The Industrial Museum* (1925) and *Industrial Art and the Museum* (1927).

7. See the *Arts and Crafts Essays by Members of the Arts and Crafts Exhibition Society* (1899), by William Morris, Walter Crane, and others.

8. A brief outline of part of the story is found in Mary R. Spain, *The Society of Arts and Crafts* (published by the Society in Boston and New York, 1924).

CHAPTER XIX

LARGE-SCALE VS. SMALL-SCALE INDUSTRY TODAY

AS WE have seen, art is not shut out of the factory, nor does it rise spontaneously in small workshops. In any balanced conception of industry we must consider the advantages and disadvantages of both large-scale and small-scale establishments. In America we are not allowed to tire of hearing the praises of the bigger units. And truly there ought to be no grudging concession made to the monstrous instruments of man.

The big factory is commonly most economical in the production of staple products.[1] The newest, most powerful, and most effective machines can be utilized. Unskilled labor can be put to work to the benefit of all concerned, that is, to both society and the individual. The machine may not lend dignity to the dull-brained individual, but it elevates him to a position of usefulness. Hitching some men to a machine is a crime, but linking others to continuous labor keeps them out of mischief in so far as it gives them a fixed place in life. The assumption is made that the hours of labor are not long and that other conditions are favorable.

Large plants can, and do, carry on research which gives them an initial advantage over their competitors and ultimately elevates the whole trade. The economies in the use of by-products introduced into industry in the last twenty years are almost beyond belief.[2] New products either in the form of substitutes or fresh creations meet us every day. Patent shingles, proprietary medicines, and the radio are diverse but significant illustrations.

In marketing, the large plant usually has a great advantage. It can advertise nationally or even internationally and within a year establish a new product or popularize an old one. Being forced to see the glaring signs and to listen to the noisy preachments of certain firms, we lose sight of the fact that much, perhaps one-half, of advertising is really educational, the other half being merely competitive. At any rate this useful thing—telling the people, even the world—is most economically done by advertising. Sometimes it is badly done as when recently a confectionary factory was so successful in advertising a commonplace concoction, to which an attractive name had been given, that it could not supply the demand which it had created. Certainly factories are of no use unless they can sell their output, and advertising enables them to do this, though even the big factories make mistakes in the way in which they advertise. While Ingersoll's slogan, "the watch that made the dollar famous," was a stroke of genius, Eastman's "Kodak" was questionable, because other concerns began to make Kodaks which Eastman was advertising for them.

To advertise takes capital, often in very large amounts. The making of improvements, such as is involved in the scrapping of old machinery, forces the manufacturer to go to the bank for loans. For these and many other purposes the large factory has an advantage. Moreover, its stocks and bonds, used for long-time financing, can find a wider market than those of some small and therefore unheard-of plants. In these days of strenuous competition, marketing and financing constitute the key to victory. It was his ability along these two lines that put John D. Rockefeller, Sr., upon the pinnacle of success.

Into the management of factories creep evils of great social import. Long hours, bad air, and inadequate lighting are among the most common. But the very evil of the situation—the concentration in a big plant—calls attention to the need of redress either by the action of the owners or by public law. The latter was the old way, the former is the new one. Accordingly we find today that factories are commonly more sanitary than the homes of the workers.

But the large factory, not necessarily the largest, has weaknesses which are not easily remedied. Labor difficulties often arise and because of the number of persons and the amount of capital involved bring about gigantic and irreparable losses. The very large establishment takes a long time to gain momentum and about as long a time to stop and start again. The change from an old to a new model in the Ford factories is an illustration of this. But of course the advantages of the old and the merits of the new momentum are not to be forgotten in any effort to judge industries by their size.

Large plants are commonly, almost always sooner or later, far from the source of raw material and sometimes from their market. The flour mills of Minneapolis have had to reach farther north and west and now to send to far-off Kansas for their supply of good hard wheat. The iron mills of Pittsburgh soon came to depend upon the distant mines of Minnesota. Many large lumber mills have cut up the forests of their district and then have been allowed to rot and rust. Around the flourishing industrial plants large cities gradually grow. Inevitably there is a rise in rents and in wages until the point is soon reached where removal elsewhere is advantageous or even necessary. But moving elsewhere just starts the process all over again: that it is no solution of difficulties the cotton manufacturers who have left Massachusetts for North Carolina already know.

Besides these large units there are many small-scale

industries that are carried on in petty establishments, far from the gaze of the casual onlooker, in out-of-the-way quarters where rents are low in the town, and in villages and scattered homesteads in the country. They are in large part the survivals of types of industry characteristic of past generations. In America they are virtually ignored; in England they have been relegated to the category of things forgotten and allowed to die; and in Germany, France, and Russia they are regarded by some as necessary evils, by others as vital parts of modern industry, at any rate neither ignored nor neglected. The factory, on the other hand, is new, a factor in dramatic contests, an issue before the courts and society, while small-scale industries just live on and occasionally manage to grow somewhat. They would be quite unnoticed by the public, were it not for social evils connected with some of them. And yet even in England, the classic home of the factory, these small-scale establishments included in 1904 over twenty per cent of industrial workers.[3]

There are at least five kinds of small-scale industries.[4] In the home a solitary individual may undertake to manufacture wares for others, as well as for the family. Sometimes the output is for a customer living near at hand; sometimes it is for a merchant or industrial entrepreneur who has only an office and a warehouse for storing, sorting, and packing. In other instances it may be an outworker for a factory, doing little bits by hand, things that require special attention but often no great skill. In 1915 in Massachusetts, for example, the making of jewelry, mesh bags, and chains at home required not a little skill and was largely confined to adults, while the stringing of tags was largely mechanical and employed many children ofter school hours.[5] Thus we see all four stages of industrial development epitomized in this one lonely worker. A good illustration is the women of the London slums making small articles of clothing for men, women, and children.[6]

A second kind is the domestic workshop, one in which several members of the family participate in manufacture. In such an establishment it is a question whether the family is more a unit of kinsmen or of workmen. This may be illustrated by the textile industry which lends itself to the various capacities of adults and children. The boys may assort the wool, the women (mother and grandmother) may card it, the women and daughters may spin it, and the father (also grandfather and oldest sons) may weave and dye it. Some such division of labor is found in this industry in widely scattered communities, from Persia to Scotland, from China to the north of Ireland. Such a workshop may illustrate any of the first three stages, as here outlined, for it may manufacture for family use, for direct sale to the user, for sale to, or on the order of, a merchant or industrial employer.

The small master's workshop is the third class of small-scale industry. It is a small shop, a room in the house of the master or in a tenement factory, or in a separate hovel, or shed, in which a few artisans are employed. Some of these workers are apprentices and some journeymen. The master works with and over his helpers. He makes goods for sale in the retail handicraft, for a customer who has ordered his specialty; he works in the wholesale handicraft type when he sells to a merchant or when he takes a commission from a factory for special commodities. The small master cutler of Sheffield is a case to the point. He usually works under the wholesale handicraft system for a merchant or entrepreneur, making pocket knives, table cutlery, scissors, scythes, and what not. In the case of steel forks, he has a virtual monopoly of the manufacture of the steel parts. He does this for a factory which simply puts on the heft and packs the finished product.[7] When such a small master employs a motor and efficient power machinery, there is, of course, some question as to whether his establishment is not a factory. Often such small shops grow into enormous factories, showing that one form may shade into another. It is well to note, however, that a common practice has grown up in various countries to regard that establishment as a workshop which employs as many as ten craftsmen, while the one with over ten is taken to be a factory. For the purpose of administration of wage and sanitation legislation, some such easy distinction is necessary, but it has little value for economic history.

The mill and small factory are other examples of small-scale industry existing at the present time. Though historically different in their origins they have come to be hardly distinguishable from one another and from the small workshop. Collectively these small units are of vast importance both in Europe and America for the manufacturing of new commodities and for the repair of old ones.

The small-scale industries may be illustrated from all the countries of the world, advanced and unprogressive, from Germany, Britain, and America as well as from China, Russia, and India. And the difference between these two groups is largely one of degree. In India the contest that is waged between the small-scale establishment and the large (cotton) factory takes on an added interest, in so far as the former is somewhat identified with Indian nationalism under the leadership of Gandhi, the latter with British imperialism. So far imperialism and the factory have won: Gandhi has been in prison and small-scale industries languish. But right in the shadow of the British factory, and often as an aid to it, the small-scale establishment holds its own. In Leeds and Bristol and especially in Leicester, shoe factories employ many home-workers. Of sixty-five factories, fifty-three give out work in the surrounding villages.[8] Watch-making has been carried on in England in the homes of the workers, especially in London, though competition with factory product has been difficult.[9] Many London women make cheap shirts at home. They buy foot-power sewing machines and pay for them out of the piece wages that they receive.[10] Chains, bits, bridles, spurs, and other metallic wares are made in small establishments in Staffordshire. In one of the small-scale industries of Nottingham a middlewoman, also found in the cheap clothing trade of London, plays a part. She takes material from an industrial employer and distributes it among the workers. Then she collects the finished goods, checks up on their quality, and delivers them to the employer. She may pay the worker in truck, for instance, in groceries if she keeps a grocery store. In many cases the profits are so high that the margin left for the worker is very low.[11] In Somersetshire, women, compelled to supplement their husbands' earnings, sew gloves—kid, suède, silk, and cotton. Whole villages in Devonshire made toothbrushes, or did before the late war.[12] In France there is a good deal of weaving done in towns and country homes and shops. This work includes cotton, wool, linen, and silk and is strongest in fancy and unusual work. Wooden spoons, briar pipes, and bric-à-brac of many kinds are also made.[13] And it should be noted that in France and elsewhere the small-scale industry is especially strong in repair work and services of various kinds. Many laundries, cobblers' shops, blacksmiths' shops, and garages come under this category.

The great evil connected with small-scale industry is summed up under the word sweating. This does not mean that the employer or merchant gets rich, but that the worker gets a miserable income from his work. Wages are low because the supply of workers is large. Little training is needed and there are many women, especially, who, because of the low earnings of their husbands or because of infirmities, have to labor at home for what they can get. The price at which the wares are sold is often determined by machine-made products manufactured in efficient factories of giant size. The long hours and unsanitary conditions are in marked contrast to conditions in the better factories of today, an eloquent tribute to our latest development in industry.

The fluctuations of the fortunes of small industrial units are very great. These units are here today and gone tomorrow—especially in America. Their coming and going have left no record of great success or failure. There are no adequate statistics that record their history or their contributions. Small grist mills have declined, as have small lumber mills. The small tailor shop has not flourished recently in America, nor the cobbler's shop. In both of these cases, however, there are factors quite apart from the large competing units. The automobile has made men get along with their old clothes and the new styles in shoes, particularly women's, do not lend themselves to much repairing. On the other hand, there are small plants that are well entrenched, particularly those producing wares which have a high transportation cost. Artificial stone is largely sand and cider is largely water. Accordingly the establishments which make them must cater to a narrow market and remain small. Automobile repair shops are thriving, more than making up for blacksmiths' shops which they replace.

It is thought that with the change from steam to electricity as the source of power there will be a fresh opportunity for the small industrial plant. The new plan of linking a great many small electrical power plants has the advantage of reducing costs and also insuring a continuous supply of current. In order to increase the consumption of electricity some of the power companies not only reduce their regular rates but offer particularly low ones during a period of a few years in order to aid prospective users when they are buying equipment—particularly motors and motor-driven machinery. The purely rural community cannot go much beyond electric milking machines and electric sewing machines, but where conditions are favorable sundry small machines could be used profitably—the lathe, the saw, various grinding machines, and so on. Where electric current is not available, there is the cheap engine driven either by gasoline or by the consumption of straw and other waste products.

Quite apart from the manufacture of goods by means of power machinery there is the work of skill which small masters can do when the general economic setting is ripe. Handmade rugs and baskets might well replace the ugly things now in common use. Wrought-iron wares are coming to have increasing favor both for houses and commercial buildings. Copper and brass wares are not far behind. Much skill is required to make furniture and pottery, but it could be gained if the market became more insistent upon the individual and the artistic and perhaps, we may add, if there were more opportunity to learn craftsmanship. Toys are even now made in the country and sold to many passing tourists. This is also true of confections, notably in Vermont where numerous signs attest the willingness of farmers' wives to part with their maple-sugar candy at various advantageous prices.

There is much to be said for the small-scale industries. There are many cultivators on very small holdings who have a great deal of leisure. There are fishermen and clammers who have much time on their hands. There are families of surplus labor in the country who wish to remain together and increase their earnings. There are women who can provide a few extras, lay up a little cash for a rainy day, and give a better education to their children. For many who are partly paralyzed or aged, home work is the alternative to the poorhouse. A stout girl works in the factory and enjoys a fair wage. Then her mother has a serious sickness. She cannot afford to hire a nurse, so she becomes a home-worker and nurse in one. This is not the ideal, but it is the most practical solution under present conditions. The widow—and there are many of them—often sees herself driven to one of two alternatives, to marry again with but little choice of a husband, or to work at home for herself and children. There are many persons who are grief-stricken and also many who have lost their reason only along certain lines who could be employed in some small isolated industry to their own great advantage. Of course we have all heard that such unfortunates should be kept in idleness at public expense. For a great many this treatment is necessary but not for all.

Marx thought that the sooner the small industrial establishment declined, the better for the workers. Factories would reign supreme and get larger and larger, until they would be taken over by the state. Socialists generally see in the small master and home-worker the bane of trade unionism, because these isolated workers cannot be organized easily, perhaps not at all by trade-union methods. On the other hand, Ruskin, William Morris, and Walter Crane regretted the loss of goods made by hand and expressing the individuality of the worker.[14] And Kropotkin, the Russian idealist, thought the world was the loser when men left the country to enter factories, when they might manufacture the same wares in their own homes. Kropotkin, like Charles Bray before him (1844),[15] regretted the loss of that happy combination of outside work in the fields and inside labor at the forge and loom. He thought the loss of independence on the part of the small master little short of calamitous.

An ideal industrial system would unquestionably include the factory for those persons who are adaptable to routine monotonous labor, who do not value the open air, who feel no regrets in the loss of personal freedom or who would regard these as more than balanced by high wages and association with large numbers of their fellows, with all the social and cultural advantages involved. The factory probably will remain indispensable for the manufacture of some commodities, such as steel rails, threshing machines, automobiles, and railroad coaches. But there are lots of things, such as small objects of individuality and changing fashion, that might well be made in the home or in the workshop, in town or country. Such work would be the willing price paid for living under the conditions liked best—fishing part of the year, or cultivating the soil, or working in the woods. The lone individual or family worker, of course, must not be exploited. We would not call into being a class of workers who, though legally free, were economic slaves. As part and parcel of the system there would be established co-operative associations to purchase raw materials and to sell the finished products. We all know the difficulties connected with co-operation, American history being strewn with the corpses of desperate efforts. But co-operative associations are beginning to take on a lease of vigorous life that is promise of relief to the small man. Without such co-operative associations we should have the wholesale handicraft system, at first the independent phase but ultimately the dependent phase with all its exploitation.

Adult education and recreation could be made available by the associations of small masters just as rapidly as members were ready for them. The post-office, parcel-post, telephone, motor car, and radio would play into their hands. Such co-operation has already made some headway in the Old World. It would seem that it deserves both the patronage of individuals and the support of governments. Much educational work would have to be done first, not only to persuade consumers to appreciate goods made by hand and with individuality graven in their lines, but to persuade the scattered workers of the need of organizing in a formal way and to educate them in the best methods of doing this. What agriculturists are doing both in the Old and the New World, small industrialists might also accomplish on a large scale, at once in Europe, more slowly in other lands. When such work is done, the public will pay extra cost, where such is incurred, in distributing raw materials and in collecting the products from scattered shops and homes. High ideals must be maintained by the workers and the consumers must be appreciative of the individual effort required to produce a fine lace collar, the best bitter-sweet marmalade, and pottery of quaint artistry.

NOTES TO CHAPTER XIX

1. See D. S. Kimball in *Recent Economic Changes*, vol. i (1929), p. 85.
2. See above, ch. xv, p. 191.
3. G. I. H. Lloyd, *The Cutlery Industries* (1913), p. 425.
4. Cf. British Parliamentary Papers, *Report from the Select Committee on Home Work* (1908), p. iv; and G. I. H. Lloyd, *op. cit.*, p. 197.
5. See *Industrial Home Work in Massachusetts*, Women's Educational and Industrial Union (1915), pp. 88 ff., 108 ff.
6. British Parliamentary Papers, *Report from the Select Committee on Home Work* (1908) pp. 86 ff.
7. G. I. H. Lloyd, *op. cit.*, p. 203.
8. G. Brodnitz, "Betriebskonzentration und Kleinbetrieb in der Englishen Industrie," *Jahrbücher für Nationalökonomie*, 3rd series, vol. xxxvii (1909), p. 152.
9. Charles Booth, *Life and Labour of the People in London,Industry*,vol. ii (1903), pp. 26–29.
10. *Report from the Select Committee on Home Work* (1907), pp. 38–39.
11. *Ibid.*, p. 23.
12. *Ibid.*, p. 34.
13. P. Kropotkin, *Fields, Factories, and Workshops* (1898, 1912), pp. 288 ff.
14. G. Brodnitz, *op. cit.*, pp. 172 ff.
15. See Bray's introduction to Mary Hennell's *An Outline of the various Social Systems and Communities which have been founded on the Principle of Cooperation* (1844), pp. lxxix–lxxxi.

INDEX

Bei Fragen zur Produktsicherheit wenden Sie sich bitte an:
If you have any questions regarding product safety,
please contact:

Walter de Gruyter GmbH
Genthiner Straße 13
10785 Berlin
productsafety@degruyterbrill.com